Konrad Becker/Fe

Deep Search
The Politics of Search beyond Google

APublication of World-Information Institute

Konrad Becker/Felix Stalder (Eds.)

Deep Search

The Politics of Search beyond Google

StudienVerlag
Innsbruck
Wien
Bozen

This publication is supported by the Austrian Federal Ministry of Science and Research.

© 2009 by Studienverlag Ges.m.b.H., Erlerstraße 10, A-6020 Innsbruck
e-mail: order@studienverlag.at
Internet: www.studienverlag.at

Corporate design by Kurt Höretzeder
Layout: Studienverlag/Walter Methlagl
Cover: World Information Institute/t0

Distributed in North America ans South America and the rest of the world excluding Austria, Germany and Switzerland by: Transaction Publishers, Rutgers - the State university, 35 berrue Circle, Piscataway New Jersey, 08854-8042, USA, www.transactionpub.com

This book is printed on acid-free paper.

Bibliographic information published by Die Deutsche Bibliothek
Die Deutsche Bibliothek lists this publication in the Deutsche Nationalbibliographie;
detailed bibliographic data is available in the Internet at http://dnb.ddb.de

ISBN 978-3-7065-4795-6

All rights reserved under International Copyright Conventions.

Table of Content

Konrad Becker, Felix Stalder
Introduction ... 7

Histories

Paul Duguid
Search before grep
A Progress from Closed to Open? ... 13

Robert Darnton
The Library in the Information Age
6000 Years of Script ... 32

Geert Lovink
Society of the Query
The Googlization of our Lives ... 45

Katja Mayer
On the Sociometry of Search Engines
A Historical Review of Methods ... 54

Liberties

Claire Lobet-Maris
From Trust to Tracks
A Technology Assessment Perspective Revisited ... 73

Joris van Hoboken
Search Engine Law and Freedom of Expression
A European Perspective ... 85

Felix Stalder & Christine Mayer
The Second Index
Search Engines, Personalization and Surveillance ... 98

Power

Theo Röhle
Dissecting the Gatekeepers
Relational Perspectives on the Power of Search Engines   117

Bernhard Rieder
Democratizing Search?
From Critique to Society-oriented Design   133

Matteo Pasquinelli
Google's PageRank
Diagram of the Cognitive Capitalism
and Rentier of the Common Intellect   152

Konrad Becker
The Power of Classification
Culture, Context, Command, Control, Communications, Computing   163

Visibility

Richard Rogers
The Googlization Question
Towards the Inculpable Engine?   173

Metahaven
Peripheral Forces
On the Relevance of Marginality in Networks   185

Lev Manovich
How to Follow Global Digital Cultures
Cultural Analytics for Beginners   198

Author Information   213

Introduction

It's hard to avoid search engines these days. They have established themselves as essential tools for navigating the dynamic, expanding informational landscape that is the Internet. The Internet's distributed structure doesn't allow for any centralized index or catalog; consequently, search engines fulfill a central task of making digital information accessible and thus usable. It's hard to imagine our lives without their ever-expanding digital dimension; and so it's increasingly hard to imagine life without search engines. This book looks at the long history of the struggle to impose order on the always-fragile information universe, addresses key social and political issues raised by today's search engines, and envisions approaches that would break with the current paradigms they impose.

At the moment, Google occupies a unique place in the field of digital search. It dominates the end-user market to a degree that it approaches a practical monopoly in many countries around the world.[1] Its ambitions far outstrip those of every other search company. Almost weekly, new initiatives are announced, many of them on a gigantic scale – from digitizing millions of books to rolling out an entire platform for mobile communication designed specifically for maximum integration with Google's wide array of services. Even a total refusal to use Google would offer no escape. So many others use it (for example, in the form of its Gmail email service) that a substantial amount of one's personal email communications will end up in its domain. And so many web sites and services are interwoven with its various offerings that it is unavoidable. Even if one insists of obtaining news in print, Google is there: reports about its offerings are everywhere, from the promotional to the critical, from the superficial to the in-depth. And, with each passing week, we hear more and more about the dangers posed by such a powerful entity inserting itself into so many aspects of our individual and collective existence. Thus, Google not only dominates markets, it also dominates our minds – to such a degree that it is difficult not to conflate the generic issue of search engines with the specific practices of Google. This is unfortunate, since the issues of search, questions of classification, and access to information run much deeper than the business model of a single company. They represent historical shifts (as well as continuities) of how we relate to the world. It is doubly unfortunate, because Google's primary business is no longer search per se; rather, it has become an advertising company (the source of 98% of its revenues[2]). "Search" is just one of the products that create an environment in which access to individual users, identified through detailed, personal data profiles, can be monetized.

Yet, no matter what the stock market momentarily thinks of the "tech sector," we are still in the just foundational phase of the digital information environment. The speed and dynamism with which search technologies are developing are testimony to that. Keeping up with even the most general details is daunting, to say nothing of the technical specifics, which in any case are often shrouded in trade secrets and opaque research. Fortunately, keeping up with this breathless innovation is the wrong approach. We need instead to shift our focus to the structural, long-term political issues that are emerging in this development. It is crucial that we acknowledge both the willful design of the tools we increasingly depend upon, and that their artifacts – most obviously hierarchies in markets and in search results – are anything neither natural nor arbitrary. Innocent utilities that blend into the routine of everyday work and leisure subtly bend our perceptions and weave their threads into the fabric of our cognitive reality. Most people accept the framing through these technologies uncritically.[3] Doing so is dangerous.

Looking into the social and technological construction of information and knowledge, we ask some basic questions: How is computer-readable significance produced? How is meaning involved in machine communication? Where is the emancipatory potential of having access to such vast amounts of information? And where are the dangers of having to rely on search engines – particularly when operated by opaque monopolies – to make use of that information? Could it all be different? These questions of culture, context, and classification in information systems are crucial: what is at stake is nothing less than how we, as individuals and collectives, find out about the world.

Though rarely thought of as a "mass medium", search engines occupy a critical juncture in our networked society. In many ways (and increasingly), their influence on our culture, economy, and politics dwarfs that of the broadcast networks, radio stations, and newspapers. Yet we still do not understand the kind of power they exert. It's clearly not reducible to classic editorial issues. Located at bottlenecks of our information infrastructures, search engines exercise extraordinary control over data flow in what otherwise are largely decentralized networks. Their resulting power is, as always, accompanied by opportunities for abuse and by concerns how to assure its legitimate and appropriate exercise.

The present volume is an attempt to contribute to the public debate of these issues. It is organized into four sections. The first deals with *histories*. Paul Duguid examines the arrangements that have framed the practice of search beginning with the first Sumerian libraries. He sees two trends working across periods: on the one hand, the need to manage expanding volumes of information, which he sees as one of the drivers in the evolution of storage, organization, and search;

and, on the other, an ongoing tension between practices of making information available more easily (in the name of freedom) and practices to restrict the ways it can be handled (in the name of quality). After this broad overview, Robert Darnton focuses on the history of how we have handled text and the transformations of the library as one of its core institutions. He begins with the observations that information has always been unstable, and that each age has been an information age in the sense that its particular ways of handling (textual) information was profoundly influential. This suggests that information never simply corresponds to an external reality but, rather, is always (also) the product of particular storage methods and retrieval procedures. Thus, Darnton asks, what is gained, and what is lost, as we move from one information processing system to another? With an eye on this instability, he concludes: "Long live Google, but don't count on it living long enough to replace that venerable building with the Corinthian columns."

Google and virtually all other search engines right now are based on link analysis, that is, they analyze the links pointing to a document in order to assess its relative importance. While this is often thought of as a major breakthrough, Katja Mayer shows that this sociometric approach itself has a long history. It was first developed in the early 20th century as a politically progressive approach to help small groups become aware of their own, often surprising internal dynamics. It was later transformed into a management technique to assess the sciences without having to deal with the intricacies of the arguments made in the ever-expanding number and size of its subdisciplines. The Science Citation Index, developed in the 1950s, seemed to offer a politically neutral, purely formal way of determining the importance of publications and scientists. This method, taken up by search engines, is now applied to all informational domains. Yet by becoming transparent, it is increasingly – like the citation index, too – subject to manipulation and its inherent limitations are exposed. The final chapter in this section is by Geert Lovink. He returns to Joseph Weizenbaum's observation that "not all aspects of reality are computable" and asks how we can, in a historically and socially informed way, think about the flood of information that search engines try to make accessible for us. His advice: Stop searching. Start questioning!

The book's second section focuses on *liberties*. Search engines empower individuals by making vast amounts of information available to them, yet their increasing centrality also makes them, voluntarily and involuntarily, an arbiter of these very freedoms. Claire Lobet-Maris examines the tradition of technology impact assessment to develop a framework of how to bring the technologies of search into the democratic debate and how to envision accountability. For her, three main questions need to be asked: one concerning equity (the equal chance to be found online), one concerning the tyranny of the majority (link analysis favoring the popular), and finally transparency (that is, the ability to assess and contest how search engines work). All this leads to a discussion of autonomy, which, as she indicates, might be reduced when search engines assume that the "clicking body", i.e., the tracks that people leave and search engines collect, is more reliable than the "speaking body", i.e. what people actually say about themselves. Joris van Hoboken approaches the question of liberties from the other side, looking at how search engines are being regulated in European law and how they are becoming targets for efforts to restrict access to information by being forced to censor their search results. Van Hoboken points out that the many legal gray zones that search engines must operate in are restricting the opportunities for new entrants in the field. One of the reasons Google can still provide its services is its large and powerful legal department, a prerequisite for working in this area. The third chapter in this section, by Felix Stalder and Christine Mayer, returns to the question of whether search engines enhance or diminish users' autonomy. They approach this question via the issue of personalization, that is, of tailoring the services – to users and advertisers – based on extensive user profiles. Will this open the way to overcome the tyranny of the majority by making information available that is not generally popular, or will it decrease autonomy by strengthening surveillance and manipulation through social sorting?

The book's third section directly examines issues of *power*. First, Theo Röhle employs concepts derived from Foucault and Actor–Network Theory to examine the subtle combination of rewards and punishment employed by Google to keep webmasters within bounds. This strategy, he argues, involves the establishment of a disciplinary regime that enforces a certain norm for web publishing. Turning to Google's relationship to the users he finds forms of power that aim at controlling differential behavior patterns by gaining an intimate statistical panorama of a population and using this knowledge as a means of predictive risk management. Bernhard Rieder observes that discussions about the power of search engines are often hampered by the considerable distance between technical and normative approaches. To counter this, he develops a technologically grounded normative position that advocates plurality, autonomy, and access as alternative guiding principles for both policy and design. His conclusions are surprising: one of the most important ways to restrain the unchecked power of search engines might be to strengthen the ability of third parties to rerank the search results. We need to demand: access to the index! This would allow a wide range of actors to take advantage of the search engines' vast infrastructure (which is extremely hard to replicate) while applying other methods of ranking (which is comparatively doable). Moving from a liberal to a more radical perspective, Matteo Pasquinelli examines how Google extracts value from individual actions and the common intellect and transforms it into network value and wealth. To frame how such value is accumulated and extracted, Pasquinelli sketches a concept of "cognitive rent", which no longer needs intellectual property but, instead, is particularly attuned to "free culture" and "free labor". The final paper in this section is by Konrad Becker. In a broad-ranging essay, he looks at the role of classification systems as techniques of power, highlighting that such "technologies of the mind are political philosophy masked as neutral code".

The final section deals with issues of *visibility*. Richard Rogers observes a creeping "googlization" of the entire media landscape, that is, how approaches made dominant by Google are now being employed beyond its realm. These approaches are never purely technical but also necessarily political, if not by intent then certainly in effect. As one way of assessing these developments, he proposes studying "how subtle interface changes imply a politics of knowledge". Metahaven, a studio for research and design, focuses again on sociometrics and the dominant paradigm underlying Google's legendary PageRank method. However, rather than concentrating on the usual link-rich nodes, they ask "how a different take on the sociability of weak ties may bring a different appreciation of their relevance to networks". Using advanced network theory, they contrast an approach focusing on the redundancy of the center with one that seeks particular positions at the periphery. They look at sites that bridge densely connected clusters and which might actually provide access to the greatest amount of information, since they bring together otherwise disconnected worlds. They use the Obama presidential campaign as well as the network structure of Al Qaeda as examples for the potential of focusing on unique weak ties rather than on redundant strong ones. The last chapter in this section is by Lev Manovich who reports on his ambitious new project. He leaves behind the dominant approach of trying to find the one right document. Rather, he argues for the need to analyze patterns hidden in large datasets. For the field of digital culture, he argues that we need to leave behind 20th century paradigms, which were developed on the basis of relatively small datasets that allowed close inspection of each item in isolation (think of a painting hanging on a white wall in a museum). Instead, he argues, we must come to terms with the fact that cultural development can no longer be reduced to a few privileged producers: it is now driven by the interactions of millions of producers, using the same tools and acting on the same information. Manovich thus abandons the logic of the results list and envisions new ways of how to follow global digital cultures.

Pointing to new technological developments and breakthroughs in the field of organizing, classifying, and analyzing large datasets, this is where history meets the future. We are thus reminded that liberties always need to be defended and renegotiated and that visibility and invisibility must be in the service of autonomy and empowerment.

Acknowledgments

Many of the papers of this volume were first presented at the Deep Search conference, which took place in Vienna on November 8, 2008. The original presentations are available online as high-quality video streams.[4] The conference was organized and conceptualized by the World-Information Institute, realized in partnership with international research network IRF (Information Retrieval Facility) and supported by Matrixware Information Services and the Austrian Federal Ministry of Education, Science and Culture.

Producing a conference and a subsequent book is a task that cannot be realized without the help and generous support of many individuals involved in the process. We would like to thank all participants for their great contributions and the enthusiasm they brought to the conference and into the making of this book. We have also benefited greatly from Patrice Riemens, who put us in contact with ongoing research and publication projects that we might have missed otherwise. Ted Byfield provided valuable input and Christine Mayer and Aileen Derieg carefully edited all the papers.

Vienna, April 2009

Konrad Becker and Felix Stalder

WORLD-INFORMATION INSTITUTE

Notes

1. In the US, Google's market share is 72%, in India 81%, in Germany, in Chile 93%, and in the Netherlands 95%. Only in EastAsia Google is not dominant, in China its share is 26%, in Taiwan it is 18% and in Korea it is as low as 3%. For details, see http://googlesystem.blogspot.com/2009/03/googles-market-share-in-your-country.html
2. Eric Schmidt, *Interview with Charlie Rose* (March 6, 2009) http://www.charlierose.com/view/interview/10131
3. Lee Rainie and Graham Mudd, "Search Engines: Project Data Memo", *Pew Internet & American Life Project* (Aug. 2004) Available at http://www.pewinternet.org/pdfs/PIP_Data_Memo_Searchengines.pdf ("The average visitor scrolled through 1.8 result pages during a typical search.")
4. http://world-information.org/wii/deep_search/

Histories

Search before grep
A Progress from Closed to Open?

Paul Duguid

In recent years the Internet has increasingly been defined by search, its resources reached primarily through a search box.[1] While the Internet is new, search of course is not. And though modern search may appear to have shrugged off much of the old apparatus to make information appear increasingly "free" and autonomous, a historical understanding of how that apparatus developed can help clarify what is and is not new and perhaps what is and is not possible for the developing world of digital search. In a highly speculative, partial, and truncated form, this essay attempts to give an idea of what such a history might look like.

The world according to grep

The separation between the short epoch of digital search and its long analogue past can be marked by two "Gs", standing for grep and Google. Grep is the enormously powerful search tool built for Unix software in 1973.[2] It allows searchers to scan digital documents for any "regular expression", any specifiable chunk or "string" (this can include letters, "wild cards", spaces, punctuation marks, or line endings) in the electronic representation of a text. Its closest antecedent was probably the cumbersome concordance, but that was word-based, a limitation left far behind by grep. Google's intervention can be measured by its difference from even its digital predecessors such as Veronica, Archie, Alta Vista, and Yahoo. These relied in varying degrees on hierarchical order for their searches. Google implicitly abandoned that approach, allowing us to hunt down strings across, and regardless of, the hierarchical boundaries that traditionally organized documents and ranking results instead by the intertexutality of the Internet.[3] Grep and Google, then, brought search into a world of information that was indifferent to semantics, syntax, and hierarchy. Search thus became both a mechanism for and an example of the shift away from ancient constraints, material, conceptual, and institutional, towards the "open" informational environment that is championed by proponents of "open source" and "Web 2.0".[4]

The vision behind open, modular, and hierarchy-free information is not entirely new. Paul Otlet, the grandfather of "information science", long ago suggested that the book was less a resource for information than a constraint upon it, arguing

> The external make-up of a book, its format and the personality of its author are unimportant provided that its substance, its sources of information and its conclusion are preserved and can be made an integral part of the organization of knowledge, an impersonal work, created by the efforts of all ... the ideal ... would be to strip each article or each chapter in a book of whatever is a matter of fine language or repetition or padding and to collect separately on cards whatever is new and adds to knowledge.[5]

Bill Mitchell, the dean of MIT's Media Lab, expressed a similar view of the book as a constraint on free-flowing ideas when he described it as no more than "tree flakes encased in dead cow" – an outdated old technology ripe for replacement by new. Elsewhere, arguments for "virtual" libraries or "libraries without walls" as well as the simple claim that the Internet is a library, indicated a desire to shake off information-constraining burdens of the past and aggregate knowledge or information, Otlet style. Stewart Brand summed up such ideas with the compelling phrase "information wants to be free".

Whatever the oddities of these claims – Mitchell seems unaware of the incongruity of leather bound books with wood-pulp paper; Brand of whether information is the sort of thing that has wants or, indeed, is capable of freedom – history, at least the history told by the victors, seems to be on their side. The tools provided by the 2 Gs have triumphed, allowing us to search in ways never possible before. String search à la grep has allowed us to follow our interests, rather than subordinating them to concordances and hierarchies formed elsewhere. And information-shucking devices such as *Google Books* have shed material and institutional constraints to provide unprecedented routes to enormous amounts of data, allowing Google, while eschewing hierarchy, to talk nonetheless of "organizing the world's information". Without detracting from the remarkable successes of these technologies, it does seem worthwhile to ask whether, as is often assumed, this progress is part of a continuing movement in the history of search from closed to open, from bounded to free information, from in sum a benighted past to an enlightened future.

A history of the world before grep and Google offers to throw some on light on this question. After all, the more we claim that present capabilities are unprecedented, the more we oblige ourselves to study the past, otherwise how do we know what is or is not unprecedented?[6] A glance over the history of search suggests that it takes a fair amount of Whiggish thinking to portray it as the linear emancipation of information wherein the cumbersome shackles of material and institutional constraints were broken by technological innovations and only set back by revanchist assaults on progress.

Such teleological accounts tend to include Darwinian or Spenserian assumptions about human behaviour. Kilgour, a more serious scholar than many who talk teleologically, offers a version of this kind of history in his *Evolution of the Book*. To account for selection and extinction in his evolutionary story, Kilgour relies on an innate human trait of information foraging. Thus, for example, he argues that "The need to find information more rapidly than is possible in a papyrus-roll-form book initiated the development of the Greco-Roman codex in the second century".[7] I hope to show that such an account of human needs, while beguiling, undersells both the complexity of the past and the challenges of the future. A human need for information is here taken as an ahistorical, acultural constant, engaged in at all times by all people, who are also taken to be forever in search of better foraging technologies. While useful in some ways, such an information-driven account can be misleading, describing what we see our distant ancestors as doing, but missing what they saw themselves as doing. Ignoring the gap between these two allows us to enroll the past in an endorsement of present interests, an endorsement which, when actually consulted, the past does not always seem prepared to give. The actual patterns of human behavior are, I hope to show, more complex than a simple evolutionary or emancipatory account claims, in part because the information constraints we so often want to overcome may simultaneously be information resources serving not necessarily to help us find, but often to help us assess, in culturally specific terms, what we find. As assessment is essential if the success of search is not to be random, such constraining-resources often have to be rebuilt in another form that impedes the conventional, progressive story.

Search, storage, organization

To get a grip on grep and Google, we need to look beyond search alone to storage and organization. Google's self-proclaimed mandate, after all, is to "organize the world's information" in order to "make it universally accessible and useful".[8] Moreover, Google's real power probably lies less now in its innovative Page Rank algorithms than in its extraordinary storehouse of open information (refined and tagged by the not-so-open information Google has accrued from searches run over this storehouse); what Battelle has called Google's "database of intentions".[9] The relationship between storage and search is important, because when we look at the distant past, much of what we see is evidence of storage from which we can only infer the historical character of search.[10]

A very early and yet oddly familiar glimpse of storage comes in the opening of the ancient *Epic of Gilgamesh*, which talks of boxes of cedar with clasps of bronze holding tablets of stone and lapis lazuli – stone being one of the first means of recording human ideas and different kinds of boxes being, as they still are, useful mechanisms not just for storing, but also for ordering. The relatively valuable materials cedar, bronze, and lapis lazuli then suggest a certain hierarchy of ordering, indicating then as now that the adventures of Gilgamesh were tales worthy of privileged preservation.[11]

In the ancient Middle East, where *Gilgamesh* is set, stone soon gave way to clay. When wet, it is the more malleable material, but when dry almost as durable. Its durability provides our insight into ancient collections of the region such as the "library" of the royal palace at Ebla (c. 2300 BC), many of whose robust clay tablets still survive.[12] These give an idea of what was stored and presumably what was searched. Accounting data, administrative records, and religious incantations dominate this and other early libraries, as well as bilingual word-lists and other forerunners of conventional reference tools. Early collections were relatively small (the room at Ebla was roughly 3.5 x 4 metres). But over this region and the next two millennia collection building became much more ambitious and the content became less pragmatic, shifting from the illiberal to the liberal arts. Great collections, such as the library at Nineveh, gathered principally by the erudite Assyrian ruler Ashurbanipal, and the iconic libraries at Alexandria, built under Ptolemy I and II, grew to embrace and give pride of place to philosophy, astronomy, and literary works like *Gilgamesh*. They also grew in absolute terms: the multiple collections at Alexandria held more than 500,000 items.

Ebla's relatively narrow range of documents seem to have been shelved by type and were probably consulted primarily by scribes who created these or similar works. Familiarity would have limited the need for "finding aids". But as collections grew and were consulted by outsiders, the need for more elaborate ordering and finding grew too. The second-millennium collection at Hattusas used a system of colophon marks to identify each record. These suggest some kind of central catalogue for users to find a way to and through particular documents, features echoed on the spines of modern library books. At Alexandria, the first director Zenodotus arranged the collection by type and introduced the idea of a catalogue ordered alphabetically. Callimachus, who may also have been a director, later provided Alexandria with a more elaborate catalogue (itself some 120 volumes) that sorted by author and category, limiting the authors to the "eminent" and breaking the categories down into subcategories, and so framing the collection within various hierarchical orderings of the sort still used to manage large, complex libraries.[13]

Immutable mobiles

That such collections could be built from different and dispersed sources (by acquisition or more aggressive appropriation), and assembled and reordered indicates the mobility, adaptability, and to some degree modular self-sufficiency of the works in these collections.[14] In the extreme case, we can contrast this mobility with, for example, the relative immobility of cave paintings, wall carvings, and the like.[15] Such collection building and organizing would have been difficult even with the stones and tablets of Gilgamesh and much easier with the papyrus and parchment of Alexandria. Latour has usefully defined documents as "immutable mobiles", and in the transition from stone to the papyrus we see a tension between this pairing emerge.[16] Increasing mobility and pliability, which allowed these great collections to develop and be organized and searched, challenged the immutability that allowed documents to stay constant over time. Stone and clay were resilient in the face of *tempus edax rerum*, but resistant to organization. Papyrus and parchment, by contrast, could be organized, rearranged, and stitched together with relative ease, but they were more easily damaged, intentionally or unintentionally. The contents of Sumerian "tablet houses", much of it the equivalent of modern ephemera, have survived remarkably intact for 5,000 years; the contents of Alexandria have all but disappeared.[17]

Despite increasing frailty, the emphasis on mobility seems to have predominated for all but monumental inscriptions. Texts moved from stone and clay to more amenable material. What material was actually used was in part a function of place. Alexandria took advantage of the plants that grew in the Nile valley to make papyrus. In Greece and Rome, where papyrus was not available, parchment (which takes its name from the great library at Pergamum) or vellum was the main support for library documents, though more ephemeral writings used wood and wax. In India, birch bark was used in the north and palm leaves in the south; in China, boards, bamboo, and silk. Place was not the sole determinant. In India, for example, the status of cattle ruled out parchment.

China's invention of paper, which can be made more or less anywhere and violates no widespread taboos, ultimately overcame all the competition as material support for all but a few documents. It endures as a type of support to this day (sometimes even used as insurance against the frailty of digital storage), though in terms of its material endurance, it is perhaps the most mutable of all the materials discussed so far except for wax, suggesting that mobility may trump immutability in Latour's dyad.[18] If printing began, as some suggest, with the Chinese tradition of copying Confucian classics by making paper rubbings from their stone engravings, that process also captures the symbolic transition of communication from the primarily immutable to the primarily mobile. Paper, which could be marked and amended, glued, stitched, and appended more easily than most of its rivals, advanced possibilities for storing, ordering, and indexing. Its introduction should not be read as a simple advance on information's linear progress towards Brand's freedom and autonomy. The salient features of paper suggest that much of its attraction came because it was particularly well behaved within institutional collections, which in turn could protect its fragility.[19] Paper undoubtedly helped underwrite more powerful search, but within, rather than in isolation from institutionally based organizational hierarchy.

Bad punctuation

The significance of this new material base for search may in part reflect the way paper helped underpin a new form for documents, the codex, the object of Mitchell's scorn. What we think of today as the modern book, with its stiff cover and sequential, individuated pages folded from larger sheets into signatures, gradually replaced the scroll more or less as paper replaced parchment. As these two seem to belong together (for paper folds more easily than papyrus or parchment, which are better adapted to the roll), it is easy to tell stories about a new technology replacing the old because of its inherent suitability for the underlying human trait of information foraging. Kilgour, who makes such an argument, explains away the long gaps in this process of replacement, in which nothing of technological interest happens, with the help of Gould's notion of punctuated equilibrium.[20]

Such stories of supersession, extinction, and equilibrium need treating with caution. Too often to make their case for the new and adaptable, they belittle the older technologies as primitive and static.[21] The scroll was in fact a highly adaptable form within which some of the most enduring features of the apparatus of search – apparatus we tend to associate with the codex and print – developed.[22] In terms of adaptability to human needs it was, moreover, particularly handy, more suited when closed to the human grip than the codex. It was thus easily carried – and concealed, leading Socrates to tease Phaedrus about what he had under his cloak (a question that also teased Derrida). Certainly, the codex unquestionably had advantages. It could import many of the features of the scroll, while adding features previously unavailable. It allowed, for example, writing on two sides of a document (as, of course, had clay tablets). It also gave the page (and the two-page spread) a more robust semantic role, and it provided an unambiguous margin, essential for concise annotations and reference markings.[23] While it was perhaps not so easy to carry, it stored and stacked more easily, suggesting again how the needs of storage and organization might take precedence over individual access. Though, unlike the scroll, the small codex or *membrana* could, as Martial argued, be held and read with just one hand (a possibility which teased Rousseau).

Even as we weigh advantages and disadvantages, it is important not to jump to simple evolutionary conclusions about survival and extinction. Given their slightly different properties and potential, it is not surprising that these two forms, the scroll and the codex, existed side by side, as illustrated by a famous painting from Pompeii in which one of the two figures holds a codex and the other a scroll. Nor was this overlap particularly brief. The original codex of wax and wood (from whence its name) was around as a convenient notebook long before it rose to prominence as a high cultural object, threatening the scroll. Moreover, as Clanchy reminds us, long after the codex was widespread, the English adopted the scroll for legal and government documents, and it survived as the principal means of recording, storing, and organizing chancery court proceedings until at least the late 19th century. Nor, as screen documents remind us, is it quite dead yet. Indeed, in Google's book project, the pages of the scanned books helpfully scroll, whereas in other more literal translations, such as *Early English Books Online*, they jump from page to page.

Casting far and wide

Even if we can see the print book emerge triumphantly to supersede the manuscript scroll, it is hard to make easy evolutionary sense of the development of the book in terms of information foraging, as even the following survey, geographically as broad as it is shallow and historically as deep as it is lacking in profundity, can show.[24] And once we look beyond Europe, the often-told story of Western triumph becomes increasingly confusing. If we take paper alone and ignore hints that it may have been around for up to 300 years before its official

Chinese birth in 105 AD, what seems to some a principal information-foraging resource takes a surprisingly long time to spread to societies that evolutionary models assume were no less information-obsessed than China. It took 500-600 years to reach India and the Middle East and a further 500 to cross the short distance from there to Western Europe. China had also developed xylography by the eighth century, and moveable type by the eleventh, yet, despite the codex and paper together forming a robust manuscript culture in Europe and Byzantium, it still took until the fourteenth century for xylography to develop and until the fifteenth for the apparently transformational appearance of moveable type. Moreover, for all its info-precociousness, China for its part proved resistant to the pure, search-friendly codex, relying on the "sutra fold" until well into the seventeenth century.[25]

Korea and Japan, though both heavily influenced by and influencing China, also reveal distinct chronologies. Korea had paper by the third century, print by the eighth, and moveable, alphabetic type 50 years before Gutenberg, yet the full panoply of the Western print codex and what Febvre and Martin see as a key information device, the newspaper, waited to be "introduced" by the Japanese until around the end of the nineteenth century. Meanwhile, Japan itself might almost appear to have put evolution into reverse. It got paper from Korea early in the seventh century and was capable of printing the celebrated charms of the Empress Shōtoku in an edition of perhaps one million copies in the eighth century, yet printing for reading (the charms were a ritual rather than a communicative act) failed to develop until the eleventh century (well before Europe). Even then it was generally ignored until typography reappeared with the Jesuits in the seventeenth century.

Indian palm-leaf books or *pothi* may have inspired the sutra fold used in China. India also had paper from the sixth century. Yet paper did not become widespread for another 700 years, while, despite the use of print by the British in India, print was barely used by Indians for themselves until the late nineteenth century. The Indian nations had thoroughly sophisticated mechanisms of communication, as Bailey points out in *Empire and Information*. Consequently, an explanation must lie "in the information order as a whole, rather than in one particular dimension of it".[26] Again, the Islamic cultures had the codex almost from their beginning, and paper by the ninth century. It was from the Islamic Middle East that paper spread slowly to Europe and Byzantium (in the latter, paper was named after its source, "Baghdad"). Moreover, though Islamic communities often had in their midst both Jewish and Christian printing centers, print did not spread through Islamic nations until the late nineteenth century. For their part, Jewish communities do not seem to have adopted the codex until the ninth century, being until then identified, at least in the eyes of Christians, by their affinity for the scroll.[27]

This historical accounting, however inadequate, makes it hard to argue for some kind of simple technological determinism or a fundamental information imperative in human nature. Rather, it suggests that the spread of communication technology is subject to many forces. It is, after all, widely acknowledged that the codex spread in the West less on the back of its communicative or search capabilities, than as a mark of religious affiliation. It spread with Christianity because Christians used it to distinguish themselves from the scroll-using religions that came before it. Much like the iphone and the ipod, the codex was a cultural marker as much as an efficient device to provide access to information.

It would be wrong, of course, to deny that the codex became enmeshed in sets of practices that look increasingly information-centered and technology driven to us. But it is important not to separate those practices from a vast array of others that do not reduce so readily. In the West the codex was a religious instrument for a long time and its development as a technology for search, organization, and storage reflected changes in the way in which texts were used in that particular confession. Developments in Christian scholarship changed the appearance and use of the codex in the long and often underestimated period between its initial spread and development as the primary medium of print in the West. In particular, in a remarkable period from the eleventh to the fourteenth century, Christian scholars devised new textual and intertextual resources to further access, search, and reference. These advances might almost be thought of as paving the way for print. Driven in part by the spread of minuscule writing in both Western Europe and Byzantium, word divisions, paragraph markers, and punctuation began to break up the text itself into more accessible chunks. Paratextual apparatus also developed, including the increasingly sophisticated gloss, running heads, shoulder notes, the table of contents and the alphabetical index, and the page number. The printed book inherited all these, though some, like the page number and the shoulder note, only with difficulty.[28] Indeed, in the early period of print, search capability does seem to go backwards, suggesting that it was less of an imperative than scholars like Kilgour or Eisenstein imagine.

Mutability, reliability, and verification

In trying to understand changing search, we need to note that in the last centuries of the manuscript era in Western Europe, the social context of the book was changing too. Both production and consumption were leaving the controlled confines of the monastery for the wilder terrain of cities and universities. In the growing professions of the book trade new centers of production arose outside the enclosed scriptoria and new readers arose outside the cloistered library. It was more in these new hands than in the old monastic ones that the new tools for search described above developed. But to go beyond simple finding tools and to help searchers assess the worth of what was found, these new sites had to address again the tension – this time of their own making – that emerges when increasing mobility of texts and textual production threatens the stability or, in Latourian terms, immutability of the text. As book production and consumption spread, the threat came not so much from individual documents decaying, but in the variation introduced between versions of the "same" text by proliferating copies.

Openings for this kind of change and corruption were numerous. On the one hand, there was legitimate change. St. Bonaventure famously distinguished four kinds of copying. The lowest involved no more than verbatim repetition of an original, but higher levels of scribal practice permitted the addition of comments from other writers, and from the scribe himself, who ultimately is acknowledged as a new author.[29] On the other hand, there were illegitimate changes, some through incompetence, and some through different kinds of forgery and falsification. Even monasteries, as Clanchy shows, were forced to forge, sometimes producing false forgeries and sometimes true ones, a distinction that complicates the mix even further.[30]

In Western Christian culture in the centuries before print, Cavallo and Stock argue, the codex developed into an authoritative form at the same time as its centers of production were spreading and its audience was growing. The mutability that came with new places and processes of production challenged the book's potential authority. Mutability – in this case less within copies than among them – presents readers, and especially new readers, with a challenge. For if a reader goes to a book searching for new ideas but without a strong background in the domain, he or she is unlikely to be able to judge reliability.[31] A kind of market for intellectual lemons may well develop.[32] A retrospective view suggests that the conflicting challenges of making works findable and making what was found reliable resulted in moves, as they might be described today, to "free" information being countered by moves to restrain it. The world of books found various ways to do this.

Islamic tradition found one solution. It did not take books, in particular religious books, as autonomous. Rather books drew their authority from particular teachers, who in turn were warranted by a "golden chain" that connected them to Muhammad.[33] Elsewhere, books developed more inherent authority, provided not by the text on its own, but by supervening institutions. Again, Alexandria provides an early precedent. Zenodotus took it as part of his role as librarian to produce exemplary texts.[34] Later, the Christian church worked to standardize its texts and remove apocrypha of one sort or another. So doing, the church also spread the carolignian minuscule as a standard script.[35] And universities, first in Byzantium and later in Western Europe, also took responsibility for the textual integrity of celebrated works. In tenth-century China, where corruption resulting from ease of print and paper was directly contrasted to the reliability imputed to the immutability of stone, the National Academy took up the task of quality control.[36] A related two-step can be perceived with the advent of print in the West. As Johns has argued, the reliability of the text, even within editions, was not a function of print alone. Here as elsewhere the institutionalization of publishing acted as a centripetal force providing reliability to counteract the centrifugal tendencies that came with the increasing mobility introduced by the new technologies.[37] Censorship and later copyright were heavy constraints, but they were excused at the time, sometimes with justification, as ways to secure reliable copy.[38]

Encircling and uncircling

Such institutionalization helped conceptually to circumscribe the text within the book, which was in turn within an institution such as the library or similar system of authorization. As we have seen with *Gilgamesh*, combinations of material and institutional constraints, from cedar boxes to the library at Nineveh, are both brought to bear on the central texts of a society. This concept of circumscription is implicit in two important scholarly words. One is *encyclopedia*, which invokes an encircled body of knowledge essential to education. And the other is search itself, which like encyclopedia, is etymologically descended from classical words for a circle and whose roots suggest an encircled body of knowledge to be examined. Search, that is, demarcates not just the needle, but also the haystack. The idea of a corpus that can be encircled and searched implies (and simultaneously deprecates), of course, a secondary body that is excluded as false, forged, ephemera, and the like.[39] Such an idea is physically inscribed in some of our main institutions of learning, in particular, as Chartier points out, in the round reading rooms of major national libraries (from the old Bibliothèque Nationale in Paris and the old British Museum reading room in London, to the Library of Congress in Washington, and Asplund's great national library in Stockholm). These evoke the circles of established knowledge in which the learner can safely and reliably search.[40]

But, like the *salons des refusés* formed by artists that the official art exhibitions of Paris had rejected, such attempts to bound information inevitably engender attempts to break the bounds. It may be chance, but it is indicative that Wikipedia kept the pedia aspect of its source, but rejected the encircling or enclosing part. Wikipedia's vision is of open and unrestricted contributions. Symbolically, at least, this speaks to a desire for search not to be circumscribed, as it had been in the past, but to be ever more open.[41] As I have tried to suggest, this impetus is far from new. The path to openness may in fact be more cyclical than linear. Attempts to break out in the name of freedom lead in turn to attempts to constrain in the name of quality, which in turn lead to new breakouts. Another imprudent canter across changes in England towards the end of the seventeenth century allows me to sketch a set of prior profoundly important attempts in politics, in business, and in science to break established boundaries of search.

Habermas indicates the change in politics in his account of the development of a "public sphere".[42] The growing bourgeoisie came to believe that citizens, by shedding their particular, personal interests and entering a sphere of open debate, could make the best political decisions. The search for political solutions now turned not to the monarch for answers, but instead to free enquiry, rational debate, and the open exchange of information. This type of search could lead not to some preordained answer, but rather, as it did with the American revolution, to a conclusion that was previously unimagined and perhaps unimaginable – an answer that was in some ways an emergent property of the process of search itself. As such, search did not involve, as it does in Socratic dialogue, uncovering something the interlocutor knows already but is not aware of; and it did not involve, as it did in most scholastic or religious enquiry, returning to what had already been written and revealed. It involved finding what had hitherto been unknown and perhaps even unknowable.[43]

In the same period, the development of stock markets produced a comparable process in the realm of commerce. The search for the price of shares and by extension the value of companies created that price in the very practices of the exchange. Price in such conditions was hitherto unknowable; only within the economic activity of the market did it emerge. By extension, and in opposition to the mercantilists of the period, free-traders suggested that the worth of the nation as a whole could only be determined by openly trading rather than by hoarding (and counting) its gold reserves. Finally, seventeenth century science can be seen as rejecting deference to prior authority and developing a similar, open-ended kind of search. Galileo, Descartes, Boyle, Hooke, Huygens and the other early modern empirical scientists, to the dismay of figures from the pope to Hobbes, interrogated nature with odd devices and open-ended searches.

Science was no longer the province of scholastic figures with ancient books, but open enquiry unfettered by institutions and claims of expertise. Experience, as Chaucer's Wife of Bath memorably claimed, and not authority was the currency of scientific endeavour.

These extraordinary revolutions broke down many of the prior bounds of search and pointed to an open landscape, addressing desires for individual freedom and distaste for existing institutions and their hierarchies of knowledge. But the story did not end there. The public sphere, as Habermas noted, was transformed and subordinated to bourgeois interests. It took institutional innovation and experimentation in different kinds of democracy to maintain the very notion of openness, to which institutions had previously been thought to be anathema. Similarly, the developing markets and their open trade met their first global shocks with the South Sea Bubble and tulip mania. Like the public sphere, they came to rely on institutional boundaries that the idea of a free market and an open search for value still holds in contempt. Most markets continue to require institutional intervention and adjustment to ensure that prices are more open than fixed. And science, as Shapin and others have shown, slowly institutionalized as well.[44] Over time, the Royal Society and its remarkably open publication the *Philosophical Transactions* became increasingly closed.

While holding admirable aspirations to freedom and openness, politics, business, and science circled the wagons, limiting legitimate search to certain endeavors, certain methods, and certain types of questions, and ruling others out as unacceptable. Dissenting voices were spun off into the realm of alchemy, antiquarianism, cabalism, necromancy, and the like. Indeed it is noticeable that many of the major encircling institutions – from the modern newspaper, the Bank of England, and the Royal Society, to modern encyclopedias were in fact constructed around the time of – and it seems plausible to suggest in response to – these three revolutions in search. And much of the success of their searches was due to the constraints that bound them. It is unsurprising, then, that succeeding centuries mark new attempts to break restrictive bounds and new countermoves to reign in unstructured behavior. Inevitably, some of the new constraints are imposed by forces of reaction, like Catholicism's response to Galileo. But not all. Some involved the building of Weberian institutions to provide the very conditions for idealized Habermasian discourse, Hayekian markets, or open science in their search for answers.

Let me take one final example from a domain that developed many powerful search tools, analogue and digital, the law.[45] The common law is in many ways an archetypal open system that over time went closed with the development of statutory law. Yet even this process is not linear. Cycles of openness and closedness are evident, for example, in the development of law reports. These published the significant case law on which courts and litigants relied for precedent. At the beginning of the nineteenth century, new printing technologies and the resulting drop in the cost of publishing led to a bustling market for law reports. The Law Amendment Society noted at the time, "it has long been considered a practicable scheme for any barrister and bookseller who united together with a view to notoriety or profit, to add to the existing list of law report". This expansion, the *History and Origin of the Law Reports* noted in the mid-century, resulted from "applying the principle of competition to correct the evils of prolixity, delay, and expense incident to the [old] system of authorized reporting". The process might be described today as having "opened" law reporting, allowing the market to work and superior contributions rising to the top. But such markets for knowledge often work the other way. With proliferating reports and no institutional standards for reporting, lawyers and judges became increasingly worried about the reliability of the reports. While old constraints were broken, the change led to "new evils [that] created confusion and uncertainty in the law". Open competition, championed in the nineteenth century much as it is today, served the interests of individual lawyers and publishers in expanding the production of legal information, but made search and the assessment of what was found more and more problematic as it was "carried on without regard to the interests of the profession or public" and produced "perplexity in the administration of justice".[46] Trying to balance conflicting imperatives, the Law Amendment Society, a reforming organization, managed to institutionalize the system and rein in the proliferating reports without entirely stifling innovation in reporting. Such processes continue to be cyclical, however. New technology has opened the system again, and consequently forward-looking lawyers are beginning to sound much like their nineteenth century counterparts: "The almost universal view among judges in England is that too much, rather than too little, is reported".[47]

Beyond the 2 Gs

As we look at modern search tools, it is easy to believe that they are contributing to a historical march away from closed and restrictive institutions to democratic openness and that amassing more information, regardless of source, and running grep-like searches across it is inherently a good thing. From its beginnings in open source software, this new idea of openness has spread to contemporary aspects of politics, of markets, and of science, as well of cultural endeavor. To speak against it seems hopelessly reactionary. As I have tried to argue, attempts to impose structure are not always attempts to return us to the past. They are often (though again not always) attempts to control what has become, like the nineteenth-century law reports, unmanageable information, information that baffles search not because it is resistant to search algorithms, but because it is not structured in any openly accessible way, and hence its findings are inscrutable or unreliable for those who want to use them. It is easy to believe that new technology replaces old institutions. Google, it is often thought, will replace the library. But technologies and institutions are not the same thing. Technology alone is often incapable of imposing useful structure and to increase reliability, but requires complementary institutions that are open and available for public scrutiny. Thus a history of search, as I have tried to illustrate, looks less like a linear progression driven by an innate appetite for information foraging than a set of almost unfathomable cycles around closed and open structures.

Indeed, and I apologize to anyone who has come this far for saying this so late, we can see these cyclical movements without undertaking such a tortuous historical journey. Wikipedia, for example, which has exemplified for many the accrual of open, searchable, and reliable information about the world, has for some time been engaged in building structures. Its early contempt for credentials and expertise and its resistance to hierarchical exclusion has given way to an understanding that claimed experience is not necessarily better than earned authority. Indeed, Wikipedia itself has started to build an institutional structure through its foundation, which is inevitably imposing constraints on the project's openness.[48] Implicitly, the *encyclo* is returning to fence around the *pedia*. More intriguingly, Google has challenged Wikipedia with its Knol project, which pays far more deference to institutions and their role in the creation of knowledge, aggregation of information, and the hierarchical ordering of ideas. Meanwhile, in the face of uncertainty as to its quality, Google's own technology-driven library project is being corralled by the Hati Trust. In this case, attempts to make search more reliable are being tempered by one of the oldest of contemporary institutions, the university.[49]

Notes

1   The same, if my own practice is representative, may be true of the personal computer: tools like Apple's "Spotlight" and Google's "Desktop" search tools are making the old, hierarchical "desktop" ordering less important.
2   According to the *Netizens* anthology, "grep" stands for "global regular expression print", and was written by Ken Thompson as a search command for Version 4 Unix in November 1973. See Michael Hauben & Ronda Hauben, *Netizens: On the History and Impact of Usenet and the*

Internet (1995) chapter 9. Online: Available at http://www.columbia.edu/~hauben/project_book.html. Visited December 22, 2008.

3   "Yahoo" stands for "yet another hierarchical officious order", a phrase which sums up the antagonism towards hierarchy and order by even those who felt they depended upon it. See http://docs.yahoo.com/info/misc/history.html. Visited December 22, 2008.

4   For a critique of anti-institutional sentiment about the Internet, see Megan Finn, Daniel Kreiss, and Fred Turner, "The Iron Cage in the Network Society: Some Reminders from Max Weber for Web 2.0," in preparation.

5   Paul Otlet, International Organization and *Dissemination of Knowledge: Selected Essays of Paul Otlet* (New York: Elsevier, 1990), quotation at p. 17; William Mitchell *City of Bits*: Space, Place and the Infobahn (Boston: MIT Press, 1996).

6   In a similar vein, the poet Kipling asked "What should they know of England, who only England know?" See Rudyard Kipling, "The English Flag" in *Writings in Prose and Verse* (New York: Charles Scribner, 1899).

7   Frederick G. Kilgour, *The Evolution of the Book* (New York: OUP, 1998), quotation at p. 5. See also "The need for readily available information, which had been steadily rising, was accelerated by the advent of Christianity", *ibid* p. 48.

8   See http://www.google.com/intl/en/corporate/, visited December 22, 2008.

9   John Battelle, *The Search: How Google and Its Rivals Rewrote the Rules of Business and Transformed Our Culture* (New York: Portfolio, 2005), chapter 1.

10 Of course, not all storage is done with later search or consultation in mind. The Hebraic *Genizah* manuscripts, for example, were stored simply to prevent the written name of God from being destroyed. Equally, storage is not always done with search primarily in mind. JSTOR, the online database of academic journals, was envisaged to reduce storage costs for libraries. It has become such a powerful resource for searching, however, that its name now seems almost inappropriate. See Roger C Schonfeld, JSTOR: A *History* (Princeton: Princeton University Press, 2003).

11 The *Epic of Gilgamesh*, trans. Andrew George (London: Penguin, 2003). The paraphernalia were, of course, more indications of hierarchy and canonization – tools of assessment rather than tools for search per se.

12 Sites like Ebla would more easily be called archives rather than libraries today, but as Clanchy reminds us, the distinction is a modern one. M.T. Clanchy, *From Memory to Written Record*: England 1066-1307 (Oxford: Blackwell, 1993).

13 For my account of early libraries, I am particularly dependent on Lionel Casson, *Libraries in the Ancient World* (New Haven: Yale University Press, 2001). Even modern hierarchical orders have long roots. The Library of Congress system, widely used in the United States, is based on the system used by Thomas Jefferson, who donated his private library to the country. Jefferson's library was in turn based on a system developed in the seventeenth century by Francis Bacon. See Francis Miksa, "The Development of Classification at the Library of Congress" Occasional Paper 164, University of Illinois, Graduate School of Library and Information Science, Champagne-Urbana, 1984.

14 The great early collections were built not only by lavish patronage of arts and science, but also by an enduring library tradition of conquest, pillage, and other kinds of forced appropriation. The emissaries sent out to track down acquisitions by fair means or foul are perhaps early antecedents of Google's crawlers, and the libraries, such as those of Babylon and Pergamum, dissolved under this kind of appropriation, the forerunners of dead links.

15 Armando Petrucci, *Public Lettering: Script, Power, and Culture* (Chicago: University of Chicago Press, 1993)

16 Bruno Latour, "Visualization and Cognition: Thinking with Eyes and Hands", *Knowledge and Society: Studies in the Sociology of Culture Past and Present* 6 (1986): 1-40.
17 Though probably not, as is usually assumed, in the famous fire. See James Raven, ed. *Lost Libraries: The Destruction of Great Book Collections Since Antiquity* (London: Palgrave, 2004).
18 It is always tempting to argue that the frailty of new kinds of support, such as for example digital documents, will prevent them supplanting the old. Trithemius makes such an argument, using the frailty of paper to suggest that print will not be able to compete with manuscript. In fact, despite the need for an immutable text, lability often trumps rigidity in such confrontations. See Johannes Trithemius, *In Praise of Scribes*, trans. R. Behrendt (Lawrence, KA: Coronado Press 1974), first published 1492.
19 Different traditions made different assessments of paper's frailties. Islamic bureaucrats adopted paper quite early, whereas European chanceries were more suspicious and slow to adapt. See Pierre-Marc de Biasi & Karine Douplitzky, *Le Saga du Papier* (Paris: Adam Biro, 2002) for Islamic enthusiasm, Lucien Febvre & Henri-Jean Martin, *The Coming of the Book: The Impact of Printing*, 1450-1800 (London: Verso, 1984) for Western hesitation.
20 These gaps usually signal that no major new technology was introduced, which, in technologically determined stories, means that nothing of interest occurred. Such accounts have to leap from paper to print and from print to the steam press, the camera, or the telegraph. For the technologically driven, the twelfth or the eighteenth century, for example, seem to be periods in which nothing happened.
21 This is a regular feature of accounts that stress the advances of the new. Hence Grafton complains of Elizabeth Eisenstein belittling scribal culture in order to enlarge the effects of print. Anthony Grafton, "The Importance of Being Printed", Journal of Interdisciplinary History 11 (2) (1980): 265-286.
22 Apart from colophons and sillyboi and the developments of Zenodotus and Callimachus, the scroll introduced markers for the beginning and end of significant textual chunks (*incipits* and *explicits*) and other important internal features.
23 For the importance of marginalia, see William H Sherman, *Used Books: Marking Readers in Renaissance England* (Philadelphia: University of Pennsylvania, 2008).
24 Along with works specifically cited, the following sections borrow extensively from Thomas Francis Carter, *The Invention of Printing in China and its Spread Westward*, 2d edition, ed. L. Carrington Goodrich, (New York: Roland Press, 1955); Guiglielmo Cavallo, "Du Volumen au Codex: La Lecture dans le Monde Romain", in Guiglielmo Cavallo & Roger Chartier, eds., *Histoire de la Lecture dans le Monde Occidental* (Paris: Éditions du Seuil, 1997), pp. 47-78; Roger Chartier, *The Order of Books: Readers, Authors, and Libraries in Europe between the Fourteenth and Eighteenth Centuries* (Stanford: Stanford University Press, 1994); Simon Eliot & Jonathan Rose, eds., *A Companion to the History of the Book* (Oxford: Blackwell, 2008); Alexandra Gillespie, *Print Culture and the Medieval Author: Chaucer, Lydgate, and Their Books*, 1473-1557 (Oxford: Oxford University Press, 2006); William A. Graham, "Traditionalism in Islam: An Essay in Interpretation", *Journal of Interdisciplinary History* 23(3)(1993): 495-522; Paul Lemerle, *Le Premier Humanisme Byzantin: Notes et Remarques sur Enseignement et Culture à Byzance des Origines au Xe Siècle* (Paris: Presse Universitaires de France, 1971); *Library of Congress, Papermaking: Art and Craft* (Washington, DC: Library of Congress, 1968); Malcolm Parkes, "The Influence of the Concepts of *Ordinatio* and *Compilatio* on the Development of the Book", in J.J.G. Alexander & M.T. Gibson, eds., *Medieval Learning and Literature: Essays Presented to R.W. Hunt* (Oxford: Oxford University Press, 1976), pp. 115-141; Francis Robinson, "Technology and Religious Change: Islam and the Impact of Print", *Modern Asian Studies* 27(1)(1993): 229-51.
25 This is a hybrid between the scroll and the codex, whereby pages fold on both their front edge

and back edge, rather like a paper blind, so that, though such books fold flat like the codex, when open they are continuous like a scroll.

26 C.A Bayly, *Empire and Information: Intelligence Gathering and Social Communication in India, 1780-1870* (Cambridge: Cambridge University Press, 1998), quotation at p. 239.
27 Emile G.L. Schrijver, "The Hebraic Book" in Eliot & Rose, *A Companion*, pp: 153-164; Lemerle, *Premiere Humanisme*, Clanchy, *Memory*.
28 Margaret M. Smith, "Printed Foliation: Forerunner to Printed Page-Numbers", *Gutenberg-Jahrbuch* 63(1988): 54-70.
29 Gerald Bruns, "The Originality of Texts in a Manuscript Culture", *Comparative Literature* 32(2)(1980): 113-129.
30 Guglielmo Cavallo, "Du Volumen au Codex"; Brian Stock, *The Implications of Literacy: Written Language and Models of Interpretation in the Eleventh and Twelfth Centuries* (Princeton: Princeton University Press, 1983). The varied practices of this period led in good part to the development of the skills of document-fraud detection known as diplomatics and the remarkable work of Mabillon.
31 This is a central challenge presented in the Plato's *Meno* and *Charmides*.
32 George A. Akerlof, "The Market for Lemons: Quality, Uncertainty, and the Market Mechanism", *Quarterly Journal of Economics* 84(1970): 488-500. The book world Johns describes would seem to embrace several such markets. See Adrian Johns, *The Nature of the Book: Print and Knowledge in the Making* (Chicago: University of Chicago Press, 1998).
33 Consequently, in Islamic cultures, biographies establishing personal connection were a particularly important form, whereas in the West the provenance-establishing bibliography was perhaps more significant. Michael Albin, "The Islamic Book" in Eliot & Rose, *A Companion*, pp: 165-176.
34 I have argued elsewhere that libraries have more to do with quality than they usually own to. See Paul Duguid, "Inheritance or Loss: A Brief Survey of Google Books", *First Monday* 12(8) 2007.
35 Michelle P. Brown, "The Triumph of the Codex: The Manuscript Book before 1100" in Eliot & Rose, A Companion, pp: 179-193
36 Carter quotes one such argument:

> During the Han dynasty, Confucian scholars were honored and the Classics were cut in stone. ... In T'ang times also stone inscriptions containing the text of the Classics were made in the Imperial School. ... We have seen, however, men from Wu and Shu who sold books that were printed from blocks of wood. There were many different texts, but there were among them no orthodox Classics. If the Classics could be revised and thus cut in wood and published, it would be a very great boon to the study of literature.
>
> (Carter, *Invention*, p. 70)

37 Some early printers signed their output as an attempt to indicate authenticity. Some print shops allied themselves with scholars. See Johns, *Nature of the Book*; Elizabeth Eisenstein, *The Printing Revolution in Early Modern Europe* (Cambridge, UK: Cambridge University Press, 1983). For the complex task of quality assurance in early publishing, see Paul Duguid, "Brands in Chains", in Paul Duguid & Teresa da Silva Lopes, *Trademarks, Brands, and Competitiveness* (London: Routledge, forthcoming 2009).
38 Loewenstein sees this as a "founding myth" of intellectual property systems, but like most myths it contained a grain of truth. Joseph Loewenstein, *The Author's Due: Printing and the Prehistory*

of Copyright (Chicago: University of Chicago Press, 2002), quotation at p. 252. For the connection between early forms of copyright and control in France and their relation to the reliability of the text see Mark Rose, *Authors and Owners: The Invention of Copyright* (Cambridge, MA: Harvard University Press, 1993) and Elizabeth Armstrong, *Before Copyright: The French Book-Privilege System 1498-1526* (Cambridge: Cambridge University Press, 1999).

39 Such an idea lies behind Caliph Omar's famous edict that if what a book says is not already in the Qu'ran, then it is heretical and the book must be rejected; and if what it says is already in the Qu'ran, then the book is redundant and can be rejected. Phrases like "useful knowledge" or "useful information", which are endemic in discussions of collections of one sort or another, similarly acknowledge the idea of boundedness. What is not useful is left beyond the pale of institutions and collections.

40 Chartier, *Order*. This argument owes much to my colleague Geoffrey Nunberg's insights into the place of information.

41 Elsewhere, I have argued that this openness loses for Wikipedia some of the useful resources that come from boundedness. See Paul Duguid, "Limits of Self-Organization: Peer Production and the 'Laws of Quality'", *First Monday* 11(10) 2006.

42 Jürgen Habermas, *The Structural Transformation of the Public Sphere: An Inquiry into a Category of Bourgeois Society* (Cambridge, MA: MIT Press, 1989). Habermas' account is undoubtedly idealized and his periodization problematic (see, for example, Craig Calhoun, ed. *Habermas and the Public Sphere* (Cambridge, MA: MIT Press, 1996)), but his claim that a significant change in politics and political debate took place around this time remains reasonable.

43 In this regard, search and learning can be ambiguous in similar ways. Both can point to what the searcher/learner did not know before but others did, or to what no one knew before.

44 Steven Shapin, *A Social History of Truth: Civility and Science in Seventeenth-Century England* (Chicago: University of Chicago Press, 1995).

45 Mead Data, for example, forerunner of LexisNexis, played an important role in the history of modern search.

46 W.T.S. Daniel, *The History and Origin of the Law Reports: Together with a Compilation of Various Documents Shewing the Progress and Result of Proceedings ...* (London: W. Clowes & Sons, 1884), quotations pp 23-4.

47 H.W. Arthurs, "A Lot of Knowledge is a Dangerous Thing: Will the Legal Professions Survive the Knowledge Explosion?", *Dalhousie Law Journal* 18(2) (1995): 295.

48 I'm grateful to Mayo Fuster Morell for conversations that have helped me understand tensions around the Wikimedia Foundation.

49 Even open source software, the exemplar of the new spirit of openness, turns out not to be the linear example of the closed going open after all. A good deal of software was quite open by contemporary standards in the 1950s before corporations enclosed it. And much of what is open now is held open by the institutions of the law (which protects "copyleft"), by the self-interest of quite hierarchical organizations from Red Hat to Sun and IBM, and by the university. For software that was open before it was closed, see Michael Schwarz & Yuri Takhteyev, "Half a Century of Public Software Institutions", in preparation.

The Library in the Information Age
6000 Years of Script

Robert Darnton[1]

Information is exploding so furiously around us and information technology is changing at such bewildering speed that we face a fundamental problem: How to orient ourselves in the new landscape? What, for example, will become of research libraries in the face of technological marvels such as Google?

How to make sense of it all? I have no answer to that problem, but I can suggest an approach to it: look at the history of the ways information has been communicated. Simplifying things radically, you could say that there have been four fundamental changes in information technology since humans learned to speak.

Somewhere, around 4000 BC, humans learned to write. Egyptian hieroglyphs go back to about 3200 BC, alphabetical writing to 1000 BC. According to scholars like Jack Goody, the invention of writing was the most important technological breakthrough in the history of humanity. It transformed mankind's relation to the past and opened a way for the emergence of the book as a force in history.

The history of books led to a second technological shift when the codex replaced the scroll sometime soon after the beginning of the Christian era. By the third century AD, the codex – that is, books with pages that you turn as opposed to scrolls that you roll – became crucial to the spread of Christianity. It transformed the experience of reading: the page emerged as a unit of perception, and readers were able to leaf through a clearly articulated text, one that eventually included differentiated words (that is, words separated by spaces), paragraphs, and chapters, along with tables of contents, indexes, and other reader's aids.

The codex, in turn, was transformed by the invention of printing with movable type in the 1450s. To be sure, the Chinese developed movable type around 1045 and the Koreans used metal characters rather than wooden blocks around 1230. But Gutenberg's invention, unlike those of the Far East, spread like wildfire, bringing the book within the reach of ever-widening circles of readers. The technology of printing did not change for nearly four centuries, but the reading public grew larger and larger, thanks to improvements in literacy, education, and access to the printed word. Pamphlets and newspapers, printed by steam-driven presses on paper made from wood pulp rather than rags, extended the process of democratization so that a mass reading public came into existence during the second half of the nineteenth century.

The fourth great change, electronic communication, took place yesterday, or the day before, depending on how you measure it. The Internet dates from 1974, at least as a term. It developed from ARPANET, which went back to 1969, and from earlier experiments in communication among networks of computers. The Web began as a means of communication among physicists in 1981. Web sites and search engines became common in the mid-1990s. And from that point everyone knows the succession of brand names that have made electronic communication an everyday experience: Web browsers such as Netscape, Internet Explorer, Safari, and search engines such as Yahoo and Google, the latter founded in 1998.

When strung out in this manner, the pace of change seems breathtaking: from writing to the codex, 4,300 years; from the codex to movable type, 1,150 years; from movable type to the Internet, 524 years; from the Internet to search engines, nineteen years; from search engines to Google's algorithmic relevance ranking, seven years; and who knows what is just around the corner or coming out the pipeline?

Each change in the technology has transformed the information landscape, and the speed-up has continued at such a rate as to seem both unstoppable and incomprehensible. In the long view – what French historians call *la longue durée* – the general picture looks quite clear – or, rather, dizzying. But by aligning the facts in this manner, I have made them lead to an excessively dramatic conclusion. Historians, American as well as French, often play such tricks. By rearranging the evidence, it is possible to arrive at a different picture, one that emphasizes continuity instead of change. The continuity I have in mind has to do with the nature of information itself or, to put it differently, the inherent instability of texts. In place of the long-term view of technological transformations, which underlies the common notion that we have just entered a new era, the information age, I want to argue that every age was an age of information, each in its own way, and that information has always been unstable.

Let's begin with the Internet and work backward in time. More than a million blogs have emerged during the last few years. They have given rise to a rich lore of anecdotes about the spread of misinformation, some of which sound like urban myths. But I believe the following story is true, though I can't vouch for its accuracy, having picked it up from the Internet myself. As a spoof, a satirical newspaper, The Onion, put it out that an architect had created a new kind of building in Washington, D.C., one with a convertible dome. On sunny days, you push a button, the dome rolls back, and it looks like a football stadium. On rainy days it looks like the Capitol building. The story traveled from Web site to Web site until it arrived in China, where it was printed in the Beijing Evening News. Then it was taken up by the Los Angeles Times, the San Francisco Chronicle, Reuters, CNN, Wired.com, and countless blogs as a story about the Chinese view of the United States: they think we live in convertible buildings, just as we drive around in convertible cars.

Other stories about blogging point to the same conclusion: blogs create news, and news can take the form of a textual reality that trumps the reality under our noses. Today many reporters spend more time tracking blogs than they do checking out traditional sources such as the spokespersons of public authorities. News in the information age has broken loose from its conventional moorings, creating possibilities of misinformation on a global scale. We live in a time of unprecedented accessibility to information that is increasingly unreliable. Or do we?

I would argue that news has always been an artifact and that it never corresponded exactly to what actually happened. We take today's front page as a mirror of yesterday's events, but it was made up yesterday evening – literally, by "make-up" editors, who designed page one according to arbitrary conventions: lead story on the far right column, off-lead on the left, soft news inside or below the fold, features set off by special kinds of headlines. Typographical design orients the reader and shapes the meaning of the news. News itself takes the form of narratives composed by professionals according to conventions that they picked up in the course of their training – the "inverted pyramid" mode of exposition, the "color" lead, the code for "high" and "the highest" sources, and so on. News is not what happened but a story about what happened.

Of course, many reporters do their best to be accurate, but they must conform to the conventions of their craft, and there is always slippage between their choice of words and the nature of an event as experienced or perceived by others. Ask anyone involved in a reported happening. They will tell you that they did not recognize themselves or the event in the story that appeared in the paper. Sophisticated readers in the Soviet Union learned to distrust everything that appeared in Pravda and even to take nonappearances as a sign of something going on. On August 31, 1980, when Lech Walesa signed the agreement with the Polish government that created Solidarity as an independent trade union, the Polish people refused at first to believe it, not because the news failed to reach them but because it was reported on the state-controlled television.

I used to be a newspaper reporter myself. I got my basic training as a college kid covering police headquarters in Newark in 1959. Although I had worked on school newspapers, I did not know what news was – that is, what events would make a story and what combination of words would make it into print after passing muster with the night city editor. When events reached headquarters, they normally took the form of "squeal sheets" or typed reports of calls received at the central switchboard. Squeal sheets concerned everything from stray dogs to murders, and they accumulated at a rate of a dozen every half hour. My job was to collect them from a lieutenant on the second floor, go through them for anything that might be news, and announce the potential news to the veteran reporters from a dozen papers playing poker in the press room on the ground floor. The poker game acted as a filter for the news. One of the reporters would say if something I selected would be worth checking out. I did the checking, usually by phone calls to key offices like the homicide squad. If the information was good enough, I would tell the poker game, whose members would phone it in to their city desks. But it had to be really good – that is, what ordinary people would consider bad – to warrant interrupting the never-ending game. Poker was everyone's main interest – everyone but me: I could not afford to play (cards cost a dollar ante, a lot of money in those days), and I needed to develop a nose for news.

I soon learned to disregard DOAs (dead on arrival, meaning ordinary deaths) and robberies of gas stations, but it took time for me to spot something really "good", like a holdup in a respectable store or a water main break at a central location. One day I found a squeal sheet that was so good – it combined rape and murder – that I went straight to the homicide squad instead of reporting first to the poker game. When I showed it to the lieutenant on duty, he looked at me in disgust: "Don't you see this, kid?" he said, pointing to a B in parentheses after the names of the victim and the suspect. Only then did I notice that every name was followed by a B or a W. I did not know that crimes involving black people did not qualify as news.

Having learned to write news, I now distrust newspapers as a source of information, and I am often surprised by historians who take them as primary sources for knowing what really happened. I think newspapers should be read for information about how contemporaries construed events, rather than for reliable knowledge of events themselves. A study of news during the American Revolution by a graduate student of mine, Will Slauter, provides an example. Will followed accounts of Washington's defeat at the Battle of Brandywine as it was refracted in the American and European press. In the eighteenth century, news normally took the form of isolated paragraphs rather than "stories" as we know them now and newspapers lifted most of their paragraphs from each other, adding new material picked up from gossips in coffeehouses or ship captains returning from voyages. A loyalist New York newspaper printed the first news of Brandywine with a letter from Washington informing Congress that he had been forced to retreat before the British forces under General William Howe. A copy of the paper traveled by ship, passing from New York to Halifax, Glasgow, and Edinburgh, where the paragraph and the letter were reprinted in a local newspaper.

The Edinburgh reprints were then reprinted in several London papers, each time undergoing subtle changes. The changes were important, because speculators were betting huge sums on the course of the American war, while bears were battling bulls on the Stock Exchange, and the government was about to present a budget to Parliament, where the pro-American opposition was threatening to overthrow the ministry of Lord North. At a distance of three thousand miles and four to six weeks of travel by ship, events in America were crucial for the resolution of this financial and political crisis.

What had actually happened? Londoners had learned to mistrust their newspapers, which frequently distorted the news as they lifted paragraphs from each other. That the original paragraph came from a loyalist American paper made it suspect to the reading public. Its roundabout route made it look even more doubtful, for why would Washington announce his own defeat, while Howe had not yet claimed victory in a dispatch sent directly from Philadelphia, near the scene of the action? Moreover, some reports noted that Lafayette had been wounded in the battle, an impossibility to British readers, who believed (wrongly from earlier, inaccurate reports) that Lafayette was far away from Brandywine, fighting against General John Burgoyne near Canada.

Finally, close readings of Washington's letter revealed stylistic touches that could not have come from the pen of a general. One – the use of "arraying" instead of "arranging" troops – later turned out to be a typographical error. Many Londoners therefore concluded that the report was a fraud, designed to promote the interests of the bull speculators and the Tory politicians – all the more so as the press coverage became increasingly inflated through the process of plagiarism. Some London papers claimed that the minor defeat had been a major catastrophe for the Americans, one that had ended with the annihilation of the rebel army and the death of Washington himself. (In fact, he was reported dead four times during the coverage of the war, and the London press declared Benedict Arnold dead twenty-six times.)

Le Courrier de l'Europe, a French newspaper produced in London, printed a translated digest of the English reports with a note warning that they probably were false. This version of the event passed through a dozen French papers produced in the Low Countries, the Rhineland, Switzerland, and France itself. By the time it arrived in Versailles, the news of Washington's defeat had been completely discounted. The comte de Vergennes, France's foreign minister, therefore continued to favor military intervention on the side of the Americans. And in London, when Howe's report of his victory finally arrived after a long delay (he had unaccountably neglected to write for two weeks), it was eclipsed by the more spectacular news of Burgoyne's defeat at Saratoga. So the defeat at Brandywine turned into a case of miswritten and misread news – a media non-event whose meaning was determined by the process of its transmission, like the blogging about the convertible dome and the filtering of crime reports in Newark's police headquarters.

Information has never been stable. That may be a truism, but it bears pondering. It could serve as a corrective to the belief that the speedup in technological change has catapulted us into a new age, in which information has spun completely out of control. I would argue that the new information technology should force us to rethink the notion of information itself. It should not be understood as if it took the form of hard facts or nuggets of reality ready to be quarried out of newspapers, archives, and libraries, but rather as messages that are constantly being reshaped in the process of transmission. Instead of firmly fixed documents, we must deal with multiple, mutable texts. By studying them skeptically on our computer screens, we can learn how to read our daily newspaper more effectively – and even how to appreciate old books.

Bibliographers came around to this view long before the Internet. Sir Walter Greg developed it at the end of the nineteenth century, and Donald McKenzie perfected it at the end of the twentieth century. Their work provides an answer to the questions raised by bloggers, Googlers, and other enthusiasts of the World Wide Web: Why save more than one copy of a book? Why spend large sums to purchase first editions? Aren't rare book collections doomed to obsolescence now that everything will be available on the Internet?

Unbelievers used to dismiss Henry Clay Folger's determination to accumulate copies of the First Folio edition of Shakespeare as the mania of a crank. The First Folio, published in 1623, seven years after Shakespeare's death, contained the earliest collection of his plays, but most collectors assumed that one copy would be enough for any research library. When Folger's collection grew beyond three dozen copies, his friends scoffed at him as Forty Folio Folger. Since then, however, bibliographers have mined that collection for crucial information, not only for editing the plays but also for performing them.

They have demonstrated that eighteen of the thirty-six plays in the First Folio had never before been printed. Four were known earlier only from faulty copies known as "bad" quartos – booklets of individual plays printed during

Shakespeare's lifetime, often by unscrupulous publishers using corrupted versions of the texts. Twelve were reprinted in modified form from relatively good quartos; and only two were reprinted without change from earlier quarto editions. Since none of Shakespeare's manuscripts has survived, differences between these texts can be crucial in determining what he wrote. But the First Folio cannot simply be compared with the quartos, because every copy of the Folio is different from every other copy. While being printed in Isaac Jaggard's shop in 1622 and 1623, the book went through three very different issues. Some copies lacked Troilus and Cressida, some included a complete Troilus, and some had the main text of Troilus but without its prologue and with a crossed-out ending to Romeo and Juliet on the reverse side of the leaf containing Troilus's first scene.

The differences were compounded by at least one hundred stop-press corrections and by the peculiar practices of at least nine compositors who set the copy while also working on other jobs – and occasionally abandoning Shakespeare to an incompetent teenage apprentice. By arguing from the variations in the texts, bibliographers like Charlton Hinman and Peter Blayney have reconstructed the production process and thus arrived at convincing conclusions about the most important works in the English language. This painstaking scholarship could not have been done without Mr. Folger's Folios.

Of course, Shakespeare is a special case. But textual stability never existed in the pre-Internet eras. The most widely diffused edition of Diderot's Encyclopédie in eighteenth-century France contained hundreds of pages that did not exist in the original edition. Its editor was a clergyman who padded the text with excerpts from a sermon by his bishop in order to win the bishop's patronage. Voltaire considered the Encyclopédie so imperfect that he designed his last great work, Questions sur l'Encyclopédie, as a nine-volume sequel to it. In order to spice up his text and to increase its diffusion, he collaborated with pirates behind the back of his own publisher, adding passages to the pirated editions.

In fact, Voltaire toyed with his texts so much that booksellers complained. As soon as they sold one edition of a work, another would appear, featuring additions and corrections by the author. Their customers protested. Some even said that they would not buy an edition of Voltaire's complete works – and there were many, each different from the others – until he died, an event eagerly anticipated by retailers throughout the book trade.

Piracy was so pervasive in early modern Europe that best-sellers could not be blockbusters as they are today. Instead of being produced in huge numbers by one publisher, they were printed simultaneously in many small editions by many publishers, each racing to make the most of a market unconstrained by copyright. Few pirates attempted to produce accurate counterfeits of the original editions. They abridged, expanded, and reworked texts as they pleased, without worrying about the authors' intentions. They behaved as deconstructionists *avant la lettre*.

Instability of text

The issue of textual stability leads to the general question about the role of research libraries in the age of the Internet. I cannot pretend to offer easy answers, but I would like to put the question in perspective by discussing two views of the library, which I would describe as grand illusions – grand and partly true.

To students in the 1950s, libraries looked like citadels of learning. Knowledge came packaged between hard covers, and a great library seemed to contain all of it. To climb the steps of the New York Public Library, past the stone lions guarding its entrance and into the monumental reading room on the third floor, was to enter a world that included everything known. The knowledge came ordered into standard categories which could be pursued through a card catalog and into the pages of the books. In colleges everywhere the library stood at the center of the campus. It was the most important building, a temple set off by classical columns, where one read in silence: no noise, no food, no disturbances beyond a furtive glance at a potential date bent over a book in quiet contemplation.

Students today still respect their libraries, but reading rooms are nearly empty on some campuses. In order to entice the students back, some librarians offer them armchairs for lounging and chatting, even drinks and snacks, never mind about the crumbs. Modern or postmodern students do most of their research at computers in their rooms. To them, knowledge comes online, not in libraries. They know that libraries could never contain it all within their walls, because information is endless, extending everywhere on the Internet, and to find it one needs a search engine, not a card catalog. But this, too, may be a grand illusion – or, to put it positively, there is something to be said for both visions, the library as a citadel and the Internet as open space. We have come to the problems posed by *Google Book Search*.

In 2006 Google signed agreements with five great research libraries – the New York Public, Harvard, Michigan, Stanford, and Oxford's Bodleian – to digitize their books. Books in copyright posed a problem, which soon was compounded by lawsuits from publishers and authors. But putting that aside, the Google proposal seemed to offer a way to make all book learning available to all people, or at least those privileged enough to have access to the World Wide Web. It promised to be the ultimate stage in the democratization of knowledge set in motion by the invention of writing, the codex, movable type, and the Internet.

Now, I speak as a Google enthusiast. I believe *Google Book Search* really will make book learning accessible on a new, worldwide scale, despite the great digital divide that separates the poor from the computerized. It also will open up possibilities for research involving vast quantities of data, which could never be mastered without digitization. As an example of what the future holds, I would cite the Electronic Enlightenment, a project sponsored by the Voltaire Foundation of Oxford. By digitizing the correspondence of Voltaire, Rousseau, Franklin, and Jefferson – about two hundred volumes in superb, scholarly editions – it will, in effect, recreate the transatlantic republic of letters from the eighteenth century.

The letters of many other philosophers, from Locke and Bayle to Bentham and Bernardin de Saint-Pierre, will be integrated into this database, so that scholars will be able to trace references to individuals, books, and ideas throughout the entire network of correspondence that undergirded the Enlightenment. Many other such projects – notably American Memory sponsored by the Library of Congress[2] and the Valley of the Shadow created at the University of Virginia[3] – have demonstrated the feasibility and usefulness of databases on this scale. But their success does not prove that *Google Book Search*, the largest undertaking of them all, will make research libraries obsolete. On the contrary, Google will make them more important than ever. To support this view, I would like to organize my argument around eight points.

1. According to the most utopian claim of the Googlers, Google can put virtually all printed books on-line. That claim is misleading, and it raises the danger of creating false consciousness, because it may lull us into neglecting our libraries. What percentage of the books in the United States – never mind the rest of the world – will be digitized by Google: 75 percent? 50 percent? 25 percent? Even if the figure is 90 percent, the residual, nondigitized books could be important. I recently discovered an extraordinary libertine novel, *Les Bohémiens*, by an unknown author, the Marquis de Pelleport, who wrote it in the Bastille at the same time that the Marquis de Sade was writing his novels in a nearby cell. I think that Pelleport's book, published in 1790, is far better than anything Sade produced; and whatever its aesthetic merits, it reveals a great deal about the condition of writers in pre-Revolutionary France. Yet only six copies of it exist, as far as I can tell, none of them available on the Internet.[4] (The Library of Congress, which has a copy, has not opened its holdings to Google.)

    If Google missed this book, and other books like it, the researcher who relied on Google would never be able to locate certain works of great importance. The criteria of importance change from generation to generation, so we cannot know what will matter to our descendants. They may learn a lot from studying our Harlequin novels or computer manuals or telephone books. Literary scholars and historians today depend heavily on research in almanacs, chapbooks, and other kinds of "popular" literature, yet few of those works from the seventeenth and eighteenth centuries have survived. They were printed on cheap paper, sold in flimsy covers, read to pieces, and ignored by collectors and librarians who did not consider them "literature". A researcher in Trinity College, Dublin recently discovered a drawer full of forgotten ballad books, each one the only copy in existence, each priceless in the eyes of the modern scholar, though it had seemed worthless two centuries ago.

2. Although Google pursued an intelligent strategy by signing up five great libraries, their combined holdings will not come close to exhausting the stock of books in the United States. Contrary to what one might expect, there is little redundancy in the holdings of the five libraries: 60 percent of the books being digitized by Google exist in only one of them. There are about 543 million volumes in the research libraries of the United States. Google reportedly set its initial goal of digitizing at 15 million. As Google signs up more libraries – at last count, twenty-eight are participating in *Google Book Search* – the representativeness of its digitized database will improve. But it has not yet ventured into special collections, where the rarest works are to be found. And of course the totality of world literature – all the books in all the languages of the world – lies far beyond Google's capacity to digitize.

3. Although it is to be hoped that the publishers, authors, and Google will settle their dispute, it is difficult to see how copyright will cease to pose a problem. According to the copyright law of 1976 and the copyright extension law of 1998, most books published after 1923 are currently covered by copyright, and copyright now extends to the life of the author plus seventy years. For books in the public domain, Google probably will allow readers to view the full text and print every page. For books under copyright, however, Google will probably display only a few lines at a time, which it claims is legal under fair use.

Google may persuade the publishers and authors to surrender their claims to books published between 1923 and the recent past, but will it get them to modify their copyrights in the present and future? In 2006, 291,920 new titles were published in the United States, and the number of new books in print has increased nearly every year for the last decade, despite the spread of electronic publishing. How can Google keep up with current

production while at the same time digitizing all the books accumulated over the centuries? Better to increase the acquisitions of our research libraries than to trust Google to preserve future books for the benefit of future generations. Google defines its mission as the communication of information – right now, today; it does not commit itself to conserving texts indefinitely.
4. Companies decline rapidly in the fast-changing environment of electronic technology. Google may disappear or be eclipsed by an even greater technology, which could make its database as outdated and inaccessible as many of our old floppy disks and CD-ROMs. Electronic enterprises come and go. Research libraries last for centuries. Better to fortify them than to declare them obsolete, because obsolescence is built into the electronic media.
5. Google will make mistakes. Despite its concern for quality and quality control, it will miss books, skip pages, blur images, and fail in many ways to reproduce texts perfectly. Once we believed that microfilm would solve the problem of preserving texts. Now we know better.
6. As in the case of microfilm, there is no guarantee that Google's copies will last. Bits become degraded over time. Documents may get lost in cyberspace, owing to the obsolescence of the medium in which they are encoded. Hardware and software become extinct at a distressing rate. Unless the vexatious problem of digital preservation is solved, all texts "born digital" belong to an endangered species. The obsession with developing new media has inhibited efforts to preserve the old. We have lost 80 percent of all silent films and 50 percent of all films made before World War II. Nothing preserves texts better than ink imbedded in paper, especially paper manufactured before the nineteenth century, except texts written on parchment or engraved in stone. The best preservation system ever invented was the old-fashioned, pre-modern book.
7. Google plans to digitize many versions of each book, taking whatever it gets as the copies appear, assembly-line fashion, from the shelves; but will it make all of them available? If so, which one will it put at the top of its search list? Ordinary readers could get lost while searching among thousands of different editions of Shakespeare's plays, so they will depend on the editions that Google makes most easily accessible. Will Google determine its relevance ranking of books in the same way that it ranks references to everything else, from toothpaste to movie stars? It now has a secret algorithm to rank Web pages according to the frequency of use among the pages linked to them, and presumably it will come up with some such algorithm in order to rank the demand for books. But nothing suggests that it will take account of the standards prescribed by bibliographers, such as the first edition to appear in print or the edition that corresponds most closely to the expressed intention of the author.

Google employs hundreds, perhaps thousands of engineers but, as far as I know, not a single bibliographer. Its innocence of any visible concern for bibliography is particularly regrettable in that most texts, as I have just argued, were unstable throughout most of the history of printing. No single copy of an eighteenth-century best-seller will do justice to the endless variety of editions. Serious scholars will have to study and compare many editions, in the original versions, not in the digitized reproductions that Google will sort out according to criteria that probably will have nothing to do with bibliographical scholarship.

8. Even if the digitized image on the computer screen is accurate, it will fail to capture crucial aspects of a book. For example, size. The experience of reading a small duodecimo, designed to be held easily in one hand, differs considerably from that of reading a heavy folio propped up on a book stand. It is important to get the feel of a book – the texture of its paper, the quality of its printing, the nature of its binding. Its physical aspects provide clues about its existence as an element in a social and economic system; and if it contains margin notes, it can reveal a great deal about its place in the intellectual life of its readers.

Books also give off special smells. According to a recent survey of French students, 43 percent consider smell to be one of the most important qualities of printed books – so important that they resist buying odorless electronic books. CaféScribe, a French on-line publisher, is trying to counteract that reaction by giving its customers a sticker that will give off a fusty, bookish smell when it is attached to their computers.

When I read an old book, I hold its pages up to the light and often find among the fibers of the paper little circles made by drops from the hand of the vatman as he made the sheet – or bits of shirts and petticoats that failed to be ground up adequately during the preparation of the pulp. I once found a fingerprint of a pressman enclosed in the binding of an eighteenth-century Encyclopédie – testimony to tricks in the trade of printers, who sometimes spread too much ink on the type in order to make it easier to get an impression by pulling the bar of the press.

I realize, however, that considerations of "feel" and "smell" may seem to undercut my argument. Most readers care about the text, not the physical medium in which it is embedded; and by indulging my fascination with print and paper, I may expose myself to accusations of romanticizing or of reacting like an old-fashioned, ultra-bookish scholar who wants nothing more than to retreat into a rare book room. I plead guilty. I love rare book rooms, even the kind that make you put on gloves before handling their treasures. Rare book rooms are a vital part of research libraries, the part that is most inaccessible to Google. But libraries also provide places for ordinary readers to immerse themselves in books, quiet places in comfortable settings, where the codex can be appreciated in all its individuality.

In fact, the strongest argument for the old-fashioned book is its effectiveness for ordinary readers. Thanks to Google, scholars are able to search, navigate, harvest, mine, deep link, and crawl (the terms vary along with the technology) through millions of Web sites and electronic texts. At the same time, anyone in search of a good read can pick up a printed volume and thumb through it at ease, enjoying the magic of words as ink on paper. No computer screen gives satisfaction like the printed page. But the Internet delivers data that can be transformed into a classical codex. It already has made print-on-demand a thriving industry, and it promises to make books available from computers that will operate like ATM machines: log in, order electronically, and out comes a printed and bound volume. Perhaps someday a text on a hand-held screen will please the eye as thoroughly as a page of a codex produced two thousand years ago.

Meanwhile, I say: shore up the library. Stock it with printed matter. Reinforce its reading rooms. But don't think of it as a warehouse or a museum. While dispensing books, most research libraries operate as nerve centers for transmitting electronic impulses. They acquire data sets, maintain digital repositories, provide access to e-journals, and orchestrate information systems that reach deep into laboratories as well as studies. Many of them are sharing their intellectual wealth with the rest of the world by permitting Google to digitize their printed collections. Therefore, I also say: long live Google, but don't count on it living long enough to replace that venerable building with the Corinthian columns. As a citadel of learning and as a platform for adventure on the Internet, the research library still deserves to stand at the center of the campus, preserving the past and accumulating energy for the future.

Notes

1 This essay was first published in *New York Review of Book*, Vol. 55, Nr. 10 (June 12, 2008)
2 It is, according to the site, "a digital record of American history and creativity", including sound recordings, prints, maps, and many other images.
3 An archive of letters, diaries, official records, periodicals, and images documenting the life of two communities – one Northern, one Southern – two hundred miles apart in the Shenandoah Valley during the years 1859–1870.
4 See my article on Les Bohémiens, "Finding a Lost Prince of Bohemia", *The New York Review of Books* (April 3, 2008)

Society of the Query

The Googlization of our Lives

Geert Lovink[1]

A specter haunts the world's intellectual elites: information overload. Ordinary people have hijacked strategic resources and are clogging up once carefully policed media channels. Before the Internet, the mandarin classes rested on the idea that they could separate "idle talk" from "knowledge". With the rise of Internet search engines it is no longer possible to distinguish between patrician insights and plebeian gossip. The distinction between high and low, and their co-mingling on occasions of carnival, are from bygone times and should not concern us. Nowadays an altogether new phenomenon is causing alarm: search engines rank according to popularity, not Truth. Search is the way we now live. With the dramatic increase of accessed information, we have become hooked on retrieval tools. We look for telephone numbers, addresses, opening times, a person's name, flight details, best deals and in a frantic mood declare the ever growing pile of grey matter "data trash". Soon we will search and only get lost. Old hierarchies of communication have not only imploded, communication itself has assumed the status of cerebral assault. Not only has popular noise risen to unbearable levels, we can no longer stand yet another request from colleagues of importance. Even the benign greeting from friends and family has acquired the status of a chore with the expectation of reply. What most concerns the educated class is that chatter has entered the hitherto protected domain of science and philosophy, when instead they should be worrying about who is going to control the increasingly centralized computing grid.

What today's administrators of noble simplicity and quiet grandeur can't express, we should say for them: there is a growing discontent with Google and the way the Internet organizes information retrieval. The scientific establishment has lost control over one of its key research projects – the design and ownership of computer networks, now used by billions of people. How did so many people end up being that dependent on a single search engine? Why are we repeating the Microsoft saga once again? It seems boring to complain about a monopoly in the making, when average Internet users have such a multitude of tools at their disposal to distribute power. One possible way to overcome this predicament would be to positively redefine Heidegger's "Gerede". Instead of a culture of complaint that dreams of an undisturbed offline life and radical measures to filter out the noise, it is time to openly confront today's trivial forms of *Dasein* in blogs, text messaging and computer games. Intellectuals should no longer portray Internet users as secondary amateurs, cut off from a primary and primordial relationship with the world. There is a greater issue at stake and it requires venturing into the politics of informatic life. It is time to address the emergence of a new type of corporation that is rapidly transcending the Internet: Google.

The World Wide Web, which should have realized Borges' infinite library, as described in his short story *The Library of Babel* (1941), is seen by many of its critics as nothing but a variation of Orwell's *Big Brother* (1948). The ruler, in this case, has turned from an evil monster into a collection of cool youngsters whose corporate responsibility slogan is "Don't Be Evil". Guided by a much older and experienced generation of IT gurus (Eric Schmidt), Internet pioneers (Vint Cerf) and economists (Hal Varian), Google has expanded so fast, and in such a wide variety of fields, that there is virtually no critic, academic or business journalist who has been able to keep up with the scope and speed with which Google has developed in recent years. New applications and services pile up like unwanted Christmas presents with increasing regularity. Just add Google's free email service *Gmail*, the video sharing platform *YouTube*, the social networking site *Orkut*, *GoogleMaps* and *GoogleEarth*, its main revenue service *AdWords* with the Pay-Per-Click advertisements, office applications such as Calendar, Talks and Docs. Google not only competes with Microsoft and Yahoo, but also with entertainment firms, public libraries (through its massive book scanning program) and even telecom firms. Believe it or not, the *Google Phone* is coming soon. I recently heard a less geeky family member saying she had heard that Google was much better and easier to use than the Internet. It sounded cute, but she was right. Not only has Google become the better Internet, it is taking over software tasks from your own computer so that you can access these data from any terminal or handheld device. Apple's MacBook Air is a further indication of the migration of data to privately controlled storage bunkers. Security and privacy of information are rapidly becoming the new economy and technology of control. And the majority of users, and indeed companies, are happily abandoning the power to self-govern their informational resources.

My interest in the concepts behind search engines was raised again while reading a book of interviews with MIT professor and computer critic Joseph Weizenbaum, known for his 1966 automatic therapy program ELIZA and his 1976 book *Computer Power and Human Reason*.[2] Weizenbaum died on March 5, 2008 at the age of 84. A few years ago Weizenbaum moved from Boston back to Berlin, the city where he grew up before escaping with his parents from the Nazis in 1935. The interviews were conducted by Munich-based journalist Gunna Wendt. A number of Amazon reviewers complained about Wendt's uncritical questions and the polite, superficial level of her contributions. This did not disturb me. I enjoyed the insights of one of the few insider critics of computer science. Especially interesting are Weizenbaum's stories about his youth in Berlin, the exile to the USA and the way he became involved in computing during the 1950s. The book reads like a summary of Weizenbaum's critique of computer science, namely that computers impose a mechanistic point of view on their users. What especially interested me was the way in which the "heretic" Weizenbaum shapes his arguments as an informed and respected insider – a position similar to the "net criticism" that I developed with Pit Schultz ever since we started the "nettime" project in 1995.

The title and subtitle of the book sound intriguing: *Wo sind sie, die Inseln der Vernunft im Cyberstrom? Auswege aus der programmierten Gesellschaft*. Weizenbaum's system of belief can be summarized something like this: "Nicht alle Aspekte der Realität sind berechenbar"[Not all aspects of reality are calculable]. Weizenbaum's Internet critique is a general one. He avoids becoming specific, and we have to appreciate this. His Internet remarks are nothing new for those familiar with Weizenbaum's oeuvre: the Internet is a great pile of junk, a mass medium that consists of up to 95% nonsense, much like the medium of television, in which direction the Web is inevitably developing. The so-called information revolution has flipped into a flood of disinformation. The reason for this is the absence of an editor or editorial principle. The book fails to address why this crucial media principle was not built-in by the first generations of computer programmers, of which Weizenbaum was a prominent member. The answer probably lies in the computer's initial employment as a calculator. Techno determinists in Berlin's Sophienstrasse and elsewhere insist that mathematical calculation remains the very essence of computing. The (mis)use of computers for media purposes was not foreseen by the mathematicians, and today's clumsy interfaces and information management should not be blamed on those who designed the first computers. Once a war machine, it will be a long and winding road to repurpose the digital calculator into a universal human device that serves our endlessly rich and diverse information and communication purposes.

On a number of occasions I have formulated a critique of "media ecology" that intends to filter "useful" information for individual consumption. Hubert Dreyfus' *On the Internet* (2001) is one of the key culprits here. I do not believe that it is up to any professor, editor or coder to decide for us what is and what is not nonsense. This should be a distributed effort, embedded in a culture that facilitates, and respects, difference of opinion. We should praise the richness and make new search techniques part of our general culture. One way to go would be to further revolutionize search tools and increase the general level of media literacy. If we walk into a book store or library our culture has taught us how to browse through the thousands of titles. Instead of complaining to the librarian or informing the owners that they carry too many books, we ask for assistance or work it out ourselves. Weizenbaum would like us to distrust what we see on our screens, be it television or the Internet. Weizenbaum fails to mention who is going to advise us what to trust, whether something is truthful or not, or how to prioritize the information we retrieve. In short, the role of mediators is jettisoned in favor of cultivating general suspicion.

Let's forget Weizenbaum's info-anxiety. What makes the interview such an interesting read is its insistence on the art of asking the right question. Weizenbaum warns against an uncritical use of the word "information". "The signals inside the computer are not information. They are not more than signals. There is only one way to turn signals into information, through interpretation." For this we depend on the labor of the human brain. The problem of the Internet, according to Weizenbaum, is that it invites us to see it as a Delphi oracle. The Internet will provide the answer to all our questions and problems. But the Internet is not a vending machine in which you throw a coin and then get what you want. The key here is the acquisition of a proper education in order to formulate the right query. It's all about how one gets to pose the right question. For this one needs education and expertise. We do not reach a higher education standard by raising the possibility to publish. Weizenbaum: "Die Möglichkeit, dass jeder etwas ins Internet stellen kann, bedeutet nicht sehr viel. Das willkürliche Hineinwerfen bringt genauso wenig wie das willkürliche Fischen." [The possibility that everyone can put something on the Internet does not mean much. Randomly throwing something out there makes as little sense as randomly fishing.] In this context Weizenbaum makes the comparison between the Internet and the now vanished CB radio. Communication alone will not lead to useful and sustainable knowledge.

Weizenbaum relates the uncontested belief in (search engine) queries to the rise of the "problem" discourse. Computers were introduced as "general problem solvers" and their purpose was to provide a solution for everything. People were invited to delegate their lives to the computer. "We have a problem," argues Weizenbaum, "and the problem requires an answer." But personal and social tensions cannot be resolved through by declaring them a problem. What we need instead of Google and Wikipedia is the "capacity to scrutinize and think critically". Weizenbaum explains this with reference to the difference between hearing and listening. A critical understanding requires that we first sit down and listen. Then we need to read, not just decipher, and learn to interpret and understand.

As you might expect, the so-called Web 3.0 is heralded as the technocratic answer to Weizenbaum's criticism. Instead of Google's algorithms based on keywords and an output based on ranking, soon we will be able to ask questions to the next generation of "natural language" search engines such as Powerset. However, we can already guess that computational linguists do not question the problem-answering approach and will be cautious about acting as a "content police force" who decide what is and what's not crap on the Internet. The same applies to Semantic Web initiatives and similar artificial intelligence technologies. We are stuck in the age of web information retrieval. Whereas Google's paradigm was one of link analysis and page rank, next generation search engines will, for instance, become visual and start indexing the world's image, this time not based on the tags that users have added, but on the "quality" of the imagery itself. Welcome to the Hierarchization of the Real. The next volumes of computer use manuals will introduce programmer geeks to aesthetic culture 101. Camera club enthusiasts turned coders will be the new polluters of bad taste.

Ever since the rise of search engines in the 1990s we live in the "Society of the Query", which, as Weizenbaum indicates, isn't that far removed from Guy Debord's *Society of the Spectacle*. Written in the late 1960s, this Situationist analysis was based on the rise of the film, television and advertisement industries. The main difference with today is that we are explicitly requested to interact. We're no longer addressed as an anonymous mass of passive consumers. Instead we are "distributed actors" who are present on a multitude of channels. Debord's critique of commodification is no longer revolutionary. The pleasure of indulging in consumerism is so wide-spread that it has reached the status of a universal human right. We all love the commodity fetish, the brands, and indulge in the glamour that the global celebrity class performs on our behalf. There is no social movement or cultural practice, however radical, that can escape the commodity logic. No strategy has been devised to live in the age of the post-spectacle. Concerns have instead been focusing on privacy, or what's left of it. The capacity of capitalism to absorb its adversaries has been such that it has been next to impossible to argue why we still need criticism – in this case of the Internet – unless all your private telephone conversations and Internet traffic become publicly available. Even then, it is difficult to make the case for critique so much as organized complaint by a consumer lobby group. Consider this "shareholder democracy" in action. Only then will the sensitive issue of privacy become the catalyst for a wider consciousness about corporate interests, but its participants will be carefully partitioned. Entry to the shareholding masses is restricted to the middle classes and above. And this only amplifies the need for a lively and diverse public domain in which neither state surveillance nor market interests have a vital say.

Already by 2005 the president of the French Biliothèque National, Jean-Noël Jeanneney, published a booklet in which he warned against Google's claim to "organize the world's information".[3] It is not up to any single, private corporation to assume such a role. *Google and the Myth of Universal Knowledge*, translated into English by the University of Chicago Press, remains one of the few documents that openly challenge Google's uncontested hegemony. Jeanneney targets only one specific project, Book Search, in which millions of books of American university libraries are being scanned. His argument is a very French-European one. Because of the unsystematic and unedited manner by which Google selects the books, the archive will not properly represent the giants of national literature such as Hugo, Cervantes and Goethe. Google, with its bias of English sources, will therefore not be the appropriate partner to build a public archive of the world's cultural heritage. Says Jeanneney: "The choice of the books to be digitized will be impregnated by the Anglo-Saxon atmosphere." While in itself a legitimate argument, the problem here is that it is not in Google's interest to build and administrate an online archive in the first place. Google suffers from data obesity and is indifferent to calls for careful preservation. It would be naïve to demand cultural awareness. The prime objective of this cynical enterprise is to monitor user behavior in order to sell traffic data and profiles to interested third parties. Google is not after the ownership of Emile Zola. Its intention is to lure the Proust fan away from the archive. Perhaps there is an interest in a cool Stendhal mug, the XXL Flaubert T-shirt or a Sartre purchase at Amazon. For Google Balzac's collected work is abstract data junk, a raw resource whose sole purpose it is to make a profit, whereas for the French it is the epiphany of their language and culture. It remains an open question whether the proposed European answer to Google, the multi-media search engine Quaero, will ever become operational, let alone embody Jeanneney's values. By the time of Quaero's launch, the search engine market will be a generation ahead of Quaero in media and device capabilities; some argue that Mr. Chirac was more interested in defending French pride than the global advancement of the Internet.[4]

Every week we see the launch of yet another Google initiative. Even for informed insiders it is next to impossible to keep up, let alone reveal a master plan. As we write, mid-April 2008, there is the Google App Engine, "a developer tool that enables you to run your web applications on Google's infrastructure". It's a perfect example of how a company that owns today's infrastructure is able to concentrate more power. App Engine will allow startups to use Google's web servers, APIs, and other developer tools as the primary architecture for building new web applications. As Richard MacManus remarks, "Google clearly has the scale and smarts to provide this platform service to developers. However, it begs the question: why would a startup want to hand over that much control and dependence to a big Internet company?" Computing infrastructure is rapidly turning into a utility and the Google App Engine is yet another example of this. So MacManus ends with the rhetorical question: "Would you want Google to control your entire end-to-end development environment? Isn't that what developers used to be afraid of Microsoft for?" The answer might be simple: it is the developers not-so-secret wish to be bought by Google. Millions of Internet users are, willingly or not, participating in this process by freely providing these companies with their profiles and attention, the currency of the Internet. A few week earlier Google patented a technology that will enhance its ability to "read the user". The intention is to decipher which page regions and topics the viewer is interested in based on the viewer's behavior *after* they have arrived at a page. This is just an example of the many analytical techniques this media company is developing to study and commercially exploit user behaviour.

It is no great surprise that Google's fiercest critics are North Americans. So far, Europe has invested surprisingly little of its resources into the conceptual understanding and mapping of new media culture. At best, the EU is the first adaptor of technical standards and products from elsewhere. But what counts in new media research is conceptual supremacy. Technology research alone will not do the job, no matter how much money the EU invests in future Internet research. As long as the gap between new media culture and major governing, private and cultural institutions is reproduced, a thriving technological culture will not be established. In short, we should stop seeing opera and the other belles artes as a form of compensation for the unbearable lightness of cyberspace. Besides imagination, a collective will and a good dose of creativity, Europeans could mobilize their unique capacity to grumble into a productive form of negativity. The collective passion to reflect and critique may as well be used in a movement of "critical anticipation" that can overcome the outsider syndrome many feel with regard to the assigned role of merely a user and consumer.

Jaron Lanier wrote in his Weizenbaum obituary: "We wouldn't let a student become a professional medical researcher without learning about double blind experiments, control groups, placebos and the replication of results. Why is computer science given a unique pass that allows us to be soft on ourselves? Every computer science student should be trained in Weizenbaumian skepticism, and should try to pass that precious discipline along to the users of our inventions."[5]

We have to ask ourselves: why are the best and most radical Internet critics US-Americans? We can no longer use the argument that they are better informed. My two examples, both following in Weizenbaum's footsteps, are Nicolas Carr and Siva Vaidhyanathan. Carr comes from the industry (Harvard Business Review) and developed himself as the perfect insider critic. His recent book, *The Big Switch*, describes Google's strategy to centralize, and thus control, the Internet infrastructure through its data center.[6] Computers are becoming smaller, cheaper and faster. This economy of scale makes it possible to outsource storage and applications at little or no cost. Businesses are switching from in-house IT departments to network services. There is an ironic twist here. As generations of hip IT gurus cracked jokes about the IBM's Thomas Watson prediction – the world only needed five computers – this is exactly the trend. Instead of further decentralizing, Internet use is concentrated in a few, extremely energy-demanding data centers.[7] Carr's specialty is amoral observations of technology, ignoring the greedy character of the dotcom-turned-Web 2.0 class. Siva Vaidhyanathan's project, The Googlization of Everything, has the ambition to synthesize critical Google research into a book that is due to come out in late 2009. In the meantime, he collects the raw material on one of his blogs.[8]

For the time being we will remain obsessed with the diminishing quality of the answers to our queries – and not with the underlying problem, namely the poor quality of our education and our diminishing ability to think in a critical way. I am curious whether future generations will embody – or shall we say design –Weizenbaum's "islands of reason". What is necessary is a reappropriation of time. At the moment there is simply not the time to stroll around like a flaneur. All information, any object or experience has to be instantaneously at hand. Our techno-cultural default is one of temporal intolerance. Our machines register software redundancy with increasing impatience, demanding installation of the update. And we are all too willing to oblige, mobilized by the fear of slower performance. Usability experts measure the fractions of a second in which we decide whether the information on the screen is what we are looking for. If we're dissatisfied, we click further. Serendipity requires a lot of time. We could praise randomness, but hardly practice this virtue ourselves. If we can no longer stumble into islands of reason through our inquiries, we may as well build them ourselves. With Lev Manovich and other colleagues I am arguing that we need to invent new ways to interact with information, new ways to represent it, and new ways to make sense of it. How are artists, designers, and architects are responding to these challenges? **Stop searching. Start questioning.** Rather than trying to defend ourselves against "information glut", we can approach this situation creatively as the opportunity to invent new forms appropriate for our information-rich world.

(Thanks to Ned Rossiter for his editorial assistance and ideas)

Notes

1   This text was first published in Eurozine (September 5, 2008). http://www.eurozine.com/articles/2008-09-05-lovink-en.html
2   Joseph Weizenbaum mit Gunna Wendt, Wo sind sie, die Inseln der Vernunft im Cyberstrom, Auswege aus der programmierten Gesellschaft, Herder Verlag, Freiburg, 2006.
3   Jean-Noel Jeanneney, Google and the Myth of Universal Knowledge, A View from Europe, The University of Chicago Press, Chicago, 2007.
4   See the Wikipedia entry: http://en.wikipedia.org/wiki/Quaero. In December 2006 Germany pulled out of the Quaero project. Instead of a multimedia search engine German engineers favored a text-based one. According to Wikipedia "many German engineers also balked at what they thought was becoming too much of an anti-Google project, rather than a project driven by its own ideals".
5   http://www.edge.org/3rd_culture/carr08/carr08_index.html.
6   Nicolas Carr, The Big Switch, Rewiring the World, From Edison to Google, W.W.Norton, New York, 2008.
7   "The blueprints depicting Google's data center at The Dallas, Oregon are proof that the Web is no ethereal store of ideas, shimmering over our heads like the aurora borealis. It is a new heavy industry, an energy glutton that is only growing hungrier." Ginger Strand, Harper's Magazine, March 2008.
8   See http://www.googlizationofeverything.com/.

On the Sociometry of Search Engines

A Historical Review of Methods

Katja Mayer[1]

This contribution traces the changing history of a method fundamental to all current search engines – measuring the authority of a website through its links, and it discusses the perspectives on society underlying this. I start out with references provided by search engine designers on the historical roots of the technologies they use. Then I follow multiple traces on a search to see how these technologies determine authority. I examine concepts of *social relationships* and how they are transformed into socio-technical forms of communication that today seem natural.

I will refer to three related forms of handling social relations:

1) Ever since the 1930s, a "sociometric revolution"[2] has been advocating group-psychological interventions and the visualization of how they are embedded in social structures as a means of self-realization. To this end, mathematical methods were developed that were designed to assign authority directly based on group behavior, without drawing on any prior scheme of classification.

2) Present-day bibliometric methods for developing and surveying the sciences continue this tradition of thought. External references were eliminated in favor of an allegedly politically independent science, and self-referential models aggregating objective authority were developed – e.g. the *Impact Factor* and the *Science Citation Index* – both of which soon became benchmarks exercising a strong influence on their objects of measurement. As automation and data archiving progressed, such measuring methods turned into behavioral instructions.

3) Search engines incorporate and expose a particular relationship between social relations and authority, although clear qualitative points of reference are missing. As mediators (and notorious data collectors) search engines produce and represent authority themselves and render this self-referentiality visible. However, this strategy is not only found in search engines, it is part of a more general tendency of social optimization.

Some selected examples from the history of sociometry and bibliometrics will be referred to in order to illustrate various forms of visualizing social relations; they will include the seemingly natural imperative of networking and the fantasies of optimization that spring from it. Social relations, the capital of the network society, are profoundly shaped by informetrics and subjected to the requirement of visibility. The algorithms of a search engine turn normative concepts into controllable, instrumental and communicative action, rendering search engines like Google into instruments of power. Their position as competent mediators in a flood of information allows them to determine the behavior of those who trust in them.

Regulating authority – legitimizing knowledge

Google's success story started at Stanford University, when Sergey Brin and Larry Page wanted to bring "order to the web".[3] Google was going to adopt an approach to hurl the most relevant sites to the top positions different from the search engines dominating the market in 1997. These search engines measured the relevance of search results by the frequency and position of key words on the websites found, while Google began to rate websites automatically on the basis of their link structure. The so-called *PageRank* qualifies a website by the hyperlinks that refer to it. However, these incoming links are not counted evenly, but weighted according to the significance of their source site; consequently, a hyperlink from a website rated as important counts more. The *PageRank* ratings of incoming links are passed on. Each indexed website in the Google archive is given a PageRank rating independently of any search enquiries.

> *PageRank* carries out an objective rating of the importance of websites, considering more than 500 million variables and 2 billion terms. Instead of counting the direct links, PageRank interprets a link provided by site A to site B as a vote cast for site B by site A. Finally, *PageRank* rates the importance of a site based on the votes cast.[4]

This is how Google explains the process. What is referred to as 'votes', without further precision, is dealt with in somewhat more clear terms in a paper by Jon Kleinberg, also known as "rebel king": "Hyperlinks encode a considerable amount of latent human judgment, and we claim that this type of judgment is precisely what is needed to formulate a notion of authority." And more precisely still:

> Specifically, the creation of a link on the www represents a concrete indication of the following type of judgment: the creator of page p, by including a link to page q, has in some measure conferred authority on q. Moreover,

links afford us the opportunity to find potential authorities purely through the pages that point to them.[5]

In his tracing of mechanisms of order in search results Kleinberg introduces the concept of "hubs and authorities". He developed a method similar to PageRank known as "hypertext-induced topic selection" (HITS). According to Kleinberg, hyperlinks contain a certain amount of a latent human judgment that can be used for rating the importance of a page. Whoever placed a link does so for a reason and decides in favor of this reference.

Just like Page, Brin and others, Kleinberg refers to bibliometric citation analysis as the immediate source of his inspiration. Furthermore, he calls attention to the social science field of sociometry, and in particular to a method developed by Katz in 1953[6] that calculates the status of a social group, further developed in Hubbell's[7] work on identifying cliques. Nearly half a century ago, in other words, there were already methods in place that could be built upon, even though they were rooted in a social science discipline that concerned itself with social networks at this early point and became known in the 1970s as Social Network Analysis.

Visualizing social structures

Social network analysis is concerned with visualizing social structures and some of the results they yield. Its main object of research are (social) relations. Actors such as people, institutions, documents, nations, phone connections, viruses, etc., are interconnected in a wide range of different modes that are subject to mathematical methods of measurement and interpretation. Today, carefully collected data may be visualized and analyzed as a network of relations at the push of a button. The techniques of social network analysis have long left the realms of science behind and settled in commerce-oriented sociology, while academic sociologists seem to cast envious looks at the enormous data sets routinely gathered by businesses over the years.[8] While studies of network analysis were extremely time-consuming and costly undertakings in the early years, the computing capacity and the amount of data available today mean that they often outrun conventional polling and social statistics in many regards. The likely behavior of the basic population does not need to be inferred and forecast through sampling. The observing institutions archive each individual transaction, which allows them to map and rate likely behavior. Data is exchanged with partner institutions within so-called data consortia,[9] and in combination with data provided by public administration units such as statistical and census offices, geo-demographical databases are established in many places.[10] While these kinds of systems were previously the reserve of utopian concepts of society, they are realities today, allowing precise and exemplary insights into social reality. Ironically, opinion research and control can now be carried out in all orders of magnitude, while one of the original ideas of the analysis of social structures was to counter ubiquitous "scopic regimes".[11]

Methodologies for studying social structures were developed within a predominantly relational style of thought in the early 20th century. Einstein recommended reading Pearson's *The Grammar of Science*,[12] and mathematics produced set theory, topology and game theory. In parallel to the growth of state power, an optimistic vision had gained ground, according to which "a rationality based on mathematics and empirical observation will lead to objectivity and hence to a transparency that will apply to both description and decisions".[13] Mathematical survey methods and statistical methods in turn gave rise to fields such as biometrics and econometrics. Expanding infrastructures such as telegraph wires and phone and transit networks enjoyed great popularity, undermining notions of the state as the centralized unit and of society as a community.

After leading social theorists had directly addressed social structures in the late 19th century, Simmel described the mission of a "pure" sociology at the beginning of the 20th century as follows: pure sociology was meant to

> extract the moment of socialization from the phenomena, separated inductively and psychologically from their contents and purposes which for themselves are nothing social, like grammar separates the pure forms of language from the contents that give live to these forms.[14]

He focused on the interactions between individuals and a society, and on the social dynamics and structures evolving from it. Simmel preferred researching "social forms" and "forms of socialization", i.e. networks of relationships in many different contexts, over research on the content of social realities, which to him belonged to a different kind of social sciences.[15] To him, the triad, the "social triangle" was the most important organizational form in analyzing social interactions:

> The number two represented the first synthesis and unification, but also the first divorce and anti-thesis; the emergence of the third meant transition, reconciliation, overcoming absolute opposition – although occasionally also the creation of such an opposition.[16]

In Simmel's view, the triad also represented the smallest social group and was therefore meant to be the basic analytical unit in sociology.

Sociometry and network metaphors

> Before the advent of sociometry no one knew what the interpersonal structure of a group "precisely" looked like.[17]

The representatives of structural approaches in social psychology, sociology and anthropology in the 1930s and 1940s, as well as their successors in the field of social network analysis, repeatedly referred to Simmel. Jakob Levi Moreno was already investigating the relationship between psychological wellbeing and the given social configurations at the beginning of the 20th century. In 1916 he submitted a proposal to the Interior Ministry of the Austro-Hungarian monarchy that would have amounted to a socio-psychological intervention based on the measuring of social relations in a group of refugees, but the proposal was dismissed. When Moreno emigrated from Vienna to New York in 1925, his objective was to further develop his socio-psychological methods of group therapy, such as role games (socio-drama) and impromptu theatre. From this point on, he called his method "sociometry" and connected it to a political goal: the "sociometrical revolution"[18] was meant to bring about equal rights among human beings. Taking part themselves in "sociometric experiments", clients and experts were able to reconfigure their situation and their structural embedding and to recreate social order according to their own perspective. Unlike statistics and survey sociology, this method was not intended to bring any pre-fabricated categories into data acquisition; instead, such categories were supposed to emerge and become visible from the observed social structures themselves.

Sociometrists continuously worked on new techniques of measurement and representation. Observation, interviews and role plays were used to learn about attraction and repulsion experienced by individuals, and social choice was displayed in matrices. In this way, following an analysis of the group and its relationship types, social cohesion could also be measured. Sociograms were introduced as important methodological tools, allowing graphic representations of group structures and relationship patterns among individuals. Dots or symbols represented individuals, while lines represented connections among individuals. The resulting visualization had the purpose of allowing social structures to be handled and reconfigured. By visualizing the embedding of the actors and thereby rendering it evident, these actors could be brought to take charge of their own social position and initiate changes or optimize order.

It was the sociogram that first allowed the experimental study and "precise exploration" of complex relationships, since that time considered as "social networks" and "places of origin of public opinion".[19] The social mapping applied in this way allowed the discovery of the so-called "sociodynamic law", the predominant choices in a group, and also the development of patterns and forms such as the "star", which would certainly be called "hub" today.

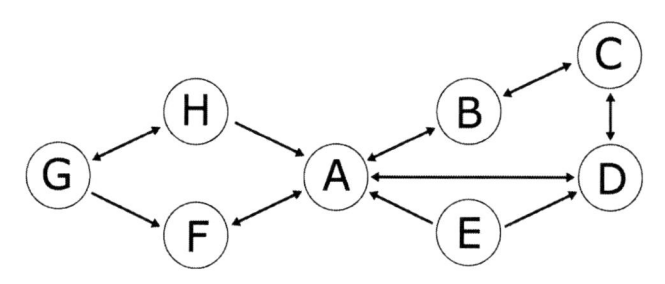

The sociogram displays a simple network based on choices of actors A – H. Actor A is called "star", because more than 4 people chose A, who holds a central position in the network. The matrix represents the same dataset.

	A	B	C	D	E	F	G	H
A	0	1	0	1	1	1	0	1
B	1	0	1	0	0	0	0	0
C	0	1	0	1	0	0	0	0
D	1	0	1	0	1	0	0	0
E	0	0	0	0	0	0	0	0
F	1	0	0	0	0	0	1	0
G	0	0	0	0	0	0	0	1
H	0	0	0	0	0	0	1	0

Mathematical networks or graphs

In the early years, the sociometrists created their sociograms manually and in an ad-hoc fashion, giving rise to widespread criticism for lack of the methodological stringency appropriate to science. In the 1940s, this continuing criticism of the intuitive sociogram led to priority being given to data displayed in matrices. The resulting standardization of data on social interaction was meant to allow a more objective handling of the data.[20] Representing data on social relations in the form of matrices promoted the mathematization of sociometry.[21] For the first time it was possible to identify sub-groups with mathematical means, and to calculate the status of a person, as well as his/her prestige within a social network, all on the basis of the measured social relations. In the 1950s and 1960s this form of notation led to the first emergence of topological and graph-theoretical approaches in sociometry. As a consequence, it was possible to topographically represent social space in the form of its relationships.

The first methods of electronically computing sociometric data paved the way to graph-theoretical sociometry. This was made possible by social matrices, while for the time being sociograms lost in importance. The advocates of sociograms[22] criticized that matrix notation made it difficult to see social patterns such as triangles, stars, and chains, and they demanded a mathematical method that would allow such techniques of visualization to be applied to matrices and result lists.

The formal processing of network data allowed the operationalization of weighted and rated connections, and, above all, the analysis of a group's structure from the point of view of each individual group member.[23] This approach was of interest to the emerging theory of group dynamics, allowing it to model group cohesion, social pressure, cooperation and relationships of dominance. However, the application of these kinds of algorithms was slow and cumbersome. Computers were virtually non-existent, and in the rare instances where they were available, the production of punch cards consumed a large amount of resources. Consequently, drafting a sociogram and computing a small network would require a lot of time,[24] if one wanted to detect particular structural patterns or test existing concepts such as "isolates", "cliques",[25] "density" and "centrality".[26]

Measuring centrality and diffusion

Centrality is one of the most widely known concepts of network analysis. Building on the topological psychology of Kurt Lewin, it was developed by the Bavelas group in psychological laboratory experiments at the MIT and applied to structures of communication.[27] The experiment consisted of five students sitting at a round table, separated from one another by screens. They were asked to jointly solve a problem, but allowed only written communications. The information comprised six symbols. Each participant had a card with five symbols, with a different one missing on each card. Through cooperation, the students were supposed to find their missing sixth symbol. At the sound of a signal, the color-coded communications could be exchanged. Following the experiment, the participants completed questionnaires on how they rated their performance and their emotional state. Frequently, the participants were purposely interrupted by interventions by the directors of the experiment, and communication channels were cut. This strongly simplified communication setting was supposed to yield data on diffusion and authority in purpose-oriented group behavior.

The study concluded that in efficient communication networks there was always one person who became the central passage point, collecting information and therefore moved into a position of power. Consequently, the flow of information in de-centralized networks was inefficient. This and similar studies were furnished with graphs that were meant to show the ideal-type patterns of communication: circle, chain, Y and wheel (X). Subsequently, these patterns could also be applied to measured values.

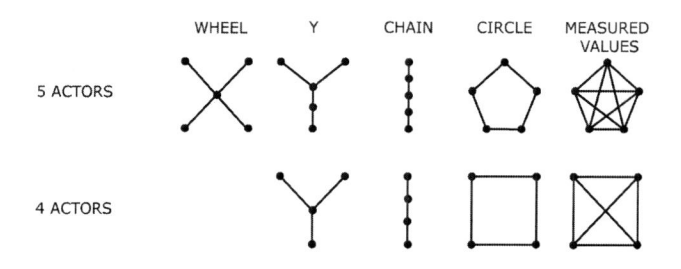

The network models most frequently used in communication studies.[28]

A central actor has many social relations, although what is decisive in terms of his/her position of power are social status and authority.[29] Control over scarce resources only manifests in the direction of the relations. If additionally a high-prestige actor positions him/herself between disconnected groups, he/she occupies a key position in the network. Calculations of centrality and social status entail a range of different formal methods to rank the nodes of a network.

Another variation of the idea of social positions and communication pathways is Stanley Milgram's well-known and much criticized "small world" experiment.[30] In an attempt to identify patterns of diffusion, participants were asked to send a package to its final destination as quickly as possible by passing it on through acquaintances. Counting the number of stops, Milgram coined the idea of "six degrees of separation", extrapolating the results of this study and subsequent ones to the US population.

As collaboration with statisticians and communication researchers increased and computers were more frequently used, the focus of social science network research shifted to the modes in which information is disseminated in society. Social groups and networks were analyzed in terms of their permeability, their social gravitation, and their different logics. In 1957 Coleman, Katz and Wenzel published a seminal paper[31] on the communication patterns that resulted in the introduction of a new pharmaceutical. The authors conducted interviews with physicians, enquiring about their professional and private contacts in relation to the introduction of the medicine. They were asked to indicate the names of three doctors with whom they were friends and with whom they consulted. This study focussed not so much on the content of the communications, but rather on the ways the communication took place and with whom, until the innovation was finally introduced. The study showed that the physicians were strongly influenced by their direct informal and professional environment: the readiness to accept the new medicine increased with the degree of the physician's networking.

Further studies[32] on cliques, elites and social movements were focused on identifying nodes of opinion formation. These studies were no longer concerned with the original demands to apply sociometry only in agreement with the clients. The progressive mathematization and the concomitant standardization not only equipped empirical observation and interviews with instruments, but also allowed it to structurally picture complex subjects by filtering documents by names and terms. The social relations of subjects, their social ties and social choices could now be determined from data collections and texts by identifying specific types of relationships. Increasingly, the analysis of social structures turned into data mining, opening interesting options to an audience located beyond the realms of the social science research community. Next to typical sociometric studies, socio-psychological interventions or anthropological investigations of rural or small-town communities, rules of marriage, social interactions in the workplace, and social conflicts, there emerged countless studies on communication behavior, opinion formation, productivity, as well as social innovation and optimization, all of them drawing on the graph-theoretical models of sociometry and social psychology.

Informetric optimization

On the other hand, socio-technical networks were the subject of both operations research and cybernetics. Flow graphs for process control and also network maps were constructed as topological graphs, suggesting analogies between the measuring of social groups and electronic networks.[33] While military logistics and the automatization of weapon systems were the initial basis of cybernetics, cybernetic theories of automatization and control of complex machine systems soon developed into a science of control and communication and the regulation and optimization of information resources.[34] Information was elevated to the constitutive principle of a progressive, telematic society and immediately became the measure of probability of social as well as machine processes. The goal of cybernetic social management was the minimization of insecurities and, consequently, the informatization of society. In this kind of vision of society, social relations are transformed into communication links. Communication behavior and information diffusion are modeled as epistemic units, while the focus is shifted away from the content towards socio-technological patterns of diffusion. The latter were also used in attempts to answer the question of knowledge and its authorization: "Who decides what knowledge is, and who knows what needs to be decided upon?"[35] The socio-informetric answer to that question might be: "This follows from successful transmission."

Recognition by reference

From the 1930s on, Robert Merton and his sociology of science sought to define the conditions for a scientific method that would be independent from politics. His studies[36] showed that the legitimization of knowledge is subject to historical transformations, that it involves specific social processes of negotiation and strategies, and that it establishes itself within social relations. Merton was convinced that the scientific system itself should be the highest authority for the knowledge produced in it. In his view, research results were common property subject to examination by peer review and to the possibility of reproducibility and criticism. Scientific research was supposed to be assessed independently of the scientist and of his/her social attributes. One of the methods that allowed this kind of assessment was bibliometry.

As a statistical examination of publication behavior and libraries, bibliometry has a long-standing tradition. Citation analysis, one specific field of bibliometry, originally used relatively simple statistical methods and indexing systems to produce one-glance visualizations of various fields of knowledge. As early as in the 16th century, passages of the Bible were marked and filtered by means of citation indexes.[37] And as early as 1926, Lotka calculated and interpreted scientific productivity in physics and chemistry by analyzing publication behavior.[38]

In the 1940s, Eugene Garfield, the founder of the Science Citation Index, was inspired by the law citation index "Shepard's" to apply a similar system to other fields of knowledge. Starting in 1873, Shepard's had collected court rulings and references to precedents in the form of a citation catalogue. This system operated with a time-based concept of authority, with the most recent ruling being the most relevant. Garfield understood the potential that such a tool could have for the vast and previously unmeasurable field of technological patents and scientific publications:

> The amazing efficiency of the citation method is such that once the starting case or statute is found, it becomes a key that unlocks the entire store of law on a given point. It is this function which it appears would be of great value in other fields. An article on any scientific subject would be the key to all others.[39]

In this way, one single scientific document could provide an entry point to the entire scientific landscape. Garfield liked to refer to himself as an "information engineer", and from the very beginning conceived of the SCI both as a tool of analysis and an instrument of evaluation like a "hyper search engine". "That's why I call it 'hypersearch'. I've said that the SCI is the ultimate hypersearch product. I think Ted Nelson is credited with the notion of hypertext, but I doubt that he knew the SCI even existed."[40] Garfield dreamed of a unified science, and consequently wanted his scientific index to cover all the disciplines. Unlike Shepard's, which depended on the expert knowledge of editors, his index was meant to generate itself on the basis of scientific journals. The peer reviews practiced by these would ensure the scientific quality of the index. The Science Citation Index does not measure and assess the contents of the cited works, but only the points of reference and thus their reputation. In as much as this is the case, the SCI produces a socio-structural model of publication behavior, turning the footnote into the most important source of information.

After the first version of the citation database was implemented using funds provided by the US National Institute of Health, an SCI for the year 1961 was extracted as early as 1963. At the same time, a patent index registering all the US patents of a particular year was set up. In 1965, the database comprised 1057 journals, nearly 50,000 patents, and more than 2 million "registered access points to the world's science and technology literature"[41], all of which were available as punch cards allowing automated processing. Thanks to automatization and the restriction of citations to their referring function, the index could be analyzed statistically. If the number of citations made within a particular year to articles published within the two preceding years is divided by the number of articles of these two years, one arrives at a number that soon was to enter the history of science, the "impact factor".

The SCI was "mainly developed in order to solve problems of information retrieval. Later additional applications were found that are of significance to historians, sociologists, administrators, etc."[42] Sociologists of science, network researchers and communication researchers frequently met with Garfield and ISI staff. The subjects discussed at these meetings went beyond the social context of knowledge production and the diffusion of innovation, often focusing on specific possibilities of assessing scientific knowledge. The SCI's impact factor represented such a possibility and today has a decisive influence on scientific career patterns. The impact factor operationalizes an evaluated social relationship, for setting a reference is equivalent to an acknowledgement of expertise.

However, at that time the impact factor was only one among several possible forms of analysis. Garfield thought up additional ways of exploring the available data:

> It is reasonable to assume that if I cite a paper that I would probably be interested in those papers which subsequently cite it as well as my own paper. Indeed, I have observed on several occasions that people preferred to cite the articles I had cited rather than cite me! It would seem to me that this is the basis for the building up of the "logical network" for the citation index service. [43]

Garfield soon found out that there was not only an interest in getting access to relevant scientific publications, but also in others' publication behavior and in the control of intellectual property. In the future, he was sure, scientists would have better possibilities of bibliographical control – and of tackling information overflow, which at the time was dramatized[44] as a crisis by many, including public institutions.

In fact, the interest in SCI data constantly increased. Citation analysis was applied as a method to historical documents, monographs, and networks of correspondence. Studies on "invisible colleges"[45] clarified a wide range of different modes of knowledge production independent from any supposed unified metanarrative. Differing from the ideal of a cumulative growth, knowledge actually combined in loosely connected configurations. Analyses of "bibliographic coupling"[46] and co-citation[47] yielded more information on the diffusion of scientific literature. Co-cited documents appeared together in a list of references of a third document, allowing for them to be counted, while bibliographic coupling only determined which works referred to the same source.

Derek de Solla Price was interested in the life cycle of a scholarly paper. "More work is urgently needed on the problem of determining whether there is a probability that the more a paper is cited the more likely it is to be cited thereafter."[48] Subsequent analyses of citations confirmed his hypothesis, according to which "the rich get richer". Price's model of a citation network consists in directional relationships and is acyclical, as only texts that already exist can be referenced. In today's terminology, such a network would be called a scale-free network, for it essentially comprises a large number of nodes with a low status, little prestige, etc., and only a few high-ranking nodes. There is a significantly greater likelihood of references being made to works that are already popular.[49] Thus, the number of references, referred to as "edges" in graph theory, generates visibility and recognition.

Merton, an advocate of a structural perspective in sociology, articulated his thesis of the "Matthew Effect"[50] on the basis of the work of Harriet Zuckerman. Within the recognition system of the scientific community, this effect means that "renowned scientists receive a disproportionate amount of recognition for their contributions, while recognition is withheld from junior scientists who have not yet established a name".[51] Merton identified citations as the "routine form" of perception in science. In addition to opening access to "borrowed" knowledge, citations act as an institution of recognition embedded in science's system of norms and rewards,[52] and in turn feed back into the system.

The SCI soon turned into a key global actor in science. The referencing of scholarly literature thus became the measurement of its reach and importance, and subsequently the indicator for evaluating scientific productivity. Consequently, citation analysis also became a tool for disciplining scientific actors. A scientific career is measured, amongst others, by the impact factors of the publications produced. Thus, epistemic citations become objectified in so far as the citing actors have come to recognize them as social capital, leading to consequences that in the long run might undermine citation analysis itself. Strategic citations, self-citations, and the so-called citation cartels, where a group of scientists continuously refer to one another, are reminiscent of search machine optimization designed to give websites greater visibility in the search results. Currently, academic search engines not only make the publications of large and dominating publishers searchable, they also list freely accessible academic publications. As the trend in scientific citation is clearly towards freely available content[53], publishers, and along with them the standard SCI and its impact factor, might become obsolete.

Networks, optimization, and control

The citation, objectifying a certain type of social relationship in science, became the guiding concept for the ordering algorithms used by current Internet search engines. The bibliometric reference provided the blueprint for the way in which hyperlinks are assigned relevance and ranked on the results pages. While early bibliometry defined a vote as a social choice to be identified within the given social embedding and involving those who choose, sociometrically informed communication research operationalized social relationships with a view to the instrumental diffusion of information. References in scientific publications in turn drove the logic of recognition within the referencing system, providing the basis for "authoritative judgement"[54] in search engine technology. Citation analysis only turned into what we understand it to be today by being assigned the explicit purpose of a tool of assessment. Its methodological authority stems from the field of science itself and is based on the norms and values that apply there.

Ranking algorithms reduce social relations to a specific dimension of communication – the placing of a reference. As communicative relationships hyperlinks connect information. Moreover, the direction taken by this connection indicates authority in the form of prestige or social status. However, in times when optimization, mash-ups and automatic feeds are common, such a concept of authority becomes questionable. Automated collective identities produce Matthew Effects, preferential attachments, etc., and one longs for the editorial teams of the Shepard's index, where each reference was exposed to a qualitative examination.

Yet the ineluctable guiding metaphors of the network, "modern capitalism's current from of socialization" obscure any perspectives beyond the "networking's claim to absoluteness".[55] "Get networked!" is not only a technological slogan, it is also directed at people's professional and private lives, requesting individuals to establish potentially beneficial contacts, to interact on social networking platforms or events, to behave flexibly in the labor market, and to locate responsibilities within the processes of the network. Individuals who are already well networked are subjected to the paradigm of optimization and challenged to improve their position both in the temporal sense and in terms of their social capital.

Today, visible networking is meant to ensure autonomy and individual responsibility as well as testimony and authority, but never social security.[56] An "audit society"[57] both incorporates and decentralizes its techniques of control and therefore remains obscure. The SCI Journal Impact Factor is an example of the systematic assumption that somewhere in the chain of relationships – in this case of references – a collective quality control has taken place. Internet search engines make use of the same kind of leap of faith, and although authorities become diffuse in an automated, networked system, they are "obligatory passage points".[58] They collect data and interpret search profiles seemingly for the purpose of optimization, but mostly for target oriented advertising. Studies such as one on understanding the spread of a flu epidemic based on search enquiries[59] are designed to ensure customers their "digital groundedness"[60], securing their trust by showing openness, transparency, and a willingness to serve society.

The sociometric art of measurement and its socio-grammatical forms of representation allow it to display search results as node-edge diagrams, to examine friendships in terms of their other friendships (friend of a friend, FOAF), to bring professional contacts a few handshakes' distance closer to one's own position, or to identify the alleged head of a terrorist group in a diagram. In a network, every relationship counts, and the "panoptic diagram"[61] allows for them to be handled. Thus, authority no longer rests in the relationships and instead migrates towards the measuring instrument and its forms of visualization. Whether the results are displayed as list, matrix, or diagram – once they appear, they both represent and establish relationships whose social content was subjected to informetrization. Search engines and their politics of visualization, then, should be understood as instruments of spectacularization and as part of a sociometric management of society. As the case of citation cartels shows, the latter is inevitably accompanied by possibilities of manipulation.

Today, the sociometric revolution is understood as network-oriented optimization: search engine optimizers construct authorities around their customers' websites in order for these to appear among the top results; search engines optimize the diffusion of their advertising customers and investigate the world of information seekers through their profiles; epidemiological studies on the spread of pathogens resemble studies on intersected financial markets not only formally, but also in terms of their appearance and rhetoric; the flexibilization of production processes, the shortening of product life cycles and the (claimed) individualization of goods result from the adaptation of mass markets to the network logic of process optimization; researchers of network economics teach structural blocking strategies against competing businesses;[62] defense departments and other executive organs around the world sponsor network research, hoping to benefit from improvements in logistics and key player analysis brought by network-centric warfare.

Locating central positions – key players – in a network in order to monitor them, act against them, circumnavigate or even eliminate them – these are interests the military and business worlds share with scientists seeking to identify the works that will allow innovative insights, to enhance their position in the scientific system, or to intervene in the field of research. Epidemiologists, financial service providers, marketing strategists, insurance representatives and election campaign consultants are also interested in key players and pursue their own strategies of network optimization. Could it be that such optimization strategies will act as cybernetic feedback cycles facilitating the systems' self-regulation, or is it more likely that they manifest the absurdity of certain systems of analysis? For the present, it seems clear that they lead to a sociometric subjectivization of actors who now understand themselves as nodes and seek to optimize their social relations.

Notes

1 This article is based on research carried out for other publications, including my PhD thesis on network visualization in social network analysis (Mayer, K. forthcoming. *Imag(in)ing Networks*. Doctoral Thesis, University of Vienna, Department of Social Studies of Science), and an article (Mayer, K. 2007. "Who shall survive? Die Netzwerke des Jakob L. Moreno"; in: Bredekamp, H., Werner G., (Eds.), 2007, *Bildwelten des Wissens. Systemische Räume*. Berlin, Akademie Verlag). I wish to express my thanks to Konrad Becker, Gerhard Dirmoser, Arno Böhler, Ulrike Felt, Lin Freeman, Thomas König, Astrid Mager, Patrick Pulsinger, Theo Röhle, Felix Stalder, Wolfgang Sützl and the contributors to the SOCnet mailing list for their valuable insights and suggestions.
2 Moreno, J.L. 1967. *Die Grundlagen der Soziometrie*. Köln u. Opladen: Westdeutscher Verlag.
3 Page, L. Brin, S., Modwani, R., and Winograd, T. 1999. *The PageRank Citation Ranking: Bringing Order to the Web*. Stanford: http//ilpubs.standford.edu:8090/422/ [1 Dec. 2008]
4 Google. 2008. *Corporate information*. http://www.google.de/corporate/tech.html [1 Dec. 2008]

5 Kleinberg, J. 1998. *Authoritative sources in a hyperlinked environment.* Proc. 9th ACM-SIAM Symposium on Discrete Algorithms. (Extended version in Journal of the ACM 46(1999). Also appeared as IBM Research Report RJ 10076, May 1997.) 2.
6 Katz, L. 1953. "A new status index derived from sociometric analysis". In: *Psychometrika*, Vol. 18, Nr.1, 39-43.
7 Hubbell, Ch. H. 1965. "An Input-Output Approach to Clique Identification". In: *Sociometry*, Vol. 28, Nr. 4, 377-399.
8 Savage, M. and Burrows, R. 2007. "The coming crisis of empirical sociology". In: *Sociology*, Vol. 41, Nr. 5, 885-599.
9 Cf. Marsh, H. 1998. "What's In Store?" In: *Marketing*, Vol. 15th October 1998, p. 37-38.
10 Evans, M. 2005. *Confidentiality, Data Protection & Marketing.* http://www.ccels.cf.ac.uk/archives/publications/2004/evanspaper.pdf (1.12.2008) (Edited version of "The data-informed marketing model and its social responsibility'" by Martin Evans in *The glass consumer: Life in a surveillance society* published by The Policy Press, June 2005.)
11 Cf. Crary, J. 1990. *Techniques of the Observer: On Vision and Modernity in the 19th Century.* Cambridge: MIT Press; Jay, M. 1994. *Downcast Eyes: The Denigration of Vision in Twentieth-Century French Thought.* Berkeley: University of California Press.
12 Pearson, K. [1892] 1957. *The Grammar of Science.* New York: Meridian Books.
13 Desrosières, A. 2005. *Die Politik der großen Zahlen. Eine Geschichte der statistischen Denkweise.* Berlin, Heidelberg: Springer. 33.
14 Simmel, G. 1917. *Grundfragen der Soziologie. (Individuum und Gesellschaft).* Berlin und Leipzig: Göschen'sche Verlagshandlung. 27. http://socio.ch/sim/gs171.htm [1 Dec. 2008]
15 Simmel, G. 1908. *Soziologie. Untersuchungen über die Formen der Vergesellschaftung.* Berlin: Duncker & Humblot.
16 Simmel 1908: 75.
17 Moreno, J.L. [1934] 1953. *Who shall survive. A New Approach to the Problem of Human Interrelations.* Washington D.C.: Nervous and Mental Disease Publishing. (2nd substantially expanded edition: *Who Shall Survive? Foundations of Sociometry, Group Psychotherapy and Sociodrama.* NY: Beacon House Inc.) lvi.
18 Moreno 1967.
19 Moreno 1967: 276.
20 Forsyth, E. and Katz, L. 1946. "A Matrix Approach to the Analysis of Sociometric Data: Preliminary Report". In: *Sociometry*, Vol. 9, No. 4 (Nov., 1946), 340-347.
21 Wasserman, S. and Faust, K. 1994. *Social Network Analysis.* Cambridge. University Press. 79.
22 Moreno, J.L. 1946. "Sociogram and Sociomatrix: A Note to the Paper by Forsyth and Katz". In: *Sociometry*, Vol. 9, No. 4 (Nov., 1946), 348-349.
23 Cf. Cartwright, D. and Zander, A. 1953. *Group Dynamics: Research and Theory.*1st ed., Evanston, IL: Row Peterson; Harary, F. and Norman, R. Z. 1953. *Graph theory as a mathematical model in social science.* Ann Arbor, Mich.: University of Michigan; Bavelas, A. 1950. "Communication patterns in task oriented groups". In: *Journal of the Acoustical Society of America*, Vol. 22, 271–282.
24 Freeman, L.C. 2004. *The Development of Social Network Analysis: A Study in the Sociology of Science.* Vancouver: Empirical Press. 98.
25 Cf. Luce, R. D and Perry, A. 1949. "A method of matrix analysis of group structure". In: *Psychometrika*, Vol. 14, 94-116; Luce, R. D. 1950. "Connectivity and Generalized Cliques in Sociometric Group Structure". In: *Psychometrika*, Vol. 15, 169-190.
26 Cf. Bavelas, A. 1948. "A mathematical model for group structure". In: *Applied Anthropology*, Vol. 7, 16-30; Leavitt, H.J. 1951. "Some effects of certain communication patterns on group performance". *Journal of Abnormal and Social Psychology*, Vol. 46, 38–50.

27 Cf. Bavelas 1948, 1950; Leavitt 1951.
28 Leavitt 1951.
29 Cf. Moreno 1953; Katz 1953; Harary, F. 1959. "Status and contrastatus". In: *Sociometry* Vol. 22, 23-43; Hubbell 1965; Freeman, L. C. 1977. "A set of measures of centrality based on betweenness". In: *Sociometry* Vol. 40, 35-41.
30 Milgram 1967. "The Small World Problem". In: *Psychology Today*, May, 60-67.
31 Coleman, J., Katz, E. and Menzel, H. 1957. "The Diffusion of an Innovation Among Physicians". In: *Sociometry*, Vol. 20, 253-170.
32 Cf. Freeman 2004.
33 Cf. Cherry, C. 1963. *Kommunikationsforschung – eine neue Wissenschaft*. Hamburg: S. Fischer Verlag; Schüttpelz, E. 2007. "Ein absoluter Begriff. Zur Genealogie und Karriere des Netzwerkkonzepts". In: Kaufmann, S. (Ed.): *Vernetzte Steuerung*. Zürich: Chronos, 25-47.
34 Cf. Wiener, N. 1961. *Cybernetics. Second Edition: or the Control and Communication in the Animal and the Machine*. New York: MIT Press.
35 Lyotard, J.-F. [1979] 2005. *Das postmoderne Wissen*. Vienna: Passagen. 35.
36 Cf. Merton, R. K. 1985. *Entwicklung und Wandel von Forschungsinteressen. Aufsätze zur Wissenschaftssoziologie*. Frankfurt am Main: Suhrkamp Verlag.
37 Weinberg, B.H. 1997. "The earliest Hebrew citation indexes". In: *Journal of the American Society for Information Science*, Vol. 48, 318-330.
38 Lotka, A. J. 1926. "The frequency distribution of scientific productivity". In: *Journal of the Washington Academy of Sciences*, Vol. 16, 317-323.
39 Letter Garfield to Adair 1954, Cf. Wouters, P. 1999. *The citation culture*. Unpublished doctoral dissertation, University of Amsterdam, Amsterdam. 26.
40 Garfield, E. 2000. "Eugene Garfield celebrates a Birthday and a Career". In: *Information Today*, Vol. 17, No. 10, November 2000.
http://www.garfield.library.upenn.edu/papers/informationtoday11172000.html [1 Dec. 2008]
41 Garfield, E. 1965. "Über den Science Citation Index (SCI) und Verwandte Entwicklungen der Jüngsten Zeit". In: *Nachrichten für Dokumentation*, Vol. 16. – Nr. 3, 130- 140. 31.
42 Garfield 1965: 136.
43 Garfield to Lederberg 1962, cf. Wouters 1999: 72.
44 Cf. Wouters 1999.
45 Cf. Crane, D. 1972. *Invisible Colleges: Diffusion of knowledge in scientific communities*. Chicago: University of Chicago Press; Kadushin, C. (1968): "Power, Influence and Social Circles: A New Methodology for Studying Opinion-Makers". In: *American Sociological Review*, Vol. 33, 685-699.
46 Cf. Kessler, M. M. 1963. "Bibliographic Coupling Between Scientific Papers". *American Documentation*, 14: 10-25; Martyn, J. (1964). "Bibliographic Coupling". *Journal of Documentation*, 20(4): 236.
47 Cf. Marshakova, I. V. 1973. *A system of document connection based on references. Scientific and Technical Information Serial of VINITI*, 6(2): 3-8; Small, H. 1973. "Co-citation in the scientific literature: A new measurement of the relationship between two documents". *Journal of the American Society of Information Science*, 24(4): 265-269.
48 Price, D. J. de Solla. 1965. "Networks of Scientific Papers". In: *Science*, Vol. 149, No. 3683, 510-515. 512.
49 Cf. "cumulative advantage" model in Price, D. J. de Solla. 1976. "A general theory of bibliometric and other cumulative advantage processes". In: *Journal of the American Society for Information Science*, Vol. 32, 280–286; or "preferential attachment" model in Barabási, A.-L. and Albert R. 1999. "Emergence of scaling in random networks". In: *Science* Vol. 286: 509-512. http://arxiv.org/abs/cond-mat/9910332 [1 Dec. 2008]

50 Cf. Merton, R. K. 1968. "The Matthew Effect in Science". In: *Science* Vol. 159, 56-63.
51 Merton 1985: 155.
52 Merton, R.K. 2000. "On the Garfield Input to the Sociology of Science: A Retrospective Collage". In: Cronin, B., Barski-Atkins, H. (eds.) 2000: *The Web of Knowledge. A Festschrift in honor of Eugene Garfield*. ASIST. 438.
53 Cf. Eprints: http://opcit.eprints.org/oacitation-biblio.html [1 Dec. 2008]
54 Cf. Kleinberg 1998.
55 Schüttpelz 2007: 25.
56 Cf. Boltanski, L. and Chiapello, E. 2006. *Der neue Geist des Kapitalismus*. Konstanz: UVK. 462.
57 Power, M. 1999. *The Audit Society*. Oxford: University Press.
58 Cf. Callon 1986, Röhle in this volume, Mager forthcoming.
Callon, M. 1986. "Elements of a Sociology of Translation: Domestication of the Scallops and the Fishermen of St Brieuc Bay". In John Law (Ed.), *Power, Action and Belief: A New Sociology of Knowledge?* London, Routledge: 196-233; Röhle, T. in this volume; Mager, A. forthcoming. "Mediated Health: Socio-technical practices of providing and using online health information". in: *New Media & Society*.
59 Google Flutrends. 2008. http://www.google.org/flutrends/ [1 Dec. 2008]
60 Cf. Richard Roger's contribution in this volume
61 Cf. Elmer, G. 2003. "A Diagram of Panoptic Surveillance". In: *New Media & Society*, Vol. 5, 231-247.
62 Cf. "blocking action" in White, H. C. 1992. *Identity and Control: A Structural Theory of Action*. Princeton, NJ: Princeton UP

Liberties

From Trust to Tracks

A Technology Assessment Perspective Revisited

Claire Lobet-Maris

The two generations of TA: From forecasting to social constructivism

Over the three last decades, technology assessment has evolved both regarding its concept of technology-society interactions and its political or societal responsibilities. Traditionally, two generations of technology assessment are differentiated. The first relied on the concept of technological options and dealt with an evaluation of social impacts and developing scenarios for social responses. The anticipation of future changes and the democratization of the political decision making process were at the core of TA activities. This first generation was marked by a sort of technological determinism that sustained a vision of an autonomous technology with its inner logic that would affect the future of our society in a predetermined and thus in a non-negotiated way. In this framework, the role of TA was understood as forecasting in order to advise political decision makers and the so-called public about sustainable and socially acceptable technological choices. This institutional organization of TA with clear and separated roles attributed to the various actors (politicians decide, engineers design, the public does or does not accept the decisions) was hard to sustain in terms of empirical evidence.

This was also underlined by Bijker, who pointed out that the clear separation between decision makers, designers and users is an illusion when considering the socio-dynamism of technological deployment.

> Since the 1980s, sociological and historical studies have developed a constructivist analysis of technology in contrast to the standard image of technology that was largely "technologically determinist". The idea that technology is socially shaped, rather than an autonomously developing

force in society or a primarily cognitive development, is not entirely new, but its present momentum and precise formulation are quite recent. Social shaping models stress that technology does not follow its own momentum nor a rational goal-directed problem-solving path, but is instead shaped by social factors. ... Demonstrating the interpretative flexibility of an artifact makes clear that the stabilization of an artifact is a social process, and hence subject to choices, interests, value judgments – in short, to politics.[1]

As is well explained by Rip, the basic idea of Constructive Technology Assessment is

to shift the focus of TA away from assessing fully articulated technologies, and introduce anticipation of technology impacts at an early stage in the development. Actors within the world of technology become an important target group then, but the insight of recent technology studies – that impacts are co-produced in the implementation and diffusion stages – implies that technology actors are not the only ones to be involved. Within the world of technology, the preferred strategy for CTA is to broaden the aspects and the actors that are taken into account. More generally, one should work towards societal learning in handling, and sometimes managing, technology in society.[2]

This CTA is clearly based on the micro analysis of technological cases and articulated on a dual vision of technology as being shaped by society and on the other hand shaping it at the same time. If determinism can be seen as the major critique of the first stage of TA, the relativism related to the analysis of micro cases is one of the major risks of the second generation, since the assessment is dependent on the values and on the interests of the various factors involved in the technological dynamics. This focus on the actors, their values and their interests together with a commitment to a descriptive methodology make this constructive assessment of technologies a bit disappointing regarding its political and ethical commitment to society. In other words, there is a sort of liberalism that clouds this approach, suggesting that the "good" or the "fair" will eventually emerge from the social network involved in the construction of a particular technology. In this constructive approach, STS scientists consider that their responsibilities only apply to the social reflexivity generated by their description of the technological dynamism and its social construction.

The third generation: a revisited and militant TA

As social scientists we demand that the next generation of technology assessment be less neutral or more political and ethical in its approach to new technologies. Following Introna, we consider every technological artifact as micro-politics, as a script that incorporates social and political orderings, norms, and values.[3] The role of this revisited TA is to make this script transparent by explaining the different closures that shape its conception. This exercise of transparency needs some support to explore the script and to assess it. To a certain extent, we have to oppose other norms and values to the normative project implicit in the technological approach. If we do not explore those scripts by adopting a clear normative principles stance, we just describe the technologies as they are decided and appropriated by actors in the field.

But is this sufficient to be sure that our society remains human? In a way, this constructive approach, by proposing that we are all actors of a technological construct, denies that those technological artifacts are dominated by vested and well organized interests, introducing an unbalanced game of power. How can we move beyond the focus on the micro scale, in which the constructive TA seems to remain, so that we can address societal issues and extend their deliberation to a larger audience? For all those reasons, we demand a more militant approach from social scientists when assessing technologies. This militant approach starts from the recognition that we have some values to defend, even if it is a very ill considered position in a general context still marked by the supposed neutrality and objectivity of science.

The first age of TA was macro and heavily marked by a technological determinism and by institutional settings; the second age was micro and strongly marked by a sort of relativism due to the constructive frame. What was missing in these two generations of TA was a "moral or ethical framing" based on defined principles to conduct the exploration of the artifact under consideration.

Let us briefly question the status and the meaning of those ethical principles.

According to Ladrière, ethics is based on ability or capability.[4] It is not abstract knowledge that is theoretical or normative and which one could define and transfer to others. Instead, it is a practice, an ability to face a situation ethically. This position is very close to that developed by John Dewey who underlines that the search of universal and fixed norms for an ethical approach can be compared to the quest for certainty in epistemology, which is at the source of so many problems that are badly defined and therefore never solved.[5] In that sense and according to Ladrière, the role of the so-called STS experts is not to decide in place of the concerned actors, but to make deliberation possible and to enlighten it by clarifying the ethical questions raised by the micro politics at work.

Ladrière and Dewey suggest that we never approach an ethical problem from a "tabula rasa", without using some ethical references or principles transmitted by the tradition. But for Dewey as for Ladrière, these principles are not fixed rules that could, as in a cooking recipe, tell us by themselves what to do, how to act, determining almost mechanically the best way or the ethical course for our decisions and actions. For Dewey, these principles are explorative or analytical tools that are useful to shed light on a particular situation and to assess the various points of view expressed by the actors concerned. Dewey admits that general ideas such as justice, dignity, or fairness, are of value as tools of inquiry to question and forecast unknown ethical puzzles. They have no intrinsic normative force, but constitute a sort of moral background that may help facing an unknown moral situation.

What should those explorative principles be?

In our TA practice, two explorative principles shape our analysis of technological artifacts: The first principle relates to the autonomy of the subject and the second to democracy, the two terms being intrinsically related by a process of co-originality, each being a necessary (but not sufficient) condition for the other.

Let us first introduce very briefly our concept of autonomy. This concept may appear very vague if we do not define it in a sort of robust and pragmatic approach. This is what Nussbaum and Sen[6] do with their concept of capability, which they define by raising the Aristotelian question: Which activities characteristically performed by human beings are so central that they seem to define the life that is truly human? They identify ten fundamental capabilities that make life human. Those capabilities help to understand the two faces of autonomy as freedom from unreasonable constraints (from the state or from others) on the construction of one's identity and autonomy as control over (some) aspects of the identity one projects to the world. The second explorative principle, democracy, is strongly related to autonomy. Here again, the concept is very broad and barely operationalized for this explorative exercise. Along with Sen, we define democracy by distinguishing three critical ways in which it enriches the lives of citizens:

> First, political freedom is a part of human freedom in general, and exercising civil and political rights is a crucial part of good lives of individuals

as social beings. Political and social participation has intrinsic value for human life and well-being. To be prevented from participation in the political life of the community is a major deprivation. Second… democracy has an important instrumental value in enhancing the hearing that people get in expressing and supporting their claims to political attention (including claims of economic needs). Third…the practice of democracy gives citizens an opportunity to learn from one another, and helps society to form its values and priorities… In this sense, democracy has constructive importance, in addition to its intrinsic value for the lives of the citizens and its instrumental importance in political decisions.[7]

According to this approach, democracy is at the same time the condition for the autonomy of human individuals and conditioned by this autonomy.

Deep search engines from democracy to autonomy

Based on these two explorative principles, let us examine the major issues related to deep search engines.

Deep search engines and democracy

Analyzing search engines as micro-politics means that this artifact is not only to be considered as a search tool, but also as an infrastructure with an embedded social or political order. This is very clear when doing any research on the web with the help of different search engines. The result is different every time, even if some websites keep on scoring on the first pages and others remain hidden, since they are not indexed at all or classified with such a low ranking that no user will ever consult them. This is not neutral and this not simply technology but mostly politics. This political vision of search engines is very accurately addressed by Introna and Nissenbaum, who state:

> Make no mistake: These are political issues. What those who seek information on the Web can find will determine what the Web consists of – for them. We fear that technological limitations and commercial interests may conspire to disenfranchise those outside the mainstream and those who lack the resources or knowledge to promote their Web presence.[8]

The social shaping of those search engines and therefore their non-neutral requirements and specifications have been very well demonstrated by Cho and Roy. Exploring different engines, they point out that

> most existing search engines use a "link-popularity" metric, called PageRank, to measure the "quality" of a page. Roughly speaking, the PageRank metric considers a page "important" or of "high quality" if the page is linked to by many other pages on the Web. For example, Google puts a page at the top of a search result (out of all the pages that contain the keywords that the user issued) when the page is linked to by the most other pages on the Web. In short, "currently popular" pages are repeatedly returned at the top of the search results by major search engines. The problem of this popularity-based ranking is that it is inherently biased against unknown pages. That is, when search engines constantly return popular pages at the top of their search results, more Web users will "discover" and look at those pages, increasing their popularity even further. In contrast, a currently unpopular page will not be returned by search engines (or ranked at the bottom), so few new users will discover those pages and create a link to it, pushing the page's ranking even further down. This "rich-get-richer" phenomenon can be particularly problematic for the "high-quality" pages that were recently created. Even if a page is of high quality, the page may be completely ignored by Web users simply because its current popularity is very low. This situation is clearly unfortunate both for Web page authors and the overall Web users. New and valuable pages are ignored just because they have not been given a chance to be noticed by people.[9]

If we approach those search engines as filters or as scripts that mediate our access to information and knowledge, and therefore our vision of the world, we can consider them, along with Giddens,[10] as structures that condition our interactions. As structures, search engines cover three dimensions: meaning, since they operate a certain ordering of the world, power, since they introduce an implicit distribution of power between information operators, and norms, since they sanction certain types of behavior by being indexed and well ranked.

How is democracy affected by those new artifacts? Three main issues are at stake when examining search engines: first, equity and respect for minorities, second the diversity of this new public sphere, and finally the question of the transparency of the regulation that supports its organization.

The equity of opportunities to exist and to be consulted on the Internet is the first and most evident issue raised by the "link popularity" metrics applied by most of the engines. This questions the diversity of the web as a public sphere and the chances for the minority's voices to be heard. Most search engine providers argue for the objectivity of their search results based on their metrics. For instance, Google invokes a sort of direct and participatory democracy that guarantees that the best sources of information are always offered to those interested.

> Google works because it relies on the millions of individuals posting websites to determine which other sites offer content of value. Instead of relying on a group of editors or solely on the frequency with which certain terms appear, Google ranks every web page using a breakthrough technique called PageRank™. PageRank evaluates all of the sites linking to a web page and assigns them a value, based in part on the sites linking to them. By analyzing the full structure of the web, Google is able to determine which sites have been "voted" the best sources of information by those most interested in the information they offer. This technique actually improves as the web gets bigger, as each new site is another point of information and another vote to be counted.[11]

But, the "good intention" of search engine operators regarding the fairness of their metrics can be disrupted by both their commercial strategy of selling good positions in their top slots and the technical strategy of some announcers using their competencies to artificially raise the ranking to the top.

Introna and Nissenbaum conclude that seekers will likely find large, popular sites whose designers have enough technical savvy to succeed in the ranking game.[12] Hence, a second critical issue is raised: that of the "tyranny of the majority" and the normalization or uniformity of social visions that could emerge from this process. Let us just recall the social network theory deployed by Granovetter that demonstrates the strength and the importance of the weak ties both for the individual and for societal wealth.[13] This issue is still reinforced by the strong concentration of the field, dominated by a very small number of major search engines.

Transparency is the last but certainly the major issue in relation to the question of how search engines affect democracy. Most users are ignorant about how ranking operates and often consider it as the true response to their queries and an "objective" vision of the world. This ignorance is still reinforced by the strict secrecy that shrouds the search algorithms and the poor public information about the metrics and methods published by search engines themselves. This information, however, is critical for the trust people have about the information they get and also for the role the web could play in sound democratic deliberation.

This brief assessment of search engines asks for a better regulation of them in order to realize their potential to support democratic debate. This regulation can follow three paths according to the regulation theory developed by Williamson: pure market regulation, state hierarchical regulation, and network regulation, namely heterarchy.[14]

Let us first examine free market dynamics regulation. This is the one currently at work and the one claimed by major operators as the best practice to warrant diversity and user satisfaction. But as demonstrated by Introna and Nissenbaum, search engines and the Internet in general are anything but a true free market where customers can access transparent information and can therefore express their preferences among clear and readable alternatives.[15] Most lay users do not have any transparent information on the workings of these engines and even less the technical capability to draw a comparison of the ranking metrics used by the operators. Moreover, as seen previously, those free market rules are routinely disrupted by opportunist attitudes both on the part of the operators and of powerful web page providers. To regulate those effects, operators usually propose self-regulation by adopting codes of conduct. But this regulation strongly depends on corporate and commercial interests and more fundamentally raises questions regarding the so-called privatization of what should be considered public space.

To restore trust, some users prefer to turn to social networks, which they believe in and to which they belong. These networks play a role of intermediaries or of gatekeepers between end users and the global information sphere. But here again, questions must be raised regarding the scattering effects of this strategy on online public space, rendering difficult inclusive and productive democratic debate between those intermediary scenes and their troops. This also raises questions regarding the risks that "replis identitaires" (in the sense of self-centered identity politics) pose for social cohesion and the development of our society.

The last regulatory path is the hierarchical one passing by the hand of democratic states. What can a national state do when confronted with a global and international scene operated by transnational actors? And should a public actor intervene in this private sector? To answer those questions, it is important to consider the World Summit on the Information Society declaration of Geneva defining the Internet as a global public good.[16] "Public", as was also underlined by Poullet, means accessible for everyone and giving to everyone a true chance to actively participate in the Information Society.[17]

So to maintain the Internet as a global public good, the Internet must be regulated. Even if this public regulation is difficult, states should at least play an active role in fostering the transparency of the patterns and metrics used by the search operators in order to make their scripts as readable as possible. This could be done through different policies, such as giving certificates to search operators that provide transparent information about their metrics and ranking processes. It could also rely on public engines helping users to compare what they get and do not get when using a specific engine, and in explaining to customers how to increase their chances to be ranked in good positions. This policy of transparency is already at work in other domains that are considered a basic service, but where provision is privatized as in the case of electricity, for instance.

Deep search and autonomy

Let us now look at the other side of the coin, the autonomy of the users as citizens. Most of the search engines now offer new devices to contextualize and personalize delivered information. One of the values added by search engines consists of all the data collected on the search habits of their end-users, which is subsequently used to shape profiles and preferences in order to push personalized and contextualized information to them. This can be considered as empowering the citizens, but also has, as always, a reverse effect. Let us just remember the story of AOL, which in 2006 accidentally allowed online access to its whole database displaying more than 36 million queries made by 650.000 AOL users. With this error, the world discovered the back end of the search engines. All this collected data serves to infer a profile from the current searching and consuming acts of an end-user in order to predict future preferences of people sharing statistical similarities to him or her. This management of profiles and preferences is always presented as a benefit for the end-users and as increasing the efficiency of their search trajectory. At the same time, however, it does constitute an obscure iron numeric cage that constrains the users' freedom and their capacities of self-determination.

Two points have to be addressed here: first, the lack of transparency in the way those profiles and preferences are generated and managed. Second, the lack of the individuals' capacity to manage their numerical tracks, which means that they increasingly become "prisoners" of a story and of a social identity over which they can no longer exert any control.

81

This issue is traditionally addressed by legal considerations regarding privacy. In a recent article, Kessous demonstrates that the traditional regulations of privacy do not appear efficient enough to address this issue.[18]

Let us consider his argument. For Kessous, this regulation first endorsed a hierarchical pattern with national and international laws and bodies aiming at protecting privacy and individual freedoms. These public regulations appear quite incoherent and often ineffective and weak in a global context marked by a strong liberalization and an absence of effective world regulation.

The second path is the market based on the free will of the actors supported by the concept of informed consent on the one hand and opt-in and opt-out mechanisms on the other. This market regulation raises political issues regarding the concept of justice, since it creates a de facto asymmetry between the "haves" and the "have nots" in terms of their capability to act in order to protect their privacy and their autonomy. But this market mechanism can also appear counter-productive for the search engine operators, since their systems of preferences and profiles usually give a clear primacy to the acting or clicking body as the ultimate access to the truth, rather than to the subject and to his or her rhetoric or expressive capacity. In this search context, the clicking bodies are considered more objective, more reliable and more informative than the thinking or speaking persons, and more revealing of the "true" personal identities, personalities and lifestyles than whatever the individuals may tell or express. This "body paradigm" introduces a sort of paradox in the regulation inspired by the liberal frame of the "free will".

The third path suggested by the author is based on the technico-political empowerment of the citizens by providing them with technical facilities to write their story and their identity themselves by managing their numerical tracks. Kessous calls these technologies "Maoïst cleaners"[19] giving people the opportunity to "reset" their profiles, to delete some out-dated or prejudicial links, to restore their intellectual rights and the principle of reversibility of their social identity and life story. In my view, the hierarchical and market paths are necessary to protect the privacy rights of people, yet they are not sufficient to restore their autonomy and capacity for self-determination. This requires new technical innovations to support an effective political empowerment of the citizens.

Conclusion

The global economy is often synonymous with the end of the national state placed in a sort of asymmetric equation confronting large and well organized transnational corporations. Does that mean that there is no more space for an effective responsibility of the national states to protect their citizens? As pointed out by Stiglitz, government definitely has a place, but it must know its place.[20] The example of deep search engines demonstrates that there are still large margins for pro-active roles of the national states in guiding their citizens in the so-called Information Society. These roles concern education and innovation: education by encouraging learning programs that help people to better understand and decode these new search windows by which they have access to information and to knowledge; innovation by investing in research programs supporting projects based on "ethical value-added" engines, but also projects to empower the citizens to manage and control their tracks... and hence returning to them their property and restoring their human right to their own identities.

Notes

1 Wiebe Bijker. "Democratization of Technology:Who are the Experts?" *World Series on Culture and Technology*. (1995) http://www.angelfire.com/la/esst/bijker.html (accessed Dec. 2008)
2 Arie Rip. "Science & Technology Studies and Constructive Technology Assessment." *European Association for the Study of Science and Technology* (1994) http://www.easst.net/review/sept1994/rip (accessed Dec. 2008)
3 Lucas Introna. "The Ethics of Things." *Working Paper*, Lancaster University Management School, WP 2003/090, (2003): 19
4 Jean Ladrière. "L'éthique dans l'univers de la rationalité". Namur: Artel / fides (1997).
5 John Dewey. Democracy and Education. The Macmillan Company (1916)
6 Martha Nussbaum and Amartya Sen (eds). *The Quality of Life*, Oxford: Clarendon Press; New York: Oxford University Press (1993)
7 Amartya Sen. "Democracy as Universal Value." *Journal Of Democracy* 10.3 (1999): 3-17
8 Lucas Introna and Helen Nissenbaum. "Shaping the Web: Why the Politics of Search Engines Matters" *The Information Society* 16,3 (2000): 169-186
9 Junghoo Cho and Sourashis Roy. "Impacts of Search Engines on Page Popularity", *Proceedings of the World-Wide Web Conference* (WWW), (May 2004): 20-29
10 Anthony Giddens. "The Constitution of Society: Outline the Theory of Structure." Berkley: University of California Press (1984)
11 http://www.google.com/corporate/tenthings.html
12 Lucas Introna and Helen Nissenbaum (2000)
13 Mark Granovetter, "The Strength of the Weak Ties: A Network Theory Revisited" *Sociological Theory*, Vol. 1, (1983): 201-233
14 Oliver E. Williamson. "The modern corporation: origins, evolution, attributes", *Journal of Economics Literature* (1981): 1537-1568
15 Lucas Introna and Helen Nissenbaum (2000)
16 WSIS (2003), "Geneva Declaration of Principles", World Summit on the Information Society, December 2003 – http:// www.itu.int/wsis
17 Yes Poullet, "Internet Governance: Some Thoughts after the two WSIS", In; *The Information Soci-*

ety: Innovation, Legitimacy, Ethics and Democracy, edited by Goujon, Philippe; Lavelle, Sylvain; Duquenoy, Penny; Kimppa, Kai and Laurent, Véronique, Springer, (2007): 203-224

18 Emmanuel Kessous. "La privacy dans les univers numériques : trois rationalités de la confiance". In *Variations sur la Confiance*, Edited by Lobet-Maris, Claire ; Six, Benjamin and Lucas, Robin. Bruxelles: Peter Lang édit. To be published 2009

19 This term was suggested to E. Kessous by F. Pallu in reference to the dethroned dignitaries of the Maoïst regime who were effaced on the official pictures of the regime.

20 Joseph Stiglitz. "The Role of Government in Economic Development". In *Annual World Bank Conference on Development Economics*. Washington DC (1996)

Search Engine Law and Freedom of Expression

A European Perspective

Joris van Hoboken[1]

Introduction

A typical exposition of the challenges to freedom of expression in the context of search engines starts with a discussion of Internet censorship in China and other countries that do not have a tradition of freedom of expression and a free press. As a result, the censorship of the Web and the suppression of search results by global search providers in China is well documented[2] and widely discussed in the media.[3] The debate about the proper implications of freedom of expression for search engine law and policy in the European context has been much less prominent. This is regrettable because a variety of issues warrant such a discussion. Before addressing these issues in more depth, it is useful to start with a few examples.

Over the last two years, Martin Leguizamon, an Argentinian attorney, secured court orders for over a hundred people to get search results removed from Google and Yahoo.[4] Some of the court orders related to searches about public officials. If anything, democratic governance and the freedom of expression imply the freedom to discuss and inform oneself about the functioning of public officials. This has led Google to publicly state its discomfort with Argentinian laws and appeal the respective court orders.[5] Remarkably, in its plea for search engine freedom, Google refers to the protection it receives in Europe. Unfortunately, this reference is mistaken. In most European countries, search engine providers receive no clear legal protection against requests for removal of search results and struggle with similar issues as in Argentina.

In 2008, an artist and a photographer successfully sued Google in Germany for showing thumbnails of their works in its image search service.[6] The material was posted online with the authors' consent, but the court in Hamburg ruled that this does not imply that Google can make it searchable through an image search engine. The possibility for webmasters to exclude material from search engines by using the robots.txt instruction is also irrelevant, according to the court in Hamburg. The court concluded that search engines need express permission of copyrights holders, in the absence of which the use of thumbnails amounts to copyright infringement. Google has appealed the German ruling for obvious reasons. If the ruling stands, Google might have to shut down or restructure its image search service in Germany. Needless to add, it would also obstruct others than Google from providing image search services in Germany in the way that seems to have arisen as a standard on the Web.

In September 2007, a French court in Paris ordered Google to hand over the IP addresses of users of its search service to an *AdWords* customer, the French company *Attractive Ltd.*[7] This developer of bars and restaurants in Paris contested the monthly Google bills for its advertisements on the Google page. An IP address with a time stamp is the key to the identification of Internet users. Although European regulators, amongst others, have started to scrutinize search engine providers for the systematic surveillance of users, it is likely they will continue to log a detailed set of non-anonymous data for lengthy periods of time. This information is available not only to the providers themselves, but, subject to conditions in national laws, also to third parties, including law enforcement and national security agencies. The effects of user surveillance on access to information and user behavior are not yet clear, but it is obvious that some users could start to self-censor themselves when considering using search engines for more controversial or sensitive subjects.

These three anecdotes clarify some of the typical challenges to freedom of expression and information in the context of Web search engines. In the following, I will give a systematic overview of these challenges and show that from the perspective of freedom of expression, which includes not only the freedom to express but also the freedom to seek and receive information and ideas, European search engine law and policy is far from ideal.

The importance of search engines

Search engines are amongst the most dominant media on the Web. Since the Web does not provide a search functionality itself, except for the limited navigational value of domain names, this gap has been filled by a variety of providers, tools and practices.[8] Parallel to the growth of the Internet and the Web, there is an ever growing need for effective mediation between information sources and audiences. The informational abundance has made effective search tools extremely important and powerful. As first points of access to the Web, general purpose search engines have become the dominant navigational tool for Internet end-users. They have also become some of the most important platforms for information, knowledge and advertisements to find their way to an audience. Thus, the Internet and effective search tools in particular provide end-users with unprecedented levels of access to information. However, new modes of suppression of the relative accessibility of information have started to interfere with such access.

Pressure on entities controlling "accessibility"

There is a general recognition that traditional intervention or strategies focusing on the governance of the availability of content have become less effective. As a result some of this attention has shifted towards intermediaries that control the accessibility to content such as search engines and internet access providers. Here, availability means that the material exists somewhere on the Internet and accessibility stands for the relative "reachability" of available material.[9] Among the reasons for this shift in focus are the abundance of information arising from the ease and variety of techniques for online publication, the global nature of the Internet with related jurisdictional problems, and the immaturity of enforcement mechanisms to tackle illegal material at its source.[10]

Internet service providers (ISPs) are amongst the primary targets to regulate the accessibility of content. Ofcom recently concluded that self-regulation by ISPs, which have strong ties with the jurisdictions of end-users, is a crucial element in a policy that aims to manage content risks for children.[11] The discussion about the censorship of a Wikipedia entry in the United Kingdom is an illuminating example as well. The *Internet Watch Foundation* (IWF) placed the Wikipedia entry about a Scorpions cover on its list of child pornographic material that is used as a black list by major ISPs.[12] The discussion in the media that followed and the widespread availability and accessibility of the targeted image caused the IWF to review its decision and remove the Wikipedia entry from its list.[13] There are various "voluntary" Internet filtering schemes directed at child pornography in Europe and the United States: quote-unquote voluntary because adopted under government pressure.[14] More recently, rights holders have started to lobby for filtering and disconnection of users by ISPs in the context of illegal file sharing. It is important to note here that the possibility of circumventing blocking and filtering by Internet access providers is well-documented, so these measures can hardly be seen as preventing access to the blocked or filtered material entirely.

Like ISPs, search engines are being pushed or asked to help to regulate the accessibility of online information. In the United States, the *Digital Millennium*

Copyright Act incentivizes search engines to remove results when receiving a notice that they link to copyright infringing material.[15] All major U.S. based search engines react to such notices by removing the results globally. In Europe, a variety of laws put search engines under legal pressure to remove results from their index. In the Netherlands, *Zoekmp3*, a search engine for mp3-files, was found to be illegal altogether because of its exploitation of infringing material on the Web.[16] Instead of using Zoekmp3 to target the source of the infringements, rights holders sued the service that made the material more readily accessible. Since 2004, major search engine providers in collaboration with government agencies in France and Germany remove some search results to illegal and harmful information from their country-specific services.[17] Others have proposed to target the interface between users and search engines. For instance, European Commissioner Frattini called on search engines to make certain "dangerous" searches impossible.[18] In all these cases the material remains available online and accessible through other means, for instance through the non-country-specific versions of the same search providers.

Freedom of expression

Without passing a definitive judgment on whether these developments are appropriate responses to what can in general be considered to be valid concerns, it is clear that freedom of expression theory should inform us about the legitimacy of this move to the suppression of accessibility of information. Whereas censorship and suppression of findability might be the logical outcome of an information environment that cannot be kept "clean" entirely, the same findability is essential for the freedom of expression in an environment that is characterized by information overload. It is not the ability to speak that is at risk as much as the ability to be found, and it is not the ability to access information that is at stake as much as the ability to locate that information. This brings us to the important question of what the right to freedom of expression actually protects.

Freedom of expression is protected as a fundamental right on the international level in United Nations Treaties,[19] at the regional level in Article 10 of the European Convention on Human Rights (ECHR)[20] and at the national level in constitutions. Broadly defined, as in Article 10 ECHR, freedom of expression stands for the freedom to hold opinions and to receive and impart information and ideas without interference by public authorities and regardless of frontiers. It is informed by democratic ideals, the search for truth and individual self-fulfillment.[21] Notably, it does not only protect the freedom to speak, but also other communicative freedoms such as the freedom to gather, look for, access, and transmit information and ideas. The freedom to seek is explicitly mentioned in the UN treaties. Freedom of expression as protected in Article 10 ECHR is not absolute, but allows for certain narrowly defined interferences that are necessary in a democratic society.[22] It is primarily a negative right, protecting private parties against state interferences such as censorship. However, freedom of expression can also place positive obligations on the state to guarantee the respect for the principle of freedom of expression in society and a minimum ability to effectively exercise one's right to freedom of expression. Under Article 10 of the European Convention, the state is for instance ultimately responsible for a pluralist information environment.[23]

Two types of legal pressure on search engines

If one analyzes the pressure that is placed on search engines to suppress information in Europe, one can make a distinction between two types. First, there is pressure that is specifically directed at search engines and meant to suppress access to certain information. Second, there is pressure, more structural in nature, caused by the lack of acknowledgment of search engines' importance for the online information environment. Both types of pressure are problematic from the perspective of freedom of expression. The first type can incentivize search engines to censor or obscure the presence of certain information on the Web, thereby obstructing legitimate information flows. The second type increases the difficulty of operating a search engines in Europe and prevents the development of a wide variety of effective services and tools that help to mediate effectively between information sources online and Internet users.

Liability of search engines for search engine results

When we look at the issue of censorship by search engines in Europe, a continuing problem is the absence of clear rules about the obligations of search engines when they are confronted with requests to remove certain results from their index.[24] A variety of national laws can make search results legally problematic, such as laws relating to copyright and trademark infringement, privacy, defamation, and certain forms of illegal speech such as hate speech or child pornography. Because of its massive automatic crawling of online information, a crawler-based search engine is bound to end up indexing illegal information published by third parties. The question is what a search engine should do, when a government agency requests the removal of a search result,[25] when a TV-hostess asks for removal of results that connect her to adult websites,[26] or when the Church of Scientology asks it to remove results that allegedly infringe its copyright.[27] Should it remove or obscure these or some of these results or should it refuse to remove material without a valid legal order? Should it inform the particular website that it has been removed from the index and provide an opportunity to the website to contest the alleged illegality of their publications and to be restored in the index? Should it make it clear to users that results are being removed or obscured and for which reasons?

The legal regime for search engines in Europe does not at all guarantee that search engines will get the answers to these questions right. The current regime and the differences in legal rules between different jurisdictions have caused search engines to navigate between three options, when asked to remove material. They can adopt the lowest common denominator and remove information globally when there is a legal request for information, they can remove results from country-specific services, or they can refuse to comply with the request without a valid court order. The first option is the simplest, but results in the suppression of legitimate speech because of overbroad requests and cultural differences regarding tolerance for the publicity of information. The second option is in some ways more nuanced, but it does not prevent access to the information for the Internet savvy and results in the fragmentation of the Internet through intermediaries.[28] As the legal obligations are unclear, the third option is currently the best from the perspective of freedom of expression. But costly litigation, legal penalties, unfavorable legal precedent and regulatory pressure can make this option unattractive.

To summarize, European laws with regard to the liability of search engine providers for unlawful references do not protect users against facing undue suppression of search results. In addition, there is a significant lack of transparency about these practices. Since one can hardly expect major search engines to thoroughly investigate every complaint they receive, the existing uncertainty is bound to lead to the removal of legitimate websites, thereby diminishing their accessibility for end-users.[29] It is fair to add that third parties that feel that certain search results harm them in their legally protected interests find themselves struggling to understand the circumstances under which they can legitimately claim to get certain information removed from a search engine. Instead of addressing the issue, the European Commission and most European legislatures have postponed dealing with the liability of search engines for nearly a decade.[30]

Legality of basic search engine operations

The basic operations of search engines are still the subject of litigation as well.[31] Crawling, indexation, archiving, the showing of parts of the index to users, and linking continue to pose difficult legal questions. The reason is that a significant part of the Web consists of copyright protected works and the basic operations of search engines involve actions that may be restricted through copyright law.

Recently, the European Commission issued a Green Paper that touched upon the legality of basic search engine operations from the perspective of European copyright law.[32] This Green Paper addresses the emergence of search engines as new successful commercial players in the online information environment and asks whether copyright law still guarantees the fair balance between rights holders and these new entities. The Green Paper seems to imply that search engines are not in full compliance with copyright law and are making their profits at the expense of rights holders, thereby increasing the pressure already placed on search engines through litigation. In a footnote, the Commission sceptically refers to one of the legal arguments search engine providers have used to claim that their basic operations are legal under copyright law. Search engines have claimed that since webmasters can opt out of indexation by a search engine by using a robot exclusion instruction such as robots.txt, webmasters implicitly give permission for the indexation of the material they publish online if they don't. [33]

The Green Paper is an excellent illustration of the ambivalent attitude of European legislatures. On the one hand, they embrace the Web and the Internet as essential for the Information Society. On the other hand, they seem unwilling to embrace the new players that have naturally emerged to make the environment work. One cause for this ambivalence may be the increasingly hostile relationship between traditional publishers and search engines in Europe. Online publishers are still struggling to establish sustainable operations on the Web. They have to make material freely accessible to reach an audience through search engines, but see a large portion of advertising revenues go to others.[34] Another explanation of this relatively unsympathetic attitude towards search engines might be found in the striking dominance of U.S. based companies in the online environment, and Google in particular.

Dominance of Google in Europe

Google's market share in Europe, ranked by searches, is around 80 percent and continues to grow.[35] This dominance makes the way Google navigates the

European legal waters particularly interesting. A website removed from Google practically ceases to exist and other search engines will be tempted to copy the practices of the leading search engine. More importantly, it raises the question of whether European law and policy is doing enough or could do more to facilitate the development of effective search tools and services and promote competition between search engines.

The government-funded *Quaero* project launched by France and Germany in 2006 has been portrayed as the European answer to Google.[36] The project soon split up into the *Quaero* and *Theseus* projects in France and Germany respectively. Both *Quaero* and *Theseus* intend to promote European search engine research and development, but the projects have not yet resulted in consumer search services with a notable user base. In particular, neither *Quaero* nor *Theseus* aims to safeguard freedom of expression and information in the search engine environment.

The point here is that instead of funding an industry that is developing incredibly fast without public spending, European legislatures could try to facilitate the search engine market by adopting laws and policies that are more favorable for new entrants. The legal uncertainty with regard to the liability and the basic operations of search engines constitutes an additional barrier to entry into the European search engine market. As this uncertainty results in significant legal overhead, a large established provider like Google is in the best position to deal with legal pressure, be it in the form of complaints, litigation, or from regulators. The more restrictive obligations are being placed on search engine providers, to negotiate with governments, to settle with publishers and to deal with complaints from third parties, the more difficult it gets for smaller providers to provide a similar service. In fact, it may be a remarkable achievement that Google, with the help of a small army of lawyers, has been able to keep its search services running in Europe.

Clearly, there is room and need for more than one general search engine, so European search engine law and policy should look beyond the dominant position of Google. The dominance of Google in combination with its central position in the ongoing legal debates about the proper responsibility of search engines and the legality of their basic operations could lead to a reinforcement of its dominance, especially if legislatures and regulators would impose additional legal obligations on search engines providers in Europe that are more difficult to fulfill for small providers.

Free access to information

Finally, if we address the freedom to search for users, it is important to reflect on search engines' collection of unprecedented amounts of user data, and the subsequent use of these data by search engines and third parties. Systematic user surveillance has been widely discussed since the *AOL* data release.[37] Privacy advocacy groups, international data privacy bodies and in particular the EU's Article 29 Working Party have reacted with recommendations that aim to minimize the processing of user data by search engines.[38]

Central to the debate has been the retention term for search engine logs, which include the IP addresses of users, unique cookie data, search queries, timestamps, and user clicks. It is important to note that even if the retention terms for search engine logs were limited to the recommended 3-6 months, users of search engines would still be placed under systematic surveillance when using the key tools to navigate the Web. Since searching the Web is for many a daily activity, the search logs of a typical Internet user over 3-6 months provides an incredibly detailed picture of that user's interests, activities, and intentions. If it is unfeasible to require search engine providers to minimize user surveillance further, the law should guarantee the confidentiality of search activity through other means.

User privacy in the context of search engines is primarily a concern related to free access to information for users. To guarantee the confidentiality of private communications and to protect the freedom of communication, communications law has traditionally placed special restrictions on the access to private communications by communications providers and third parties. The rules relating to access to the postal mail and wiretapping can serve as examples. Libraries also tend to highly value the privacy of their patrons to guarantee free access to information and ideas. In reality search activity is partly displacing the browsing through libraries and their catalogues, and it may be of an equally private nature as communications over the mail or the telephone. People may be "asking" things of search engines they might not even ask their colleagues, partners or best friends. The laws that regulate search surveillance and access to search engine logs by third parties have yet to adapt to this reality.

Ideally, search engine law and policy would not only minimize the collection of user data by search engines, but also place special restrictions on the access to search engine logs and guarantee a minimum level of transparency with regard to access to search logs by third parties. Without such restrictions, government agencies and other third parties will continue to line up to get access to these incredibly rich collections of data about the interests, intentions and online navigation of Internet users. In the meantime, Google regularly complies with valid legal requests for user data and gives no information about them as a matter of company policy.[39]

Conclusion

Search engines are amongst the most used services by Internet users and are central to the navigation of the Web. In fact, they are an indispensable component of the Internet's promise of democratizing access to information. Search engine law and policy should react by making freedom of expression a dominant concern underlying legal and policy choices with regard to Web search engines.

Unfortunately, legislatures across Europe are lagging behind in facilitating the search engine environment in this manner. In particular, they have failed to provide the legal framework for search engines to develop and provide their services in a way that is consistent with the right to freedom of expression. The effective ability of users to find valuable information online without undue interference, the ability of online sources to reach an audience, and the ability to provide search services, to locate, select and evaluate information, are restricted in manners that are suboptimal from the perspective of freedom of expression.

Therefore, in many ways, the current levels of access to information exist despite the law and not because of it. If one accepts that freedom of expression should be one of the dominant concerns underlying any law or policy for the Internet,[40] this situation calls for a change.

Notes

1 The author would like to thank the organizers and participants of the Deep Search conference in Vienna for the opportunity to present and discuss the ideas that led to this contribution. All online sources were last consulted on 5 January 2009.
2 See Ronald Deibert, John Palfrey et al. (ed.), *Access Denied: The Practice and Policy of Global Internet Filtering* (Cambridge MA: The MIT Press) 2007. See also Nart Villeneuve, 'Search Engine Monitor', Citizen Lab Occasional Paper #1, 2008, http://www.citizenlab.org/papers/searchmonitor.pdf.
3 See for instance Clive Thompson, "Google's China Problem (and China's Google Problem)", *The New York Times*, April 23, 2006, http://www.nytimes.com/2006/04/23/magazine/23google.html; Wolfgang Pomrehn, "Das Dilemma der Zensur in China", *Telepolis*, February 12, 2006, http://www.heise.de/tp/r4/artikel/22/22091/1.html; Dan Sabbagh, "No Tibet or Tiananmen on Google's Chinese site", *Times Online*, January 25, 2006, http://business.timesonline.co.uk/tol/business/markets/china/article719192.ece; Bruno Philip, "Google se plie à la censure de Pékin pour percer sur le marché de l'Internet chinois", *Le Monde*, January 27, 2008.

4 See Christopher Soghoian & Firuzeh Shokooh Valle, "Adiós Diego: Argentine judges cleanse the Internet", OpenNet Initiative, November 11, 2008, http://opennet.net/blog/2008/11/adi%C3%B3s-diego-argentine-judges-cleanse-internet; Uki Bonim, "Can A Soccer Star Block Google Searches?", *Time Magazine*, November 14, 2008, http://www.time.com/time/world/article/0,8599,1859329,00.html.
5 See Pedro Less Andrade, "La censura previa nunca es un buen modelo", El Blog Official de Google para América Latina, October 8, 2008, http://googleamericalatinablog.blogspot.com/2008/10/la-censura-previa-nunca-es-un-buen.html.
6 "Google Loses Court Battle Over Image Searches", Deutsche Welle, October 14, 2008, http://www.dw-world.de/dw/article/0,2144,3710342,00.html. See Landgericht Hamburg, 26 September 2008 – Az.: 308 O 42/06, and Landgericht Hamburg, 26 September 2008 – Az.: 308 O 248/07. Available at http://www.suchmaschinen-und-recht.de/urteile/Landgericht-Hamburg-20080926.html.
7 Tribunal de Commerce de Paris, September 6, 2007, Attractive Ltd. v. Google France, Google Ireland. Available at http://www.legalis.net/jurisprudence-decision.php3?id_article=206. It seems that Google itself proposed to hand over the IP addresses of users as a second line of defense.
8 For an overview, see Alex Halavais, *Search Engine Society*, Digital Media and Society Series (Cambridge: Polity) 2008, 5-31; Joris van Hoboken, "Legal Space for Innovative Ordering: On the need to Update Selection Intermediary Liability in the EU", *International Journal for Communications Law & Policy*, 2009.
9 Compare, Eszter Hargittai, "Open Portals or Closed Gates? Channeling content on the World Wide Web", Poetics, 27, 2000, 233-253; Eszter Hargittai, "Content Diversity Online: Myth or Reality?", in: *Media Diversity and Localism: Meaning and Metrics*. Ed. Philip Napoli. (Mahwah, NJ: Lawrence Erlbaum, 2007), 349-362.
10 This is not to say that the enforcement of national laws is impossible. See Jack L. Goldsmith, Tim Wu, *Who Controls the Internet?: Illusions of a Borderless World*, (New York: Oxford University Press US, 2006).
11 Ofcom – Office of Communications, Ofcom's Response to the Byron Review, March 27, 2008, 50-51. Available at http://www.ofcom.org.uk/research/telecoms/reports/byron/byron_review.pdf.
12 "British ISPs restrict access to Wikipedia amid child pornography allegations", Wikinews, 7 December 2008, http://en.wikinews.org/wiki/British_ISPs_restrict_access_to_Wikipedia_amid_child_pornography_allegations; Richard Clayton, "Technical aspects of the censoring of Wikipedia", Light Blue Touchpaper, December 11, 2008, http://www.lightbluetouchpaper.org/2008/12/11/technical-aspects-of-the-censoring-of-wikipedia.
13 Internet Watch Foundation, IWF statement regarding Wikipedia webpage, December 9, 2008, last modified 18 December 2008, http://www.iwf.org.uk/media/news.251.htm.
14 David Chartier, "alt.blocked: Verizon blocks access to whole USENET hierarchy", *Ars Technica*, June 16, 2008, http://arstechnica.com/news.ars/post/20080616-alt-blocked-verizon-blocks-access-to-whole-usenet-hierarchy.html; Karin Spaink, "Child pornography: fight it or hide it?", February 19, 2008, http://www.spaink.net/2008/02/19/child-pornography-fight-it-or-hide-it/, "Familienministerin will Kinderporno-Sperren bald umsetzen", Heise Online, November 30, 2008, http://www.heise.de/newsticker/Familienministerin-will-Kinderporno-Sperren-bald-umsetzen--/meldung/119663.
15 See J.M. Urban & L. Quilter, "Efficient Process or 'Chilling Effects'? Takedown Notices Under Section 512 of the Digital Millennium Copyright Act", *Santa Clara Comparative & High Technology Law Journal*, 22 (2006): 621.

16 Court of Appeals Amsterdam, June 15, 2006, TechnoDesign v. BREIN. Translation available at http://www.book9.nl/getobject.aspx?id=2778Zoekmp3. For a discussion in Dutch, see Joris van Hoboken, De aansprakelijkheid van zoekmachines. Uitzondering zonder regels of regels zonder uitzondering?, *Computerrecht* 1 (2008): 15-22.

17 For the German search engine self-regulation, see "Subcode of Conduct for Search Engine Providers of the Association of Voluntary Self-Regulating Multimedia Service Providers" ("Freiwillige Selbstkontrolle Multimedia-Diensteanbieter" – FSM) (VK-S), April 21, 2004, http://www.fsm.de/en/Subcode_of_Conduct_for_Search_Engine_Providers. For a discussion of the agreement see Wolfgang Schulz & Thorsten Held, "Der Index auf dem Index? Selbstzensur und Zensur bei Suchmaschinen", in Marcel Machill & Markus Beiler (ed.), *Die Macht der Suchmaschinen / The Power of Search Engines* (Cologne: Halem, 2007), 71-87.

18 Ingrid Melander, "Web search for bomb recipes should be blocked: EU", *Reuters*, September 10, 2007, http://www.reuters.com/article/internetNews/idUSL1055133420070910.

19 Article 19 of the United Nations Universal Declaration of Human Rights, adopted and proclaimed by General Assembly resolution 217 A (III) of 10 December 1948; Article 19(2) The United Nations International Covenant on Civil and Political Rights, adopted and opened for signature, ratification and accession by General Assembly resolution 2200A (XXI) of 16 December 1966.

20 Council of Europe, Convention for the Protection of Human Rights and Fundamental Freedoms, 4 November 1950, Europ.T.S. No. 5 (hereinafter ECHR).

21 For an overview, see Frederick Schauer, *Free speech: a philosophical enquiry* (Cambridge: Cambridge University Press, 1982)

22 See generally Van Dijk, Van Hoof, et al. (eds), *Theory and Practice of the European Convention on Human Rights*, 4th edition (Antwerpen: Intersentia, 2006)

23 European Court of Human Rights 24 Nov. 1993, *Lentia v. Austria* (labeling the state as the "ultimate guarantor of pluralism"). See generally Aernout Nieuwenhuis, "The Concept of Pluralism in the Case-Law of the European Court of Human Rights", *European Constitutional Law Review*, 3 (2007): 367–384.

24 For a detailed discussion see Van Hoboken, 2009.

25 Decision no.: R/01046/2007 of the Spanish Data Protection Authority (AEPD) (Mr. X.X.X v. Google Spain, S.L.) dealing with a request of removal from Google's index results in the following administrative order: "*calling on Google to adopt the necessary measures to withdraw the data from its index and block future access to it.*" The order is remarkable because the source of the information, an official publication by a local Spanish authority, is considered to be lawful.

26 See Van Hoboken, 2009.

27 See Urban & Quilter 2006. Interestingly, Scientology's takedown notices to Google have been cited as a reason for Google to participate in the Chilling Effects Clearinghouse, a United States based initiative that tries to make the takedown practices by online intermediaries more transparent.

28 See Soghoian & Valle, 2008.

29 Major search engines and other Internet companies have recently entered into a Global Network Initiative, which contains a set of principles for dealing with requests to censor information. It is possible that this self-regulatory framework will also prove to be of value in the European context. For more information, see the Global Network Initiative at http://www.globalnetworkinitiative.org.

30 See Van Hoboken, 2009. The review of the E-commerce directive that is supposed to address the issue is long overdue. Search engine liability and intermediary liability more generally are highly controversial issues, so from the perspective of the European Commission it is not very tempting

to address the current status quo. In fact, there is a considerable effort to shift intermediary responsibility in the other direction, making it mandatory for ISPs to help to enforce copyright laws. See e.g. Monica Horten, "2009 – the year of the throttled user", iptegrity.com, available at http://www.iptegrity.com/index.php?option=com_content&task=view&id=226&Itemid=9.
31 See for instance Court of First Instance Brussels, February 13, 2007, Copiepresse v. Google; LG Hamburg, 26 September 2008 – Az.: 308 O 42/06 and LG Hamburg, September, 26 2008 – Az.: 308 O 248/07.
32 European Commission, Green Paper on Copyright in the Knowledge Economy, Brussels, COM(2008) 466/3, http://ec.europa.eu/internal_market/copyright/docs/copyright-infso/greenpaper_en.pdf.
33 See European Commission 2008, p. 9.
34 Interestingly, in a recent competitive move against Google, Microsoft has taken sides with the publishers. See Scott Fulton, "Microsoft's IP chief: 'Information wants to be free' is a 'disaster'", BetaNews, November, 26, 2008, http://www.betanews.com/article/Microsofts_IP_chief_Information_wants_to_be_free_is_a_disaster/1227206366.
35 comScore, "comScore Releases March 2008 European Search Rankings", March 2008, http://www.comscore.com/press/release.asp?press=2208.
36 "Attack of the Eurogoogle", *The Economist*, March 9, 2006.
37 Michael Barbaro and Tom Zeller jr., "A Face Is Exposed for AOL Searcher No. 4417749", *New York Times*, August 9, 2006, http://www.nytimes.com/2006/08/09/technology/09aol.html.
38 Article 29 Data Protection Working Party, "Opinion on Data Protection Issues Related to Search Engines", April 4, 2008, http://ec.europa.eu/justice_home/fsj/privacy/docs/wpdocs/2008/wp148_en.pdf.
39 See Google Inc., "Log Retention Policy FAQ", March 2007. Interestingly, Google has tried to defend its user data collection policies with a reference to the usefulness of these data for the prevention and prosecution of crime, thereby effectively asking for data retention obligations.
40 For an excellent defense of this premise, see Jack Balkin, "Digital Speech and Democratic Culture: a Theory of Freedom of Expression for the Information Society", *New York University Law Review* 79, 1, (2004)

The Second Index

Search Engines, Personalization and Surveillance

Felix Stalder & Christine Mayer[1]

Introduction

Google's well-known mission is "to organize the world's information". It is, however, impossible to organize the world's information without an operating model of the world. Melvil(le) Dewey (1851-1931), working at the height of Western colonial power, could simply take the Victorian world view as the basis for a universal classification system, which, for example, put all "religions other than Christianity" into a single category (no. 290). Such a biased classification scheme, for all its ongoing usefulness in libraries, cannot work in the irreducibly multi-cultural world of global communication. In fact, no uniform classification scheme can work, given the impossibility of agreeing on a single cultural framework through which to define the categories.[2] This, in addition to the scaling issues, is the reason why internet directories, as pioneered by Yahoo! and the Open Directory Project (demoz)[3], broke down after a short-lived period of success.

Search engines side-step this problem by flexibly reorganizing the index in relation to each query and using the self-referential method of link analysis to construct the ranking of the query list (see Katja Mayer in this volume). This ranking is said to be objective, reflecting the actual topology of the network that emerges unplanned through collective action. Knowing this topology, search engines favor link-rich nodes over link-poor outliers. This objectivity is one of the core elements of search engines, since it both scales well and increases the users' trust in the system.

Yet, this type of objectivity has its inherent limits. The index knows a lot about the information from the point of view of the providers who create the topology of the network (through creating links), but knows nothing about the searcher's particular journey through the informational landscape. What might be relevant on an aggregate, topological level could well be irrelevant on the level of the individual search interest. This problem is compounded by the fact that the actual customers of the search engines, the advertisers, are not interested in the topology of the network either, but in the individual users journeying through the network. These two forces, one intrinsic to the task of search engines themselves, the other intrinsic to what has become their dominant business model – advertising – drive the creation of the second index. This one is not about the world's information, but about the world's users of information. While the first one is based on publicly available information created by third parties, the second one is based on proprietary information created by the search engines themselves. By overlaying the two indexes the search engines hope to improve their core tasks: to deliver relevant search results to the users, and to deliver relevant users to advertisers. In the process, search engines create a new model of how to organize the world's information, a model composed of two self-referential worlds: one operating on the collective level – one world emerging from the interactions of everyone (at least in its ideal version) – and the other operating on the individual level – one's world as emerging from one's individual history. Both of these levels are highly dynamic and by interrelating them, search engines aim to overcome the problem of information overload (too much irrelevant information), which both users and customers constantly encounter, the former when being presented with hundreds of "hits" while looking for just a handful (maybe even just one), the latter when having to relate to a mass of people who don't care, rather than just a few prospective customers. Speaking about the user's problem, Peter Fleischer, Google's global privacy counsel, writes:

> Developing more personalized search results is crucial given how much new data is coming online every day. The University of California Berkeley estimates that humankind created five exabytes of information in 2002 – double the amount generated in 1999. An exabyte is a one followed by 18 noughts. In a world of unlimited information and limited time, more targeted and personal results can really add to people's quality of life.[4]

Fleischer and others usually present this as a straightforward optimization drive – improved search results and improved advertising. While this is certainly part of the story, it is not everything. This development also raises a number of troubling issues, ranging from surveillance, understood both as individual tracking and social sorting, to a potentially profound loss of autonomy. The latter is related to the fact that we are presented with a picture of the world (at least how it appears in search results) made up of what someone else, based on proprietary knowledge, determines to be suitable to one's individual subjectivity.

In the following, we will try to address these issues. First, we will provide a sense of the scale of this second index as it is being compiled by Google, the most prolific gatherer of such data. Given the sensitive and proprietary nature of that index, we can only list some publicly visible means through which this information is generated and look at the particular types of information thus gathered. We have no inside knowledge about what is being done with that information. Based on this overview, we will discuss some aspects of surveillance and of personalization. It is key to note that these are not issues we can reasonably opt out of. The pressures that are working to create and use the second index are real, and they are also driven by legitimate user needs. Thus, the question raised at the end of this text is how to address these challenges in an adequately nuanced way.

Gathering Data

Since its inception, Google has been accumulating enormous amounts of information about its users. Yet surveys have shown that most users are not aware of the wide range of data collected; many still have an understanding of Google as a search engine rather than a multi-million dollar corporation making large profits from devising personalized advertising schemes.[5]

While we concentrate on Google, it is important to note that it does not differ from its competitors in principle. Other search engines like Yahoo! and Live also enable cookies to track users' search histories; stores like Amazon.com also store information on their customers' shopping habits or credit card numbers; social networking sites like Facebook have had their own share of privacy problems, such as when users found out they could not permanently delete their accounts.[6] Cloud computing is promoted by companies like Microsoft or Dell, too. The case of Google, however, is special because of the sheer quantity of data that is gathered, because of the enormous variety and quality of this information, and because of Google's growing market dominance in the fields of web search, advertising, and cloud computing.

Google employs manifold methods to collect data on its users. *Click tracking* has long enabled Google to log any click made by anyone on any of its servers. *Log files* store any server request ever made to any of Google's servers and always save basic details like the user's IP address, location, date, time, time zone, language, operating system, and browser ("standard log information"). Additional information is also sent back to Google and logged thanks to *JavaScript* and *Web Beacons* being embedded in websites.[7] *Cookies* are used on all Google sites. Originally, these cookies were set to expire in 2038. In 2007 the system was changed so that currently Google cookies have a life expectancy of two years – unless you use a Google service in that time, which prompts a renewal by another two years, thereby rendering the cookie virtually immortal. Cookies reporting back to Google are not only used on sites that are on Google's web properties, but also on seemingly unrelated sites which use *AdSense*, *AdWords*, or *DoubleClick* ads or the statistics tool *Google Analytics*. Most users, and even many web-administrators, are not aware of technical implications of those services, i.e. that these cookies help to collect data on the users' movement around a large percentage of existing off-Google websites. In addition to these fairly opaque techniques, which are known only to Google's more tech savvy audience, there are also data sets provided by the users themselves. *Users voluntarily fill in forms* in order to sign up for accounts, which results in a log of those very personal details. It was only by employing this function and by combining information collected from its wide range of services and from third parties that Google could begin to accumulate the expansive knowledge about its users that has made it so powerful and attractive to advertising partners.

For purposes of analysis we can differentiate between three types of profiles, which together create a comprehensive profile of each user. First, users are tracked as "knowledge beings" and, in a second step, as "social beings", exploiting their real identities, contacts, and interaction with those contacts. A final data set captures the users as physical beings in real space.

The following survey is by no means a comprehensive collection of Google's services, not least of all because they are constantly expanding. Yet we believe that the services which will be added in the future will further contribute to increasing the scope of any (or all) of these three profiles.

Layer 1: Assembling a Knowledge Profile

The basic service of *Google Search* has never required its users to register for an account or to actively provide any personal details. Standard log information (see above) is, however, always gathered in the background. In addition, Google servers record information specific to the search function: the search query itself, default language settings, the country code top-level domain (whether google.com or google.at is being used), the search engine result pages and the number of search results, as well as settings like safe search (filtering and blocking adult content), or additional search options like file type, and region.

Various other services can arguably be placed in the same category, firstly because they let users search for web information provided by third parties – be it websites, magazines, books, pictures, or products – and secondly because Google employs them to gather similar sets of data about its users. These services include

Google Directory, Image Search, News Search, News Archive Search, Google Scholar, Google Books, Google Video, Blog Search, the *LIFE photo archive* hosted by Google, or *Google Product Search* (the service formerly known as Froogle).

Hal Roberts from the Berkman Center for Internet & Society at Harvard University writes that,

> [i]n fact, it is likely that this collection of search terms, IP addresses, and cookies represents perhaps the largest, most sensitive single collection of data extant, on- or offline. Google may or may not choose to do the relatively easy work necessary to translate its collection of search data into a database of personally identifiable data, but it does have the data and the ability to query personal data out of the collection at any time if it chooses (or is made to choose by a government, intruder, disgruntled worker, etc).[8]

The conception of services like *AdSense, AdWords, AdPlanner,* or *Analytics*[9] has helped Google to spread even further: *Google Analytics* can be installed on any website for free, but in exchange Google is entitled to collect information from all sites using its tool. Some estimates say that "the software is integrated into 80 percent of frequently visited German-language Internet sites".[10] The same principle governs Google's advertising schemes. Visitors to off-Google sites are usually not aware that Google servers could nevertheless be logging their online activities because "[w]eb companies once could monitor the actions of consumers only on their own sites. But over the last couple of years, the Internet giants have spread their reach by acting as intermediaries that place ads on thousands of Web sites, and now can follow people's activities on far more sites."[11]

Google's new web browser *Chrome*, a good example of the development towards the Google Cloud, must also be seen as a tool to construct the user's knowledge profile – with the additional benefit that it blurs the distinction of what the user "knows" online and offline. "*Chrome*'s design bridges the gap between desktop and so-called 'cloud computing'. At the touch of a button, *Chrome* lets you make a desktop, *Start menu,* or *Quick Launch* shortcut to any Web page or Web application, blurring the line between what's online and what's inside your PC."[12] *Chrome*'s "Omnibox" feature, an address bar which works like a Google search window with an auto-suggest function, logs every character typed by its users even without hitting the enter button.[13] Faced with severe criticism, Google maintained that the data collected by this keystroke logging process (keystrokes and associated data such as the user's IP address) would be rendered anonymous within 24 hours.[14] Concerns have also been voiced regarding *Chrome*'s history search feature, which indexes and stores sensitive user data like personal financial or medical information even on secure (https://) pages.[15]

New services are introduced to systematically cover data which has not previously been included in the user profile. In the process, basic personal data is enriched by and may be combined with information covering virtually each and every aspect of a user's information needs: Google servers monitor and log what users search for (*Google Search, Google Toolbar, Google Web History*), which websites they visit (*Google Chrome, Web Accelerator*), which files (documents, e-mails, chat, web history) they have on their computers (*Google Desktop*), what they read and bookmark (*Google Books* incl. personalized library, *Google Notebook, Google Bookmarks, Google Reader*), what they write about in e-mails (*Gmail*), in work files and personal documents online (*Google Docs*) and off-line (*Google Desktop*), in discussion groups (*Google Groups*), blogs (Blogger), or chats (*Google Talk*), what they want translated and which languages are involved (*Google Translate*).

Layer 2: Constructing the User as a Social Being

With the advent of Web 2.0 it became clear that users are not just knowledge-seeking individuals, but also social beings intensely connected to each other online and offline. Google's services have been expanding and more personalized programs have been added to its portfolio to capture the social persona and its connections.

Signing up for a Google Account allows users to access a wide range of services, most of which are not available "outside" the account. If you choose to edit your profile, basic personal details gleaned by Google from your account are not only the number of logins, your password, and e-mail address, but also your location, real-life first name and last name, nickname, address, additional e-mail address(es), phone number(s), date and place of birth, places you've lived in, profession, occupations past and present, a short biography, interests, photos, and custom links to online photo albums, social network profiles, and personal websites.

In addition, Google acquired previously independent sites like YouTube and Blogger, "migrated" their account information, and launched additional social networks like *Orkut* and *Lively*, Chat, Calendar, mobile phones and other social services.

On top of monitoring all the contents of communications (e-mails, postings, text messages sent or received), services like *Google Groups, Gmail, Google Talk*,

Friends Connect, or *Orkut* store *any* external text, images, photos, videos, and audio files submitted, contact lists, groups a user joins or manages, messages or topics tracked, custom pages users create or edit, and ratings they make. Google servers also record who users network with (*Orkut*), where, when, and why they meet friends and work contacts, which friends replied to invitations or what these contacts' e-mail addresses are (*Google Calendar*), where they do their online shopping and which products they look for (*Catalog Search*, *Product Search*, *Google Store*), which credit cards they use and what their card expiration date(s) and card verification number(s) are, where they buy from, where they want their purchase shipped, how much they bought and at what price, who they bought from, and which type of payment was used (*Google Checkout*, *Google Video*). In addition, stock portfolio information, i.e. stocks selected, the amount of a user's shares, and the date, time, and price at which they were bought, is collected as well (*Google Finance*).

All of these services transmit information, such as account activity, passwords, login time and frequency, location, size and frequency of data transfers, preferred settings, and all clicks, including UI elements, ads, and links. All this information is subsequently saved and stored in Google's log files. This monitoring of the users' social interactions gives Google the means to create ever more personalized data profiles. It is important to note that Google originally denied intentions that it was already connecting or planning to connect information from its various services.[16] In 2004, however, the company was forced to make its privacy policy more understandable due to a new Californian law[17] and the new wording included a passage stating that Google was allowed to "share the information submitted under [any Google] account among all of [their] services in order to provide [users] with a seamless experience".

Layer 3: Recreating the User's Real-Life Embodiment

For efficient advertising, the process of constructing the user increasingly tries to capture information about the individual as an embodied person and as an agent within a real-life environment. In order to add such data to its burgeoning second index, Google collects such disparate data as its users' blood type, weight, height, allergies, and immunizations, their complete medical history and records such as lists of doctors appointments, conditions, prescriptions, procedures, and test results (*Google Health*). Google already knows where its users live (*Google Account*, *Google Checkout*, *Google Maps* default location) and where they want to go (*Google Maps*), which places they like (annotated maps with photos of and comments about "favorite places" in *Google Maps*), what their house looks like (*Google Maps* satellite function, *Google Street View*), which videos they watch (*Google Video*, YouTube), what their phone numbers are (*Google Checkout*), which mobile carrier and which mobile phones they use, and where (*Dodgeball, GrandCentral, G1/ Android, MyLocation*).

New data-rich sources are accessed through mobile phones, which store their owner's browsing history and sensitive personal data that identifies them, and combine these with new functions such as location tracking. *Android*, Google's new mobile phone platform, offers applications like *Google Latitude* and *MyLocation*, which are used to determine a user's position; *MyTracks* is used to track users over time.[18] Google will thereby be able to assemble even closer consumer profiles; by targeting users with geo-located ads, Google is creating a virtual gold mine for associated advertisers.[19] This foray into the mobile market enables Google to collect mobile-specific information, which can later be associated with a *Google Account* or with some other similar account ID. *Google Latitude* also offers an option to invite a "friends" list to track the inviter. Privacy groups have drawn attention to the problem that user-specific location data can also be accessed by third parties without a user's knowledge or consent and that the victim may remain unaware of being tracked[20], thereby rendering ordinary mobile phones useful tools for personal surveillance.[21]

The development of *Android* is perhaps the clearest example for the amount of resources Google is willing to invest in order to generate and get access to data for expanding its second index; an entire communication infrastructure is being created that is optimized for gathering data and for delivering personalized services, which are yet another way of gathering more data.

Thus, Google systematically collects data to profile people in terms of their knowledge interests, social interaction, and physical embodiment. Outsiders can only observe the mechanism of gathering this data, which allows conclusions about the scope of the second index. What we cannot know is what precisely is being done with it, and even less what might be done with it in the future. What we can assess, though, are some issues arising from the mere existence of this index and the published intentions for its use.

Surveillance and Personalization

Considering the scope and detail of personal information gathered by Google (and other search engines), it is clear that very significant surveillance capacities are being generated and privacy concerns have been voiced frequently.[22] As we are trying to unravel the potential of that surveillance, it is important to distinguish three kinds of surveillance. While they are all relevant to search engines, they are actually structured very differently and subject to very different influences. First is surveillance in the classic sense of Orwell's Big Brother, carried out by a central entity with direct power over the person under surveillance, for example the state or the employer. Second is surveillance in the sense of an increasing capacity of various social actors to monitor each other, based on a distributed "surveillant assemblage" where the roles of the watchers and the watched are constantly shifting.[23] Finally, there is surveillance in the sense of social sorting, i.e. the coding of personal data into categories in order to apply differential treatment to individuals or groups.[24]

In the first case, powerful institutions use surveillance to unfairly increase and exercise their power. Search engines, however, have no direct power over their users which they can abuse. Assuming that search engines are concerned with their reputation and do not provide data from their second index to third parties, their surveillance capacities of this type appear to be relatively benign. Of course, this assumption is deeply questionable. Complex information processing systems are always vulnerable to human and technical mistakes. Large data sets are routinely lost, accidentally disclosed, and illegally accessed. Just how sensitive such search engine data can be was demonstrated in August 2006, when AOL made available the search histories of more than 650,000 persons. Even though the search histories were anonymized, the highly personal nature of the data made it possible to track down some of the users whose data had been published.[25] We can assume that large search engine companies have extensive policies and procedures in place to protect their data, thereby decreasing the likelihood of accidents and breaches. However, the massive centralization of such data makes any such incident all the more consequential, and the pull exerted by the mere existence of such large surveillance capacities is more problematic. Given the insatiable demands of business rivals, law enforcement and national security agencies, requests to access these data will certainly be made.[26] Indeed, they have already been made. In August 2005, all major search engines in the US received a subpoena to hand over records on millions of their users' queries in the context of a review of an online pornography law. Among these, Google was the only one who refused to grant access to these records.[27] While this was the only publicized incident of this kind, it is highly unlikely that this was the only such request. The expanded powers of security agencies and the vast data sets held by search engines are bound to come in close contact with one another. Historically, the collaboration between telecom companies and national security agencies has been close and extensive. Massive surveillance programs, such as ECHELON, would have been impossible without the willing support of private industry.[28] It is thus well possible that search engines are already helping to expand big-brother surveillance capacities of the state, particularly the US government.

Another more subtle effect of surveillance was first utilized by Jeremy Bentham in the design of a correctional facility (1785) and later theorized as a more general governmental technique by Michel Foucault. In a *Panopticon*, a place where everything can be seen by an unseen authority, the expectation of being watched affects the behavior of the watched. It is normalized, that is, behavioral patterns which are assumed to be "normal" are reinforced simply by knowing that the authority could detect and react to abnormal behavior.[29] This has also been shown to occur[30] in the context of CCTV surveillance. In the case of search engines, the situation is somewhat different because the watching is not done by a central organization; rather, the search engines provide the means for everyone to place themselves at the center and watch without being watched (at least not by the person being watched). It is not far-fetched to assume that the blurring of private and public spheres on the web impacts on a person's behavior. It is much too early to say anything systematic about the effects of this development, not least because this surveillance does not try to impose a uniform normative standard. Thus, it is not clear what normalization means under such circumstances. However, this is not related to the surveillance carried out by search engines themselves, but rather to their function of making any information accessible to the public at large and the willingness of people to publish personal information.

What is specific to the second index is the last dimension of surveillance, social sorting. David Lyon develops the concept in the following way:

> Codes, usually processed by computers, sort out transactions, interactions, visits, calls and other activities. They are invisible doors that permit access to, or exclude from participation in a myriad of events, experiences and processes. The resulting classifications are designed to influence and manage populations and persons thus directly and indirectly affecting the choices and chances of data subjects.[31]

Rather than treating everyone the same, social sorting allows matching people with groups to whom particular procedures, enabling, disabling or modifying behavior, are assigned. With search engines, we encounter this as personalization. It is important to note that, as David Lyon stresses, "surveillance is not itself sinister any more than discrimination is itself damaging."[32] Indeed, the basic purpose of personalization is to help search engines to improve the quality of search results. It enables them to rank results in relation to individual user preferences, rather than to network topology, and helps to disambiguate search terms based on the previous path of a person through the information landscape. Personalization of search is part of a larger trend in the informational economy towards "mass individualization", where each consumer/user is given the impression, rightly or wrongly, of being treated as a unique person within systems of production still relying on economies of scale.

Technically, this is a very difficult task for which vast amounts of personal data are needed, which, as we have seen, is being collected in a comprehensive, and systematic way. A distinction is often made between data that describes an individual on the one hand, and data which is "anonymized" and aggregated into groups on the basis of some set of common characteristics deemed relevant for some reason. This distinction plays an important role in the public debate, for example in Google's announcements in September 2008 to strengthen user privacy by "deleting" (i.e. anonymizing) user data after nine rather than 18 months.[33] Questions have also been raised about how easily this "anonymization" can be reversed by Google itself or by third parties.[34] In some cases, Google offers the option to disable cookies or use *Chrome*'s Incognito mode ("porn mode" in colloquial usage), but instructions how to do this are well hidden, difficult to follow, and arguably only relevant for highly technologically literate users. Moreover, the US-American consumer group *Consumer Watchdog* has pointed out that "Chrome's Incognito mode does not confer the privacy that the mode's name suggests", as it does not actually hide the user's identity.[35] It is important to note that even if Google followed effective "anonymizing" procedures, this would matter only in terms of surveillance understood as personal tracking. If we understand it as social sorting, this has nearly no impact. The capacity to build a near infinite number of "anonymized" groups from this database and to connect individuals to these small groups for predictive purposes re-integrates anonymized and personalized data in practice. If the groups are fine-grained, all that is necessary is to match an individual to a group in order for social sorting to become effective. Thus, Hier concludes that "it is not the personal identity of the embodied individual but rather the actuarial or categorical profile of the collective which is of foremost concern."[36] In this sense, Google's claim to increase privacy is seriously misleading.

Like virtually all aspects of the growing power of search engines, personalization is deeply ambiguous in its social effects. On the one hand, it promises to offer improvements in terms of search quality, further empowering users by making accessible the information they need. This is not a small feat. By lessening the dependence on the overall network topology, personalization might also help to address one of the most frequently voiced criticisms of the dominant ranking schemes, namely that they promote popular content and thus reinforce already dominant opinions at the expense of marginal ones.[37] Instead of only relying on what the majority of other people find important, search engines can balance that with the knowledge of the idiosyncratic interest of each user (group), thus selectively elevating sources that might be obscure to the general audience, but are important to this particular user (set). The result is better access to marginal sources for people with an assumed interest in that subject area.

So far so good. But where is the boundary between supporting a particular special interest and deliberately shaping a person's behavior by presenting him or her with a view shaped by criteria not his or her own? As with social sorting procedures in general, the question here is also whether personalization increases or decreases personal autonomy. Legal scholar Frank Pasquale frames the issue in the following way:

> Meaningful autonomy requires more than simple absence of external constraint once an individual makes a choice and sets out to act upon it. At a minimum, autonomy requires a meaningful variety of choices, information of the relevant state of the world and of these alternatives, the capacity to evaluate this information and the ability to make a choice. If A controls the window through which B sees the world—if he systematically exercises power over the relevant information about the world and available alternatives and options that reaches B—then the autonomy of B is diminished. To control one's informational flows in ways that shape and constrain her choice is to limit her autonomy, whether that person is deceived or not.[38]

Thus, even in the best of worlds, personalization enhances and diminishes the autonomy of the individual user at the same time. It enhances it because it makes information available that would otherwise be harder to locate. It improves, so it is claimed, the quality of the search experience. It diminishes it because it subtly locks the users into a path-dependency that cannot adequately reflect their personal life story, but reinforces those aspects that the search engines are capable of capturing, interpreted through assumptions built into the personalizing algorithms. The differences between the personalized and the non-personalized version of the search results, as Google reiterates, are initially subtle, but likely to increase over time. A second layer of intransparency, that of the personalization algorithms, is placed on top of the intransparency of the general search algorithms. Of course, it is always possible to opt out of personalization by simply signing out of the account. But the ever increasing range of services offered through a uniform log-in actively works against this option. As in other areas, protecting one's privacy is rendered burdensome and thus something few people are actively engaged in, especially given the lack of direct negative consequences for not doing it.

And we hardly live in the best of all worlds. The primary loyalty of search engines is – it needs to be noted again – not to users but to advertisers. Of course, search engines need to attract and retain users in order to be attractive advertisers, but the case of commercial TV provides ample evidence that this does not mean that user interests are always foregrounded.

The boundary between actively supporting individual users in their particular search history and manipulating users by presenting them with an intentionally biased set of results is blurry, not least because we actually want search engines to be biased and make sharp distinctions between relevant and irrelevant information. There are two main problems with personalization in this regard. On the one hand, personalization algorithms will have a limited grasp of our lives. Only selective aspects of our behavior are collected (those that leave traces in accessible places), and the algorithms will apply their own interpretations to this data, based on the dominant world-view, technical capacities and the particular goals pursued by the companies that are implementing them. On the other hand, personalization renders search engines practically immune to systematic, critical evaluation because it is becoming unclear whether the (dis)appearance of a source is a feature (personalization done right) or a bug (censorship or manipulation).

Comparing results among users and over time will do little to show how search engines tweak their ranking technology, since each user will have different results. This will exacerbate the problem already present at the moment: that it is impossible to tell whether the ranking of results changes due to aggregate changes in the network topology, or due to changes in the ranking algorithms, and, should it be the latter, whether these changes are merely improvements to the quality, or attempts to punish unruly behavior.[39] In the end, it all boils down to trust and expediency. The problem with trust is that, given the essential opacity of the ranking and personalization algorithms, there is little basis to evaluate such trust. But at least it is something that is collectively generated. Thus, a breach of this trust, even if it affects only a small group of users, will decrease the trust of everyone towards the particular service. Expediency, on the other hand, is a practical measure. Everyone can decide for themselves whether the search results delivered are relevant to them. Yet, in an environment of information overload, even the most censored search will bring up more search results that anyone can handle. Thus, unless the user has prior knowledge of the subject area, she cannot know what is not included. Thus, search results always seem amazingly relevant, even if they leave out a lot of relevant material.[40]

With personalization, we enter uncharted territory in its enabling and constraining dimensions. We simply do not know whether this will lead to a greater variety of information providers entering the realm of visibility, or whether it will subtly but profoundly shape the world we can see, if search engines promote a filtering agenda other than our own. Given the extreme power differential between individual users and the search engines, there is no question who will be in a better position to advance their agenda at the expense of the other party.

The reactions to and debates around these three different kinds of surveillance are likely to be very different. As David Lyon remarked,

> Paradoxically, then, the sharp end of the panoptic spectrum may generate moments of refusal and resistance that militate against the production of docile bodies, whereas the soft end seems to seduce participants into stunning conformity of which some seem scarcely conscious.[41]

In our context, state surveillance facilitated by search engine data belongs to the sharp end, and personalization to the soft end where surveillance and care, the disabling and enabling of social sorting are hard to distinguish and thus open the door to subtle manipulation.

Conclusion

Search engines have embarked on an extremely ambitious project, organizing the world's information. As we are moving deeper into dynamic, information-rich environments, their importance is set to increase. In order to overcome the limitations of a general topological organization of information and to develop a personalized framework, a new model of the world is assumed: everyone's world is different. To implement this, search engines need to know an almost infinite amount of information about their users. As we have seen, data is gathered systematically to profile individuals on three interrelated levels – as a knowledge person, a social person, and as an embodied person. New services are developed with an eye on adding even more data to these profiles and filling in remaining gaps. Taken together, all this information creates what we call the *second index*, a closed, proprietary set of data about the world's users of information.

While we acknowledge the potential of personalized services, which is hard to overlook considering how busy the service providers are in touting the golden future of perfect search, we think it is necessary to highlight four deeply troublesome dimensions of this second index. First, simply storing such vast amounts of data creates demands to access and use it, both within and outside the institutions. Some of these demands are made publicly through the court system, some of them are made secretly. Of course this is not an issue particular to search engines, but one which concerns all organizations that process and store vast amounts of personal information and the piecemeal privacy and data protection laws that govern all of them. It is clear that in order to deal with this expansion of surveillance technology / infrastructure, we will need to strengthen privacy and data protection laws and the means of parliamentary control over the executive organs of the state. Second, personalization is inherently based upon a distorted profile of the individual user. A search engine can never "know" a person in a social sense of knowing. It can only compile data that can be easily captured through its particular methods. Thus, rather than being able to draw a comprehensive picture of the person, the search engine's picture is overly detailed in some aspects and extremely incomplete in others. This is particularly problematic given the fact that this second index is compiled to serve the advertisers' interests at least as much as the users'. Any conclusion derived from this incomplete picture must be partially incorrect, thus potentially reinforcing those sets of behaviors that lend themselves to data capturing and discouraging others. Third, the problem of the algorithmic bias in the capturing of data is exacerbated by the bias in the interpretation of this data. The mistakes range from the obvious to the subtle. For example, in December 2007 *Google Reader* released a new feature, which automatically linked all one's shared items from Reader with one's contact list from Gmail's chat feature, *Google Talk*. As user banzaimonkey stated in his post, "I think the basic mistake here [...] is that the people on my contact list are not necessarily my 'friends'. I have business contacts, school contacts, family contacts, etc., and not only do I not really have any interest in seeing all of their feed information, I don't want them seeing mine either."[42] Thus, the simplistic interpretation of the data – all contacts are friends and all friends are equal – turned out to be patently wrong. Indeed, the very assumption that data is easy to interpret can be deeply misleading, even the most basic assumption that users search for information that they are personally interested in (rather than someone else). We often do things for other people. The social boundaries between persons are not so clear cut.

Finally, personalization further skews the balance of power between the search engines and the individual user. If future search engines operate under the assumption that everyone's world is different, this will effectively make it more difficult to create shared experiences, particularly as they relate to the search engine itself. We will all be forced to trust a system that is becoming even more opaque to us, and we will have to do this based on the criterion of expediency of search results which, in a context of information overload, is deeply misleading.

While it would be as short-sighted as unrealistic to forgo the potential of personalization, it seems necessary to broaden the basis on which we can trust these services. Personalized, individualized experience is not enough. We need collective means of oversight, and some of them will need to be regulatory. In the past, legal and social pressure were necessary to force companies to grant consumers basic rights. Google is no exception: currently, its privacy policies are not transparent and do not restrict Google in substantial ways. The fact that the company's various privacy policies are hard to locate and that it is extremely difficult to retrace their development over time, cannot be an oversight – especially since Google's mission is ostensibly to organize the world's information and to make it more easily accessible to its users. But regulation and public outrage can only react to what is happening, which is difficult given the dynamism of this area. Thus, we also need means oriented towards open source processes, where actors with heterogeneous value sets have the means to fully evaluate the capacities of a system. Blind trust and the nice sounding slogan "don't be evil" are not enough to ensure that our liberty and autonomy are safeguarded.

Notes

1   All links were last accessed on 25 Mar 2009. A comprehensive list to all footnotes, including links to Google Privacy sites, can be found on the online version of this article located on the Deep Search project site. http://world-information.org/wii/deep_search/
2   Shirky, Clay, "Ontology is Overrated: Categories, Links, and Tags", 2005 http://shirky.com/writings/ontology_overrated.html
3   Demoz.org. http://www.demoz.org
4   Fleischer, Peter, Google's search policy puts the user in charge. FT.com, May 25, 2007. http://www.ft.com/cms/s/2/560c6a06-0a63-11dc-93ae-000b5df10621.html

5   Electronic Privacy Information Center. "Search Engine Privacy", 3 Feb 2009. http://epic.org/privacy/search_engine
6   Aspan, Maria, "How Sticky Is Membership on Facebook? Just Try Breaking Free", New York Times Online, 11 Feb 2008. http://www.nytimes.com/2008/02/11/technology/11facebook.html
7   Dover, Danny, The Evil Side of Google? Exploring Google's User Data Collection, SEOmoz.org, 24 Jun 2008. http://www.seomoz.org/blog/the-evil-side-of-google-exploring-googles-user-data-collection#list
8   Roberts, Hal, "Google Privacy Videos", 6 March 2008. http://blogs.law.harvard.edu/hroberts/2008/03/06/google-watching-personal-data-collection/
9   Bogatin, Donna, "Google Analyitcs: Should Google be minding YOUR Web business?", ZDNet blogs, 9 May 2007. http://blogs.zdnet.com/micro-markets/?p=1324
10 Bonstein, Julia, Marcel Rosenbach and Hilmar Schmundt, "Data Mining You to Death: Does Google Know Too Much?" Spiegel Online International, 30 Oct 2008. http://www.spiegel.de/international/germany/0,1518,587546,00.html
11 Story, Louise, "To Aim Ads, Web Is Keeping Closer Eye on You", New York Times.com, 10 Mar 2008. http://www.nytimes.com/2008/03/10/technology/10privacy.html?_r=1
12 Mediati, Nick, "Google's streamlined and speedy browser offers strong integrated search and an intriguing alternative to Firefox and Internet Explorer", PCWorld.com, 12 Dec 2008. www.pcworld.com/article/150579/google_chrome_web_browser.html
13 Fried, Ina, "Google's Omnibox could be Pandora's box", CNet.com, 3 Sep 2008. CNet.com http://news.cnet.com/8301-13860_3-10031661-56.html
14 Cheung, Humphrey, "Chrome is a security nightmare, indexes your bank accounts", TGDaily.com, 4 Sep 2008. http://www.tgdaily.com/content/view/39176/108
15 ibid.
16 Electronic Frontier Foundation, "Google's Gmail and Your Privacy –What's the Deal?" EFFector Vol.17, No.12, 09 Apr 2004. http://w2.eff.org/effector/17/12.php#I; Liedtke, Michael, "Consumer watchdogs tear into Google's new e-mail service", USAToday.com, 07 Apr 2004. http://www.usatoday.com/tech/news/internetprivacy/2004-04-07-gmail-bad-karma_x.htm; Hafner, Katie, "In Google We Trust? When the Subject is E-Mail, Maybe Not", New York Times online, 08 Apr 2004. http://www.nytimes.com/2004/04/08/technology/circuits/08goog.html?ei=5007&en=e4bdc743c5602e3e&ex=1396756800&partner=USERLAND&pagewanted=all&position
17 Olsen, Stefanie, "California privacy law kicks in", CNet.com, 06 July 2004. http://news.cnet.com/California-privacy-law-kicks-in/2100-1028_3-5258824.html
18 Hodgin, Rick C., "Google launches My Tracks for Android", TGDaily.com, 13 Feb 2009. http://www.tgdaily.com/content/view/41439/140/
19 Greenberg, Andy, "Privacy Groups Target Android, Mobile Marketers", Forbes.com, 13 Jan 2009. http://www.forbes.com/2009/01/12/mobile-marketing-privacy-tech-security-cx_ag_0113mobilemarket.html
20 Privacy International.Org, "Privacy international identifies major security flaw in Google's global phone tracking system", 05 Feb 2009. http://www.privacyinternational.org/article.shtml?cmd[347]=x-347-563567
21 Electronic Privacy Information Center: "Personal Surveillance Technologies", 24 Nov 2008. http://epic.org/privacy/dv/personal_surveillance.html
22 For a summary, see Alexander Havalais, *Search Engine Society* (Cambridge UK: Polity Press) 2009, 139-159
23 Kevin D, Haggerty and Richard V. Ericson, "The Surveillant Assemblage", British Journal of Sociology, December 2000, Vol. 51 No. 4, pp. 605–622
24 See, Gandy, Jr., Oscar H., *The Panoptic Sort. A Political Economy of Personal Information* (Boulder:

Westview Press), 1993; Lyon, David (ed.), *Surveillance as Social Sorting: Privacy, Risk and Automated Discrimination,* (London, New York: Routledge) 2002

25 "A Face Is Exposed for AOL Searcher No. 4417749", NYT.com (August 9 2006)
26 Jonathan Zittrain, professor of Internet law at Harvard, explains: "This is a broader truth about the law. There are often no requirements to keep records, but if they're kept, they're fair game for a subpoena." Quoted in: Noam Cohen, "As data collecting grows, privacy erodes", International Herald Tribune (February 16 2009.)
27 Hafner, Katie, Matt Richtel, "Google Resists U.S. Subpoena of Search Data", NYT.com (January 20 2006.
28 Final Report on the existence of a global system for the interception of private and commercial communications (ECHELON interception system), European Parliament Temporary Committee on the ECHELON Interception System, approved September 5 2001
29 Vaz, Paulo, and Fernanda Bruno, "Types of Self-Surveillance: from abnormality to individuals 'at risk'", *Surveillance & Society,* Vol. 1, No. 3, 2003.
30 Norris, Clive, Gary Armstrong, *The Maximum Surveillance Society: The Rise of CCTV,* Oxford, UK, Berg, 1999
31 Lyon, David, 2002, p.13
32 Ibid.
33 Fleischer, Peter, "Another step to protect user privacy", Official Google Blog, 8 Sep 2008, http://googleblog.blogspot.com/2008/09/another-step-to-protect-user-privacy.html
34 Soghoian, Chris, "Debunking Google's log anonymization propaganda", Cnet.com, 11 Sep, 2008. http://news.cnet.com/8301-13739_3-10038963-46.html
35 Find videos at http://www.consumerwatchdog.org/corporateering/corpact4/
36 Hier, Sean P., "Probing the Surveillant Assemblage. On the dialectics of surveillance practices as processes of social control", *Surveillance & Society,* Vol. 1: 3, 2003, 399–411
37 Among the first to voice this critique was Lucas Introna and Helen Nissenbaum, "Shaping The Web: Why The Politics of Search Engines Matters," *Information Society* 16, No. 3 (2000): 169-185
38 Pasquale, Frank A.; Bracha, Oren (2007), "Federal Search Commission?: Access, Fairness and Accountability in the Law of Search",.. Public Law and Legal Theory Research Paper No. 123 July: 30 Social Science Research Network at http://ssrn.com/abstract=1002453
39 Greenberg, Andy, "Condemned To Google Hell", Forbes.com (April 30, 2007)
40 Bing Pan et.al., "In Google We Trust: Users' Decisions on Rank, Position, and Relevance", *Journal of Computer Mediated Communication,* Vol.12, 3, 2007
41 Lyon, David, "Introduction", In: David Lyon (ed.) *Theorizing Surveillance. The Panopticon and Beyond,* Devon, UK, Willian Publishing, 2006, 8
42 Google Reader Help, "New Feature: Sharing with Friends", 14 Dec 2007 ff. http://groups.google.com/group/google-reader-howdoi/browse_thread/thread/318c4559e2ac5bbe/e2a7a7d782571c38

Power

Dissecting the Gatekeepers
Relational Perspectives on the Power of Search Engines

Theo Röhle

The advent of new media technologies is almost inevitably accompanied by discourses that oscillate between technological and social determinism. In the utopian version of these accounts, technology is seen as supporting democratic social dynamics, in the dystopian version it instead becomes a colonizing force that pre-structures individual and group behavior. Search engines, once heralded as empowering tools to navigate online spaces, now increasingly described as "evil" manipulators and data collectors, have been no exception to this rule.

In light of the important role that search engines play in the online information environment, the growing concern about their power is certainly justified. It is questionable, though, whether dystopian technological determinism can provide adequate answers to these concerns. Due to their position in the midst of conflicting interests of users, advertisers and content producers, search engines represent an area of especially dynamic and ambivalent power relations. The determinist image of search engines as extremely powerful entities drastically reduces the complexity of these relations to a set of unidirectional effects.

In order to avoid such reductionist accounts, a more thorough reflection on the concept of power itself is required. Here, a relational perspective on power is advocated, drawing on the writings of Michel Foucault and recent approaches in Science and Technology Studies informed by Actor-Network-Theory. Rather than treating search engines as stable technological artifacts, the analysis seeks to map how different actors are involved in negotiating the development of search technology.

After outlining the theoretical framework, the paper engages in an in-depth discussion of the search engine Google, focusing on its relationship to webmasters and users. Due to its domination of the search market, Google plays a special role for directing the users' attention towards the webmasters' content. Attempts by webmasters to game the ranking system in order to boost the position of their websites are met by Google with a subtle combination of rewards and punishment. It is argued that this strategy involves the establishment of a disciplinary regime that enforces a certain norm for web publishing.

Google's relationship to the users, on the other hand, is characterized by less invasive forms of power. By inserting itself deeply into the users' information environment, Google can collect and analyze unprecedented amounts of user data. Google plans to use this data in increasingly sophisticated advertising schemes. It is argued that the modeling of segmented consumption behavior that these schemes are based upon involves a governmental form of power. It is a kind of power that aims at controlling differential behavior patterns by gaining an intimate statistical knowledge of a population and using this knowledge as a means of predictive risk management.

"Cut off the king's head" – A reversal of perspectives

Following Michel Foucault, power needs to be treated as a relational concept. His demand that political theory needs to "cut off the king's head"[1] involves a critique of mechanistic, centralistic and linear notions of power. Analyses subscribing to such notions usually seek to describe how certain powerful actors manage to enforce their intentions against the will of others. Their aim is to discern sources of power and the effects that emanate from these sources.[2] A relational perspective on power involves a reversal of this perspective – instead of identifying fixed points of sovereignty it seeks to map the relations that render the powerfulness of these entities possible in the first place.

Actor-Network-Theory (ANT) has been one of the primary vehicles for introducing relational concepts of power into the study of science and technology. Its advocate Bruno Latour sees sociology in danger of being "drunk with power", since there are scholars "who confuse the expansion of powerful explanations with the composition of the collective."[3] According to Latour, instead of explaining social relations by picking out powerful entities, power has to be explained by the acts that constitute actors as powerful.[4]

The move to abandon mechanistic, centralistic and linear concepts of power opens up socio-technological environments for a subtler enquiry into their inner dynamics. Rather than simply addressing the effects of technology on society or vice versa, "[i]t is possible to say that techniques and actors [...] evolve together."[5] This shift of perspective produces a topological view on the relations between actors. Both the relations and the characteristics of the actors are seen as inherently dynamic. The current state of things is perceived as a temporary stabilization of these actor-networks. Stability is not taken for granted but is a phenomenon that needs to be explained.

Bowker/Star advocate this kind of "gestalt switch" in their analyses of technological infrastructure: "Infrastructural inversion means recognizing the depths of interdependence of technical networks and standards, on the one hand, and the real work of politics and knowledge production on the other."[6] ANT has been criticized for losing sight of power relations when merely reiterating success stories of technology adoption.[7] However, as Bowker/Star show, ANT-inspired analyses do not have to be limited to this kind of consensus-oriented approach. Rather, the concepts of "stabilization" and "irreversibility" can be employed analytically in order to reveal the micro-political negotiations between actors.

Lucas D. Introna's call to "maintain the reversibility of foldings"[8] adds a more explicit normative stance to this discussion. He envisions an analysis of technology whose task is

> [n]ot merely to look at this or that artifact but to trace all the moral implications (of closure) from what seems to be simple pragmatic or technical decisions – at the level of code, algorithms, and the like – through to social practices, and ultimately, to the production of particular social orders, rather than others.[9]

The "disclosive ethical archaeology" advocated by Introna aims at examining the kinds of agencies that are involved in points of (technological) closure and what developments are fostered by these constellations. The normative goal is to create a situation where these points of closure can be scrutinized and re-opened in order to allow other developments to emerge.

While the stabilization of an actor-network means that alternative trajectories are abandoned[10], this does not mean that power only appears in the guise of suppressing these alternative trajectories. Again in line with Foucault, power should not exclusively be treated as inhibiting, as something that constrains the free unfolding of relations and discourse, but rather as a productive force that fosters certain kinds of relations rather than others. In ANT terminology, this productive aspect of power is contained in the concept of "translation". Actors constantly seek to recruit other actors into their networks and to render them productive within the scope of their own "program of action".[11]

Search engines as sites of the co-constitution of agency

Against the backdrop of the theoretical perspective outlined above, the following discussion takes a closer look at the search engine Google as a specific site of the co-constitution of socio-technological agency. To start with, some of the main actors involved in this negotiation process can be made out, along with their distinct "programs of action".

The World Wide Web has considerably lowered the entry barriers to content production and dissemination, resulting in a substantial proliferation of available information. As Herbert Simon[12] pointed out, such proliferation of information renders attention a scarce resource. Content producers devise different strategies in order to boost the visibility of their content. Depending on the type of content – e.g. private, scientific or commercial – this attention can be turned into different kinds of currency – social, scientific or actual currency.

The struggle for attention results in an abundance of information, threatening to destroy the users' feeling of control over their information environment. The urge to avoid this kind of "narcissistic injury" creates a demand for technological interfaces that re-instate the user in a position of control (or at least create this illusion).[13]

Search engines enter the conflicting interests between webmasters and users by diverting both kinds of actors through their own network. Google has been most successful in this enrollment process, not least because its clean interface and comparatively spam-free results effectively re-installed the illusion of control for the users. In the language of ANT, Google has established itself as an obligatory passage point – both webmasters and users need to pass this point if they want to continue moving on in their program of action. However, such traveling through other actors' networks involves a translation – a change of the conditions that constitute an actor.

Search engines' position as intermediaries between content and users has called forth comparisons to gatekeeping processes in earlier media settings.[14] Considering the above discussion on the question of power, however, the notion of the gatekeeper as an embodied entity, be it human or technical, seems oversimplified. By looking at the way actors negotiate the reciprocal recruitment processes, it is possible to arrive at a more nuanced picture of the power relations involved. The following sections focus on the negotiation process on the part of the webmasters and the users respectively.

Disciplining the webmasters

In recent years, Google has intensified its efforts to establish means of communication with webmasters. In August 2006, "*Webmaster Central*"[15] was introduced, a collection of services and information aimed especially at webmasters. The site is accompanied by the "*Webmaster Central Blog*" as well as by forums where webmasters can post questions and discuss a range of issues relating to their content.

"Webmaster Tools" is one set of services included in the Webmaster Central. Here, Google makes some of the information they keep about websites available to the respective webmasters. They can access basic statistics about crawling frequencies and potential errors during the crawling process, and they receive information on how to adapt their content in order to make it more accessible to the Google crawlers.

One adaptation, which is encouraged within the *Webmaster Tools*, is the creation of a Sitemap, an XML-file that lists the URLs of a domain. Sitemaps provide the search engine with information about URLs they otherwise cannot know about, either because there is no link to them or because they are created dynamically from a database. Thus, by providing this information in a machine-readable format, webmasters partly compensate the shortcomings of the crawler technology.

Another service that is part of the *Webmaster Tools* is called "How Googlebot sees your site". It allows webmasters to check the visibility of keywords within their content. The *Webmaster Tools* also provide a list of in-links, which lets webmasters check who linked to their content.

Questions like keyword visibility and link building belong to the practices of search engine optimization (SEO). Ever since the inception of search engines, webmasters have tried to devise techniques in order to improve the position of their content in the results. SEO techniques range from simple text adaptations to elaborate linking schemes and methods to direct crawlers and human visitors in different directions.[16] For search engines, these practices are a cause for concern, since they disturb the models of relevancy that are incorporated within their ranking algorithms.

Instead of condemning SEO practices altogether, though, Google has been increasingly apt in advocating a certain version of content optimization that fits its own agenda. The company's own SEO guide, published in November 2008, focuses on ways to adapt content which ultimately benefit the crawling, indexing and display capacities of Google itself.[17] A sharp line is drawn between these "google-friendly" practices and more outright manipulative SEO techniques. In their quality guidelines, Google puts forth a set of rules for webmasters, which prohibit the use of SEO techniques such as doorway pages, redirects, hidden text and keyword stuffing.[18] A violation of these guidelines is punished with a temporary ban from the index. If the content is not changed within a certain time frame, this ban is made permanent.

The *Webmaster Tools* can be seen as part of a strategy to associate webmasters and to normalize their behavior. The crawling statistics are used as an incentive to establish a communication channel between Google and the webmasters. Using this channel, the webmasters are encouraged to adapt their content in a way that is advantageous for Google. Further, webmasters are asked to report sites that do not comply with the rules set up by Google. For this purpose, the *Webmaster Tools* provide forms where webmasters can report spam and link selling.

Google comments on the success of this reporting scheme in the "*Webmaster Central Blog*":

> We are proud of our users who alert us to potential abuses for the sake of the whole internet community. We appreciate this even more, as Page-Rank™ (and thus Google search) is based on a democratic principle, i.e. a webmaster is giving other sites a "vote" of approval by linking to it. In 2007 as an extension and complement of this democratic principle, we want to further increase our users' awareness of webmaster practices that do or do not conform to Google's standards. Such informed users are then able to take counter-action against webspam by filing spam reports.[19]

Due to its domination of access to online information, Google is able to delineate a norm for web publishing. The specific blend of cooperation and punishment observable in the *Webmaster Tools* is akin to establishing a disciplinary regime. Involving the webmasters themselves in the identification of spam reminds them of their own risk to get "caught", should they engage in the wrong SEO practices. It thereby reinforces Google's demarcation between "legitimate" optimization and "illegitimate" manipulation.

The crossing of this line is monitored and punished automatically, using formal definitions of spam that are developed by Google's web spam team. Current research indicates that such automatic processing is bound to produce false positives, so that websites are banned from the index even when adhering to Google's guidelines.[20] Due to the high market share of Google these will remain invisible for most Internet users as long as the ban is in effect.

When taking the allusions to "democratic principles" in the *Webmaster Central Blog* at face value, the webmasters' reporting of spam would have to be interpreted as a mandate for Google to enforce quality standards on the web. However, without any transparency in the processing of these reports and the way they are turned into algorithmic sorting criteria, this is hardly a coherent line of reasoning. While it could be argued that the web requires some kind of mechanism to identify spam in order to remain navigable, it is certainly questionable whether a commercial outfit like Google should be entrusted with this kind of task.

Governing the users

As has been amply demonstrated by Michael Zimmer[21], Google is able to collect very large amounts of user data via a wide range of services. Considering the user base of the search engine itself, the reach of the advertising network *DoubleClick* and the statistics service Google Analytics as well as the depth of user data available via services like *Gmail* and *Orkut*, it seems evident that today, Google's ability to track users online is unmatched by any other Internet company.

Perhaps as a reaction to growing scrutiny by privacy advocates[22], Google has recently become more outspoken about their reasons to collect user data. One of these stated reasons is that user data can be drawn upon in order to enhance ranking algorithms.[23] Search providers are increasingly trying to determine what the users "really" want to know, in order to improve the subjective relevance of results.[24] Since many search queries are poorly formulated, more and more data is taken from the context of the search query, allowing for a range of additional "signals" to be incorporated into the ranking algorithm.

From event-based data to derived data

Completely personalized ranking models like those implemented in *Google Web History*[25] involve the most elaborate matching techniques. Personalized search involves setting up a personal profile for an individual user and ranking results according to this profile.[26] A patent application for Google's personalized search services[27] reveals what kind of data is stored in these profiles. The individual log entries that are collected during the use of Google's search engine are termed "event-based data" and include:
- search queries
- IP addresses
- result clicks (i.e., the results presented in a set of search results on which the user has clicked)

- ad clicks (i.e., the advertisements presented to the user on which the user has clicked)
- browsing data (e.g., which locations a user visits; an image that the user views) and
- product events (e.g., searches for product reviews)

Additionally, other kinds of user activity, which is not part of searching itself, can be tracked. This includes:
- advertisement presented and clicked on during an email session
- instant messaging
- word processing
- participation in chat rooms
- software application execution
- Internet telephone calls

These individual data items are connected in different ways in order to create a model of the individual user's preferences, which can be employed to re-rank results. As an example of what Google calls "derived data", the patent application describes how search queries can be matched to the topics of the *Open Directory Project*. By aggregating the queries over time, they can be processed into a weighted set of topic descriptors. This set serves as a model for topical user preferences and results are ranked accordingly.

From individual to collective

As has been shown in the case of AOL search queries that were released to the public in 2006, data gathered by search engines can reveal intimate details about real-life individuals.[28] It therefore involves many potential abuse scenarios, not only by Google itself, but also by other actors, such as governments, criminals, hackers, etc. Such abuse scenarios serve as important argumentative tools to gauge the potential impact of surveillance practices and to devise adequate policy strategies. On the other hand, these scenarios are often limited to individualistic concepts of privacy. They are fuelled by a concern that surveillance makes it possible to compile dossiers on individuals and to use this information in a discriminatory manner.

However, data collection on a scale like Google's is problematic even if it is not used in order to trace individuals. The collected data allows Google to run extensive statistical evaluations in order to construct models of user behavior and preferences. Surveillance scholar Oscar Gandy draws a historical analogy between such kinds of data mining techniques that are made possible by large-scale computing infrastructures and the invention of the microscope in the natural sciences. In both cases, the technical infrastructure involves a change of perspective that renders new kinds of classifications and typologies possible.[29]

In its corporate blog, Google stresses the advantage of modeling user behavior for ranking purposes.[30] A simple model of user behavior that has been in use for a long time involves the assumption that users prefer results in their own language. Thus, results are re-ranked based on an analysis of the user's IP address and the language of the query. Other models involve time as a factor. For example, if the collected data shows that most users prefer fresher results for a certain query, these kinds of results are ranked higher for subsequent queries.[31]

Information Retrieval and ad targeting

While Google has made an effort to explain why user data is needed for the development of ranking algorithms, they have been rather quiet about the commercial use of the collected data. In one of their earliest papers, the Google founders rejected such use, stating that they "believe the issue of advertising causes enough mixed incentives that it is crucial to have a competitive search engine that is transparent and in the academic realm."[32] In the course of Google's development from an academic experiment to the world leader in online search, there has been a remarkable shift in this attitude. Today, Google-CEO Eric Schmidt wants people to think of Google "first as an advertising system".[33]

The basis of Google's economic success is contextual advertising. Initially developed by *Goto.com*, a search engine for consumer goods, the system lets advertisers place bids for certain keywords. Whenever someone enters a search query containing the keyword, their ad is displayed.[34] When Google adopted the practice of contextual advertising, they chose to display these sponsored results separately from the so-called "organic", algorithmically selected results. It is questionable, though, whether this separation has made the problem of "mixed incentives" disappear. A study of search engine users in 2005 found that 62 percent of them were not actually aware of the distinction between paid and unpaid results.[35]

Contextual advertising thus inserts itself into the flow of online information behavior and facilitates the real-time translation of information needs into consumption needs. This translation is possible because search queries are reasonably good representations of information needs. If the ad is matched well enough to the query, the hope is that the user will accept the commercial message as an adequate answer to their information need. However, poorly formulated search queries pose a problem for the functionality of this system as well. Even if ads are matched very well to the search query, they might not be matched very well to the user's actual information need. The search providers' answer is, again, to draw on the aggregated user data in order to alleviate this problem.

Modeling and predicting behavior

As in the context of ranking, the way to determine what the user "really" wants to know is to construct models out of the aggregated user data. Individual event-based log entries are bundled together according to certain models of individual and collective behavior. As Eric Picard points out, these kinds of segmented models present advertisers with new ways to reach particular audiences:

> Tracking what someone is searching for online or which sites they visit will create an anonymous profile of that person's interests. Those interests can be segmented out and compared to advertiser goals. Then the ads can be delivered to the right person across all media.[36]

The technique to first construct segmented models of user interests and behavior and then match tracked user data to these segmented models is known as "behavioral targeting". While it has been employed by large search providers like Yahoo since 2000, Google arrived relatively late at the scene with the acquisition of *DoubleClick* in 2007. In their privacy information, Google emphasizes that these techniques are "new territory" for the company.[37] However, two patent applications reveal extensive plans to explore this territory in the future.

Firstly, Google wants to give advertisers the choice of a range of "targeting criteria" for the display of their ads. These include, among others, "geographic location, the language used by the user, the type of browser used, previous page views, previous behavior, user account, any Web cookies used by the system, user device characteristics, etc.".[38] While it would be technically feasible to let advertisers choose all these criteria individually, behavioral targeting usually implies selecting certain combinations of them. These segments, e.g. topical clusters or behavior patterns, can then be reached with specially targeted ads.

A patent application describing "network node targeting" provides more details about the operational layout of such systems. Based on social network data, the aim of this targeting method is to discover communities of users with shared interests and then to identify the most influential members of these communities. By letting advertisers place their ads on the profile pages of these influential members, the idea is that they can "target the entire community by displaying advertisements on the profile of member 1 alone". There can also be additional incentives for the influential members to maintain their position in the network: "An influencer may receive financial incentives from advertisers in exchange for permission to display advertisements on the member's profile."[39]

This example reveals several key aspects of behavioral targeting practices. Firstly, it shows how targeting involves a specific topological ordering of a continuous information space. "Network node targeting" implies that user data is analyzed according to a particular model of what a community looks like and how influence is distributed within a community. Choosing this model of analysis thus involves focusing on certain relations between data items and ignoring others. Secondly, this kind of ordering involves ascribing a specific kind of meaning to certain combinations of data items. The influential members are addressed primarily as efficient disseminators of commercial messages. Such role ascriptions have social relevance, since they are components of individual and collective subjectivation processes. Thirdly, this example shows how the model reinforces itself. By financially encouraging the influential users to consolidate their position within the network, "network node targeting" in the long run confirms the assumptions about sociality it was built upon in the first place.

"Continuity with difference"

Behavioral Targeting thus involves tracking users, constructing segmented models out of the aggregated data and feeding these models back to the users. This kind of segmentation for marketing purposes has been discussed from different angles by scholars of surveillance studies.[40] Instead of portraying surveillance as an exclusively disciplinary endeavor, these scholars have stressed the dispersed and networked characteristics of current surveillance practices.

The kinds of power relations at stake in segmentation can best be understood by drawing on Foucault's later writings on governmentality. Here, he describes power in terms of the "conduct of conduct". Rather than simply enforcing a norm, this more indirect mode of power involves structuring a field of possibilities. It aims at an intimate statistical knowledge of a population in order to be able to predict behavior and adapt control strategies accordingly.[41]

Consequently, surveillance scholar Bart Simon argues that the creation of "databased selves" involves a shift from discipline to control. Drawing on Deleuze[42], he remarks:

Discipline as a mode of power relies primarily on enclosures, be they material, cultural or psychical. Control however encourages mobility in an attempt to manage the wider territory and not just the social space of enclosures.[43]

Compared to discipline, control thus allows for a greater flexibility towards difference. The governing of consumers is less concerned with imposing forms of behavior on them and more with capturing their actions within a controllable framework.

The flexibility towards difference enables what Tom Hespos[44] calls "marketing to the unmassed". Whereas the loss of social cohesion and the differentiation of consumption patterns could pose a threat to the continuity of capitalist accumulation, the constant flow of user data into search engines and the corresponding segmented targeting techniques provide an interface for ensuring consumer predictability. It is part of a risk management strategy where the subjects are "fully integrated into a living machine that functions not against their will, their thoughts, their desire, their body, etc., but through those."[45]

Conclusions

The analysis of Google as a site of the co-constitution of socio-technological agency has revealed the emergence of two different kinds of power relations. On the one side, webmasters are enrolled into a disciplinary regime where transgressions of the norm are punished by exclusion from user attention. Encouraging conforming behavior and letting webmasters participate in identifying deviations amounts to a strategy that aims at the internalization of this norm.

On the other side, the constant monitoring of user behavior as the basis of segmented targeting techniques represents a governmental form of power. The behavioral models that are constructed out of the aggregated data locate users within certain kinds of consumption patterns. Feeding these models back to the users renders this "statistical inclination" productive.[46] It creates a more predictable and controllable field of possible actions, ensuring continuity while accepting difference.

Returning to the initial question of stabilization and irreversibility, it has to be asked whether the different actors have accepted the role ascriptions offered to them or whether they manage to keep up a process of negotiation. While webmasters hardly have another choice than using Google to reach an audience, their ongoing attempts to game the ranking through SEO techniques show that Google's publishing norm is a contested norm. Rather than being able to induce technological closure, Google has to devise flexible strategies to react and adapt to these challenges.

Considering their involvement in reporting spam, webmasters have to ask themselves whether they want Google to be the institution responsible for enforcing quality standards on the web. This also involves the question of whether there could be different solutions to this problem and how they would fit into the development of non-commercial search alternatives.

The collection of user data, on the other hand, can be placed in the context of a broader re-negotiation of the boundaries between private and public as well as commercial and non-commercial on the Internet. Again framing this process in terms of the stabilization of role ascriptions, the first question is on what basis negotiations can take place at all. Users are usually left in the dark about the ways value is created from their data. Without technical means to access, edit and erase the data, they are not in a position to withdraw, either partially or completely, from the collection process.

Technically speaking, there is a need for interfaces that provide users with a greater level of interaction with their data. On the level of discourse, these developments should be accompanied by a new privacy vocabulary (e.g. as suggested by Helen Nissenbaum[47]) in order to be able to address privacy concerns on a more granular level. For users who prefer to opt out completely, the development of privacy enhancing techniques, e.g. those that obfuscate data traces or help to avoid tracking altogether, should be encouraged.

A combination of such technical and discursive measures could be a starting point for strengthening the users' position in the negotiation process vis-à-vis search engines and advertisers. Depending on the sophistication of these measures, they might even be able to show escape routes out of the controlled spaces of user segmentation and targeting.

Notes

1   Michel Foucault, *Power/Knowledge. Selected Interviews and Other Writings 1972-1977* (Brighton: Harvester Wheatsheaf, 1980), 121.
2   Stewart R. Clegg, *Frameworks of Power* (London: Sage, 1989), 153-159.
3   Bruno Latour, *Reassembling the Social. An Introduction to Actor-Network-Theory* (Oxford; New York: Oxford University Press, 2005), 261. As Jens Schröter argues, this danger of overly "powerful" explanations also applies to parts of German media theory when, after de-centering the human subject, it seeks to reinstate media technology itself as a new "technological subject".

(see Jens Schröter, "Der König ist tot, es lebe der König. Zum Phantasma eines technologischen Subjekts der Geschichte", in Reale Fiktionen, fiktive Realitäten: Medien, Diskurse, Texte, ed. Johannes Angermüller, Katharina Bunzmann and Christina Rauch (Hamburg: LIT, 2000), 13-24.)

4   Bruno Latour, "The Powers of Association," in *Power, Action, and Belief: A New Sociology of Knowledge?*, ed. John Law (London: Routledge & Kegan Paul, 1986), 264-80.
5   Michel Callon, "Variety and Irreversibility in Networks of Technique Conception and Adoption", in *Technology and The Wealth of Nations. The Dynamics of Constructed Advantage*, ed. Dominique Foray and Christopher Freeman (London, New York: Pinter Publishers, 1993), 250.
6   Geoffrey C. Bowker and Susan Leigh Star, *Sorting Things Out: Classification and its Consequences* (Cambridge, MA: MIT Press, 1999), 34.
7   Thomas Berker, "The Politics of 'Actor-Network Theory'. What can 'Actor-Network Theory' Do to Make Buildings More Energy Efficient?", *Science, Technology and Innovation Studies* 1 (2006): 61-79, http://www.sti-studies.de/fileadmin/articles/berker-politicsofant-2006.pdf (accessed December 20, 2008).
8   Lucas D. Introna, "Maintaining the Reversibility of Foldings: Making the Ethics (Politics) of Information Technology Visible", *Ethics and Information Technology* 9 (2007): 11-25.
9   Introna (2007): 16.
10 Callon (1993)
11 Bruno Latour, "Technology is Society Made Durable", in *A Sociology of Monsters. Essays on Power, Technology and Domination*, ed. John Law (London: Routledge, 1991), 103-131.
12 Herbert Simon, "Designing Organizations for an Information-Rich World," in *Computers, Communications, and the Public Interest*, ed. Martin Greenberger (Baltimore, London: Johns Hopkins Press, 1971), 39-72.
13 Hartmut Winkler, "Search Engines: Meta-Media on the Internet?" in *Readme! Filtered by Nettime: ASCII Culture and the Revenge of Knowledge*, ed. Josephine Bosma (New York: Autonomedia, 1999), 29-37.
14 For example: Jens Wolling, "Suchmaschinen – Gatekeeper im Internet," *Medienwissenschaft Schweiz* 2 (2002): 15-23.
15 Google. "Google Webmaster Central." http://www.google.com/webmasters (accessed December 20, 2008).
16 Elizabeth van Couvering, "The Economy of Navigation: Search Engines, Search Optimisation and Search Results," in *Die Macht der Suchmaschinen. The Power of Search Engines*, ed. Marcel Machill and Markus Beiler (Cologne: Herbert von Halem Verlag, 2007), 115-119.
17 Google. "Search Engine Optimization Starter Guide" http://www.google.com/webmasters/docs/search-engine-optimization-starter-guide.pdf (accessed December 20, 2008).
18 Google. "Webmaster Guidelines – Webmaster Help Center" http://www.google.com/support/webmasters/bin/answer.py?answer=35769&topic=15260 (accessed December 20, 2008).
19 Google, "An update on spam reporting", Official Google Webmaster Central Blog, posted March 28, 2007 http://googlewebmastercentral.blogspot.com/2007/03/update-on-spam-reporting.html (accessed December 20, 2008).
20 See Richard Rogers in this volume.
21 Michael Zimmer, "The Gaze of the Perfect Search Engine. Google as an Infrastructure of Dataveillance", in *Web search. Multidisciplinary Perspectives*, ed. Amanda Spink and Michael Zimmer (Berlin; Heidelberg: Springer, 2008), 77-99.
22 For example: Center for Democracy and Technology. "Search Privacy Practices: A Work In Progress. CDT Report – August 2007" http://www.cdt.org/privacy/20070808searchprivacy.pdf (accessed December 20, 2008).

23 Hal Varian, "Why Data Matters", Official Google Blog, posted April 3, 2008 http://googleblog.blogspot.com/2008/03/why-data-matters.html (accessed December 20, 2008).
24 In a study of concepts of "quality" among search engine producers, Elizabeth van Couvering observes: "Relevance has changed from some type of topical relevance based on an applied classification to something more subjective." (Elizabeth Van Couvering, "Is Relevance Relevant? Market, Science, and War: Discourses of Search Engine Quality", *Journal of Computer-Mediated Communication* 12 (2007), http://jcmc.indiana.edu/vol12/issue3/vancouvering.html (accessed December 20, 2008). See also Zimmer (2008) on the broader context of what he calls "the quest for the perfect search engine".
25 Google, "Web History" www.google.com/psearch (accessed December 20, 2008).
26 Kevin Keenoy and Mark Levene, "Personalisation of Web Search," in *Intelligent Techniques for Web Personalization*, ed. Sarabjot Singh Anand and Bamshad Mobasher (Berlin, Heidelberg, New York: Springer, 2005), 201-28.
27 Andrew Fikes et al., *Systems and methods for analyzing a user's web history*, US Patent Application: 11097883 (2005)
28 Michael Barbaro and Tom Zeller jr., "A Face is Exposed for AOL Searcher No. 4417749", *New York Times*, August 9, 2006.
29 Oscar H. Gandy, *The Panoptic Sort. A Political Economy of Personal Information* (Boulder, Colorado: Westview, 1993), 83.
30 Google, "Introduction to Google Search Quality", Official Google Blog, posted May 20, 2008 http://googleblog.blogspot.com/2008/05/introduction-to-google-search-quality.html (accessed December 20, 2008).
31 Anurag Acharya et al., *Information retrieval based on historical data*, US Patent No 7346839 (2003)
32 Sergey Brin and Lawrence Page, "The Anatomy of a Large-Scale Hypertextual Web Search Engine", http://infolab.stanford.edu/~backrub/google.html (accessed December 20, 2008).
33 Fred Vogelstein, "As Google Challenges Viacom and Microsoft, Its CEO Feels Lucky," *Wired*, (2007), http://www.wired.com/print/techbiz/people/news/2007/04/mag_schmidt_qa (accessed December 20, 2008).
34 The procedure for determining the position of particular ads is more complicated, since it partly depends on an analysis of the landing page and click-through-rates. (see Google, "How are ads ranked?" http://adwords.google.com/support/bin/answer.py?hl=en&answer=6111 (accessed December 20, 2008).)
35 Deborah Fallows, "Search Engine Users. Internet Searchers are Confident, Satisfied and Trusting – But They are also Unaware and Naïve", http://www.pewinternet.org/pdfs/PIP_Searchengine_users.pdf (accessed December 20, 2008)
36 Eric Picard, "Hyperlinking and Advertising Strategy", in *The Hyperlinked Society: Questioning Connections in the Digital Age*, ed. Joseph Turow and Lokman Tsui (Ann Arbor: The University of Michigan Press, 2008), 163.
37 Google, "Privacy at Google", https://services.google.com/blog_resources/google_privacy_booklet.pdf (accessed December 20, 2008).
38 Jayesh Sharma, *Using search query information to determine relevant ads for a landing page*, US Patent Application: 11323303 (2005)
39 Terrence Rohan et al., *Network Node Ad Targeting*, US Patent Application: 0080162260 (2006)
40 Kevin D. Haggerty and Richard V. Ericson, "The surveillant assemblage", *The British Journal of Sociology* 51 (2000): 605-22; Greg Elmer, *Profiling Machines. Mapping the Personal Information Economy* (Cambridge, Mass.: MIT Press, 2004)
41 Nikolas Rose and Peter Miller, "Political Power Beyond the State: Problematics of Government", *British Journal of Sociology* 43 (1992): 173-205.

42 Gilles Deleuze, "Postscript on the Societies of Control," *October* 59 (1992): 3-7.
43 Bart Simon, "The Return of Panopticism: Supervision, Subjection and the New Surveillance," Surveillance & Society 3 (2005): 15 http://www.surveillance-and-society.org/Articles3(1)/return.pdf (accessed December 20, 2008). In a similar vein, Adam Arvidsson identifies a paradigm shift from "containment" to "control" in the development of marketing during the 1950s. After this shift, the role of marketing "was no longer understood primarily as that of disciplining consumer demand, but rather as that of observing and utilizing ideas and innovations that consumer's [sic] themselves produced." (Adam Arvidsson, "On the 'Pre-history of the Panoptic Sort': Mobility in Market Research," Surveillance and Society 1 (2003): 456-74 http://www.surveillance-and-society.org/articles1(4)/prehistory.pdf (accessed December 20, 2008).)
44 Tom Hespos, "How Hyperlinks Ought to Change the Advertising Business", in *The Hyperlinked Society: Questioning Connections in the Digital Age,* ed. Joseph Turow and Lokman Tsui (Ann Arbor: The University of Michigan Press, 2008), 149.
45 Frédéric Vandenberghe, "Deleuzian Capitalism," *Philosophy & Social Criticism* 34 (2008): 877.
46 Jordan Crandall, "Between Tracking and Formulating", *Vector* 21 (2008), http://www.virose.pt/vector/b_21/crandall.html (accessed December 20, 2008).
47 Helen Nissenbaum, "Privacy as Contextual Integrity", *Washington Law Review* 79 (2004): 119-57.

Democratizing Search?

From Critique to Society-oriented Design

Bernhard Rieder

Many things have changed since 1995, when engineers at the *Digital Equipment Company* introduced AltaVista, the first large scale search engine for the World Wide Web. The Web in 2009 is the dominant stage for all things related to information and communication. On a single technological platform, it hosts a wide variety of activities that were formerly distributed over many different channels. With 1.5 billion users, over a trillion pages and a diversity of services ranging from the simple display of text-based information to elaborate online applications that combine databases and sophisticated multimedia, the contemporary Web is an informational behemoth and central to a capitalist economy, whose mode of value production is shifting from industrial to *cognitive*[1]. Without any kind of built-in indexing or cataloguing system, it falls to search engines to make the rather unruly structure of the Web manageable for human users. These complex tools are surprisingly easy to use: a search query composed of one or several search terms will bring up an ordered list of pages that contain the specified words. It is no wonder that search engines are among the most popular services on the Internet.[2]

This central role of search engines has brought a considerable amount of critical attention to these technical artifacts and, more recently, to the companies that build them. Despite its reassuring (informal) corporate motto – "don't be evil" – Google Inc.[3], the undisputed market leader, has somewhat replaced Microsoft as the favorite target for scrutiny and critique by Internet researchers and activists. What initially seemed to be a purely technical matter concerning only computer and information scientists has slowly been engulfed in a rich debate[4] that includes social, political, cultural, economic, and even philosophical considerations. Search is increasingly theorized in terms of representation[5] and power[6]; matters of privacy, equality, plurality, and commercialization are taken into account. At the lower levels of normative reasoning, however, a lot of work remains to be done. This article will therefore consider two problems. First, while much of the critique directed against search engines relies on a set of particular values, the discourse on search is rarely very explicit when it comes to anchoring these values in larger normative frameworks; the arguments put forward may therefore at times appear unconnected. Second, both design and policy recommendations often remain, as a result, vague and unspecific. This is due in part to the fact that expert technical knowledge on Web search remains elusive in the humanities; C. P. Snow's "two cultures" remain separate for the time being. But it is also related to the first problem: without a clear normative standpoint, it is difficult to formulate suggestions about how search *ought* to work. After a short summary of the most common points of criticism directed at Web search and an account of the two dominant values embodied in current general-purpose search technology, popularity and convenience, I will therefore develop a rather explicit normative position that advocates plurality, autonomy, and access as alternative guiding principles for both policy and design. The concluding recommendations are probes into the question of how these principles may be applied in practice.

Web Search as Normative Technology

As the question mark in the title suggests, "democratizing search" is by no means a trivial matter and this essay is necessarily informed by the values and limitations of its author. It is meant as a contribution to the political debate on Web search; the necessary starting point, then, is a closer look at the arguments that are commonly made.

Common Critique

Most strikingly, the discussion surrounding web search has been resolutely *critical*. But although many of the central issues have been raised in two early papers,[7] the stabilization of clear lines of critique was a longer process. Today, we can identify three subject areas that have caused the most contention:

The fact that search engines habitually store personal search data for their many users has led to an interest in matters of *privacy* and its counterpart, *surveillance*. Search engine companies cooperating with totalitarian regimes on repression and censorship, data retention (and erasure) policies, and the problem of cross-database profiling have been some of the main points of critique. However important, these problems are not specific to search engines but concern all systems that store personal data. I will therefore leave them aside.

When in the nineties search engine companies started to include paid links in their result lists, *advertisement policy* quickly became a major issue, which lead to the 2002 disclosure recommendations by the US Federal Trade Commission

(FTC), which demanded that "any paid ranking search results are distinguished from non-paid results"[8]. The tension between public interest and commercial gain continues to be a permanent issue,[9] albeit typically in the context of the latter subject area.

The question of *ranking* – the ordering of search results – has certainly been the most popular topic of debate. Winkler noted early on that search engines divide the Web into "main and side roads"[10] and Introna & Nissenbaum argued that they reshape the Web in favor of commercial interests by directing "prominence" to big sites rather than small ones.[11] Hindman et al. coined the term "Googlearchy" to describe a Web that is dominated by a few highly ranked sites.[12] The question of hierarchy is at the core of search and this article will concentrate on the matter.

There are, however, two additional issues that run through all of the three subject areas:

First, critics commonly point out the lack of *transparency* when it comes to privacy, advertisement, and ranking. Modern IT systems are largely black boxes – or "black foam"[13], as I have suggested elsewhere;[14] we can never know for sure what actually happens behind the interface, which renders informed critique quite difficult. Disclosure of technical specifications and corporate policy has consequently been the most frequent demand by researchers and activists. Second, with Google Inc. controlling an overwhelming portion of the search market[15] and the crucial online advertisement business – the most important revenue stream for free online services – the question of *monopoly* is raised with increased frequency.

Behind each of these five points lurks a normative debate that is framed by the political conflicts of contemporary capitalism, including the questions of how to balance public and private interest, how to ensure equal rights to participation and expression, how to govern multinational companies, and how to keep markets open to competition. Established political positions are not left behind when discussing Web search, and the question is inseparable from larger issues concerning the politics of IT. At the same time, Web search is part of a specific research tradition, the field of *information retrieval* (IR), and in order to understand the normative dilemmas we face, we have to consider some of its specifics.

General-purpose Search

The field of IR emerged over the course of the 20th century as an answer to the problems associated with the acceleration of information production in all sectors of western society. While the first half of the 20th century was marked by library innovators like Paul Otlet and increasingly finer-grained classification systems, the emergence of automatic sorting devices and general-purpose computers opened up new directions in thinking about information. The work by pioneers like Hans Peter Luhn and others led up to Gerard Salton's monumental book "Automatic Information Organization and Retrieval" in 1968, which firmly defined computer algorithms as the logical way to meet the problem of finding information. But IR was developed at a time when information was mostly stored in well-structured form in thematic databases. Many of the conceptual ambiguities associated with Web search come from the fact that data on the Web is neither structurally nor thematically consistent.

The Web can be understood as an address space for document access. In principle, every unit of information is accessible via a *Uniform Resource Locator* (URL).[16] At least the *surface Web*[17] is, from a purely technical perspective, a homogeneous space of informational resources, stored in the form of HTML documents. Web search, by which I mean the *general-purpose* type epitomized first by AltaVista and then *Google Search*, is a technical artifact that treats the Web as this uniform address space and does not make any distinctions between different types of information beyond abstract categories such as file type, date, or language. Search engines use a "one size fits all" approach to brokering access to a wide variety of resources; contextual precision, e.g. the distinction between shopping for a book and looking for a summary, has to be provided by the user in the form of additional search terms.

This universality is in fact one of the major difficulties when it comes to conceptualizing Web search in non-technical terms. Framing the Web purely in terms of topological (a network of documents and links), syntactical (documents as containers of markup language), and statistical (word occurrences) structure radically departs from our human habit of ordering information into subject matters, areas of activity, context, and so on. We would intuitively concur that a restaurant address, the latest gossip on a Hollywood starlet, the price of a laptop, a blog post on weight loss, a scientific paper, and a newspaper article on some political candidate's stance on international politics do not embody the same *type* of information, that they belong to different domains of existence. We will probably also agree that each one of these items can be linked to a set of distinct activities – from diversion to research – that might imply specific acts of decision-making such as settling on where to have dinner or who to vote for in an election. We might even come to a rough consensus on the importance or triviality of each one of these items. These (informal) levels of differentiation belong to what Clifford Geertz defined as *culture*, "webs of significance", order based on *meaning*, not on statistics and graph theory.[18] I do not want to argue that these methods do not capture certain semantic dimensions, nor that research into semantic techniques is necessarily a dead end. But the fact remains that current general-purpose search engines treat the Web as a single whole and use the same techniques to search and rank pieces of information that pertain to a wide variety of domains. Their relative agnosticism to meaning is their brand of objectivity – which still implies a particular cultural logic and normative orientation.

Popularity and Convenience

In 1963, after a series of preliminary projects, Eugene Garfield published the first edition of the *Scientific Citation Index* (SCI), a complete index to the 1961 volume of 613 scientific journals containing an ordered list of over 1.4 million citations. Since then, the SCI has allowed scientists to search for relevant papers by following the "trails of association" – a term coined by Vannevar Bush – established through the scientific practice of citation. Starting with any given publication, a scientist can easily find all the papers citing it and techniques like co-citation analysis (two articles citing the same sources may be thematically related) turn the SCI into a powerful tool for information retrieval.[19]

The SCI is of interest here for several reasons. First, it anticipated an important development in the history of the Web, namely the move away from hand-selected and classification based directories like Yahoo towards the completely automatic search methods epitomized first by AltaVista and now by *Google Search*. Its arguments were almost identical to those of the later search engine: that there was too much information to be handled by human editors, that manual classification was slow and expensive, and that controlled vocabularies were inflexible, burdensome, and ultimately subjective. Second, the SCI represented a real paradigm-shift away from content-based organization towards topological analysis built on graph theory. Web search engines later made a similar transition: AltaVista's ranking was still mainly based on document properties, meaning that a search term's frequency of occurrence, position in the document, presence in the URL, etc. would be the dominant factors in ranking. According to Page et al., "[i]t is obvious to try to apply standard citation analysis techniques to the web's hypertextual citation structure",[20] and AltaVista did in fact count the links that pointed toward a document but did not attribute a dominant role to the link-factor. The success of *Google Search*, however, was mostly built on an explicit link-topological method, where every citation is attributed a specific "weight" (*PageRank*) depending on the "importance" of the site it comes from, which is itself based on a recursive calculation of the whole graph. A third point about the SCI is that its "impact factor" (a citation count for papers, individual scientists or institutions based on the SCI), which has become the dominant means for evaluating scientific productivity, has long been a target of the same sort of criticism that is now directed at search ranking. Researchers have argued that quality is not the same as notoriety and that citation-based ranking might stifle innovation by installing a star system and reducing diversity.[21]

This equation of importance with popularity is indeed the central critique of link analysis as the dominant method of ranking search results – *bias* in search engines is generally understood in this sense.[22] Instead of favoring a particular opinion, political party or company, the worldview embedded in link analysis is much more abstract and, in a sense, delegates ranking *to the Web itself*, as the links that will determine *PageRank* or other topological measures have not been placed by the search engine, but by the people who create websites, blogs, and other types of online content. It is not surprising that Google's own rhetoric strongly relies on "democratic" imagery and equates links with "votes".[23] The search engine then functions as a mere (vote) counting mechanism and the company used to pride itself that "no human involvement" taints this process, "which is why users have come to trust Google as a source of objective information".[24] Ranking is nonetheless targeted at emulating human agents' judgments, and the closer the equation between the machine view and the users' appreciations, the higher the "quality" of results. Search engine companies therefore employ teams of human evaluators that test changes in algorithms and decide whether they are beneficial or not.[25] A study by Pan et al. suggests that most users are willing to place great trust in the competence of this process.[26]

Generally speaking, link analysis turns the power-law link structure of the Web, where a small number of hubs dominate a large number of scarcely linked sites [cf. Hindman et al. 2003], into a measure of importance. The underlying principle has been called "cumulative advantage", "preferential attachment" or "Matthew effect", but the consequence is simply that already well-ranked sites have a higher visibility and therefore get linked more often, leading to yet better rankings. In other words, the rich get richer. Using popularity as measure for quality is, of course, a normative decision. The *logic of the hit*, combined with the fact that search engine optimization (SEO), link campaigning, and classic marketing allow economically potent actors to skew the game in their favor, is effectively responsible for both centralization[27] and commercialization[28] tendencies. But there is a second *core value* informing the current design of search engines.

The success of *Google Search* has been, in part, attributed to its simple, uncluttered interface. Apart from the basic query language, the user has few means to influence the search process, and ranking parameters are completely off-limits. Following the recommendations of user-oriented design – a design philosophy mostly based on cognitive psychology – the goal is to make the search process as *simple and convenient* as possible. That this is where research is continuing to head has recently been made clear by Marissa Mayer, Vice President of Search Products & User Experience at Google Inc., in her definition of the "ideal search engine":

> Your best friend with instant access to all the world's facts and a photographic memory of everything you've seen and know. That search engine could tailor answers to you based on your preferences, your existing knowledge and the best available information.[29]

The goal of personalization is to make search yet more convenient by using personal search histories and session profiles to disambiguate queries. If a user has been surfing shopping sites for the last hour, a query for a book title might automatically favor bookstores over informational or scholarly documents. The search experience becomes faster and simpler.

Both popularity and convenience are derived from user-oriented design principles where "reducing the cognitive effort and time costs for searchers"[30] is the main objective. Despite the "democratic" rhetoric, design decisions are based on perceived benefits to individual end-users; reasoning on the level of society rarely comes into play. But if search engines are indeed powerful gatekeepers and therefore central social institutions, we may legitimately ask ourselves what a more "society-oriented" approach that goes beyond the values of popularity and convenience would look like.

Alternative Guidelines

What I have called "society-oriented design"[31] is not a detached form of normative speculation, but the attempt to bridge the gulf between the contextualized practice of technical creation and considerations of social benefit that go beyond efficiency, control, and material prosperity. Normative reasoning, here, is *bounded* by feasibility. Therefore, if Herbert Simon was right in 1971 when he declared *attention* a scare resource consumed by an overabundance of information, we have to recognize that ranking is not only very useful but also inevitable. If there is more than one result for a query – and most often, there are many more – the only way to bypass ranking would be to order results randomly, most probably rendering the system incredibly frustrating. As Winkler argued,[32] there is no anti-hierarchic medium – just like there is nothing outside of power (Foucault) and no freedom in detachment (Latour). Any system of ranking will favor certain sites over others; the question is which ones. The goal, then, can neither be the abolition of ranking in search, nor the design of the "perfect search engine" (Larry Page). But between these two extremes lies a series of possibilities for design and policy that do indeed merit our – however scarce – attention.

Wikia Search as Society-oriented Design

Looking at some of the Web 2.0 rhetoric, one might get the impression that larger social and political considerations have already found their way into the mindset of designers. The term "democracy" has indeed become omnipresent in the Web 2.0 age. It is by and large defined as the user's ability to vote – on whatsoever; from ideas to video clips and from news items to search rankings. Jimmy Wales, the co-founder of Wikipedia, has recently attracted a lot of attention with *Wikia Search*, a new "social" search engine that tries to make use of this simple logic in its attempt to "democratize search".[33] The idea of "social" search, where user ratings replace link analysis as the dominant mode of ranking, has been implemented several times over the last years – *Eurekester, Mahalo, Wink*, etc. – but the effort lead by Wales stands out not only because of its leader's celebrity, but also because of the very explicit discussion of the norms and values that (should) guide its technical design. The project's internal mailing list is an interesting source, because it is through this channel that four principles have been decided on:
- *Transparency* has been one of the central lines of critique for search engine providers, and *Wikia Search* has decided very quickly to strive for openness on the technical level (all software is open source), on the database level (the index can be downloaded), and on the organizational level (decision-making and corporate functioning should happen in the open).
- *Community* is directly derived from Wales' most successful project, Wikipedia, and implies that ranking and other tasks will rely on user labor. The goal is to attract a sufficiently large number of active users and involve them both in the task of sorting out results and collective governance of the project.
- *Quality* would seem obvious as a goal, but it is very interesting that the *Wikia Search* project explicitly aims at results that are useful to a very high number of people. The quality principle implicitly acknowledges that ranking is not

merely a problem of values or worldview, but embedded in users' trajectories of activity and therefore more or less *useful*.
- *Privacy* is the second element that is directly related to common critique concerning search and other services on the Web. Here, the *Wikia Search* project is quite conscious of the fine line that exists between the very useful gathering of data and the users' right to protect their identity. The consensus that seems to emerge is to store as little user data as possible and to make user identification (which is crucial to transparency and community decision-making) an opt-in feature.

For the time being, *Wikia Search* is a work in progress and it remains to be seen how the guiding principles will be applied in a more definitive version of the search engine. But there are at least two observations that can be made at this point: first, it is quite reassuring to see that a deep discussion of values can be productively brought *into* the process of technical design. This is obviously not a straightforward matter of coming up with a set of values and *implementing* them, but a rather difficult process in which technical, commercial, and ethical demands are in constant conflict. Second, when looking more closely at the guiding principles of *Wikia Search*, we find that while some common criticism of traditional search engines is taken into account, the central tenant of the project – users adding, rating, and deleting results – neither addresses the problem of equality in search results, nor questions popularity as the central expression of importance. *Wikia Search*, in its current stage, produces the same top-down list of results as established search engines; when looking at some of the result pages, it becomes quite obvious that the problem of spam is nowhere near solved and, more importantly, that dominant opinions in the community will lead to imbalanced results. While researching for this article the query "John McCain" brought up a list that, below the obligatory Wikipedia entry, essentially pointed to sites criticizing or ridiculing the republican presidential candidate. It is entirely possible that further versions of the engine will be less easily controlled by dominant user groups, but this will probably entail a fine grained system of governance, which, similar to Wikipedia, will have to rely on administrators, result policing, and banning certain users.

Wikia Search is certainly a fascinating experiment in society-oriented design, but its primary concern is the *social governance of the object itself* and not the relevance of search as part of a larger *socio-technical configuration*. This has something to do with the specific interpretation of democracy as *community* that informs even the more sophisticated Web 2.0 projects.

Two Concepts of Democracy

Using the common sociological distinction between *community* and *society* – habitually traced to Tönnies, but certainly prefigured in Durkheim's distinction between organic and mechanic solidarity – we can roughly distinguish between two ideas of a "government of the people, by the people, for the people". Without going into detail, I believe that the *democracy as community* idea can be found most explicitly in certain forms of protestant doctrine (e.g. Puritanism) and in American social thinking in the tradition of Emerson and Whitman. Highly skeptical of political institutions, it holds that humans are rational beings capable of self-governance. When people come together in good will, consensus will inevitably emerge, and as Howard Zinn argues, "[t]o depend on great thinkers, authorities, and experts is [...] a violation of the spirit of democracy".[34] There is, however, considerable doubt that this ideal can (or should) be applied to the governance of contemporary nation-states:

> I believe that a democratic society is not and cannot be a community, where by a community I mean a body of persons united in affirming the same comprehensive, or partially comprehensive doctrine.[35]

For political philosopher John Rawls, the pluralistic composition of modern societies demands a concept of democracy that takes into account that certain interests and opinions cannot be easily reconciled. The idea of *democracy as society* is therefore built upon complex political institutions and processes, separation of power, and guaranteed constitutional rights that protect citizens from state control. While there is considerable disenchantment with the political maneuvering and compromises that seem to dominate liberal democracy and a longing for the warmth of community, we should be highly cautious when it comes to writing off society – the coexistence of people that neither agree nor resemble each other – as a locus for democratic governance. As Vedel points out, the community ideal tends to perceive key political institutions – parties, unions, media companies – as perversions of the democratic ideal.[36] But how can we imagine governance of very large groups without mediation? The Web 2.0 discourse provides an answer: instead of slow and intransparent institutions we now have software that allows us to scale the community ideal to the level of society; the resulting transfer of power to the companies providing these tools – which thereby become social institutions themselves – is rarely addressed.

Curiously, both understandings of democracy seem to lead to a common normative concept when it comes to Web search, namely some variant of Habermas' ideal of the public sphere as a space of egalitarian expression. The background of virtually all critique directed at ranking is the worry that the Web might lose its capacity to provide a means of expression to formerly excluded voices and to function as "a valuable collision space between official and unofficial accounts of reality".[37] Depending on the favored ideal of democracy, there are subtle but important variations. While the "community" version, which informs most Web 2.0 rhetoric (and many recent scholarly publications), insists that each voice has equal value, the "society" tradition emphasizes that "[all citizens] should have a fair chance to add alternative proposals to the agenda for political discussion".[38] Again, the second stance does not banish mediation, selection, and weighing as long as they are based on the argument made and not status, wealth, or power. Habermas not only accepts a certain level of "critical filtering" – the task of the journalist – but explicitly warns of the "fragmentation" that a public sphere would fall victim to without central mediators.[39] If we see selection and hierarchization as necessary functions for democracy, the whole question is how to define Rawls' "fair chance" to add an opinion to the debate. And if search engines indeed function as "media gatekeepers",[40] the first objective is to ask how their filtering is affecting this "fair chance" and, if necessary, to correct its course. The particular process that produces search results becomes less important than the question of whether this process furthers "reasonable pluralism" or not. This does not exclude community as a value and deep participation as a mode of governance; but the application of voting to ranking can no longer be seen as the obvious and uncontested way to "democratize search".

Before turning to alternative recommendations, I would like to point out that the Web can be seen as something other than a *mass medium*, e.g. as a huge library, a repository for cultural representation or a tool for education. This perspective opens up alternative sources for normative reasoning, including the following:

- *Ethical guidelines for librarians and documentation professionals*: Besides the usual niceties, the ethical codes of professional associations such as the European Council of Information Associations (ECIA) or the American Library Association (ALA) establish specific ethical guidelines such as confidentiality and unbridled *access to information*, which not only means rejecting censorship but actively helping users in their search.
- *Cultural diversity policy*: International declarations such as the UNESCO "Convention on the Protection and Promotion of the Diversity of Cultural Expressions", ratified in 2005 by all UN member states except for the US and Israel, expressively names cultural diversity as worth protecting and the famous *exception culturelle* clause, added in 1993 to the GATT (now WTO)

agreements, allows countries to exempt cultural products from free-trade agreements. These are efforts to extend the principle of *plurality* from the level of opinion to that of cultural expression.
- *Education and empowerment*: In the spirit of enlightenment and education reformers like Paulo Freire, we can think of the Web as a tool for empowerment and a means for individuals to gain *autonomy*. This cannot mean abandoning users to their own devices, but devising "critical pedagogy" whose goal is to help users to look behind the surface of Web search.

When combining these lines of thought with the public sphere model, three principles emerge: (reasonable) plurality, autonomy, and access.

Proposals and Perspectives

In the context of society-oriented design, normative reasoning is necessarily oriented towards application. Following the three principles established in the previous section, what follows is a series of proposals that try to go beyond the often heard demand for more transparency. Having more information about the inner workings of search engines would surely make informed critique of ranking mechanisms easier, but even now, we have a relatively good idea of how search engines produce their results.[41] Critics ask for more transparency to further social control and to impede the arbitrary exercise of power; but the problem with the current search configuration is not simply the potential for abuse, but rather the one-sided focus on popularity and convenience. The following suggestions aim at reorienting the search configuration according to the principles of plurality, autonomy, and access, which, in practice, form a coherent whole.

Regulation and Stimulus

While it is uncontested that search engines provide an immense social utility, the overwhelming dominance of the global search market by a single company is indeed a problem. Without accusing Google Inc. of any wrongdoings, the sheer concentration of power over visibility on the Web should give us pause. From the standpoint of the public sphere model, the Web is part of the media system and if search engines perform similar functions to media outlets, we can argue that the measures put in place by western democracies to thwart media concentration may apply here as well. Even without any malicious manipulation of search results, Google Inc. gains tremendously from its privileged gatekeeper status. The huge amounts of data that users leave behind in the different services provided by the company are invaluable market intelligence that can either be sold or used to optimize corporate strategy. Prominent links on the main search page direct users to the company's entire product line, a considerable advantage when introducing a new service, and with complete knowledge of ranking procedures Google Inc. has the best possible SEO a company can hope to have. As Kawaguchi and Mowshowitz argue, we need to make sure that alternatives exist and from a policy standpoint there are two strategies to do that: states can either limit the dominant actor or help the competition.[42]

Concerning the first possibility, telecommunication laws in most democracies regulate, often in precise percentages, the part of the media market a company may control and limit so called "cross-ownership", e.g. a television network acquiring a newspaper company. While such regulations may not be easily applied to the search market in letter, they may be in spirit. The 2002 FTC case already established a link between search and media legislation, and the European Commission's Article 29 Working Party is actively investigating[43] matters of data protection concerning search engines. The 2004 European Union vs. Microsoft competition case might also provide guidelines, specifically concerning the use of the dominant position in search to control other markets. However, given the complexity of such cases we should not rely solely on constraining measures; stimulating competition in the search market might be a more viable strategy.

Again, there is precedent in the context of media law. Especially European countries grant considerable benefits to newspaper companies, either through direct financial aid (Austria, France, Spain, etc.) or via reduced taxes or fees for delivery (Germany, UK, Switzerland, etc.). The French *Quaero* (€99M) and the German *Theseus* (€90M) projects are pioneer attempts to publicly fund R&D in the field of search. These sums, despite being doubled by the private consortium partners, are of course nowhere close to the major search companies' resources, and the projects, realistically, do not target general-purpose application but multimedia search (*Quaero*) and semantic approaches (*Theseus*). It is somewhat regrettable that these funds are not directly applied to areas that are central to liberal democracy. Because if we perceive the Web as a heterogeneous infrastructure, we may conclude that "more egalitarian and inclusive search mechanisms"[44] are perhaps not needed in all areas, but only in those that pertain directly to public interest, such as the representation of politically relevant information. Why not fund research in automatic news aggregation that, instead of ranking stories by popularity, the principle behind *Google News*, tries to represent the complexity and heterogeneity of the media debate? Applying the principle of plurality to general-purpose search has its limits, and as Pieter van der Linden, the coordinator of the *Quaero* project, pointed out in personal conversation, search will have to increasingly focus on niches to make progress. A public strategy for research funding should select projects not only according to industrial potential, but take into account larger questions of public interest. But this is not the only field where the state can play a productive role.

Exploration and Re-ranking

By furthering users' autonomy we can increase plurality, even with the general-purpose logic that is prevalent today. If *convenience* means shortening interaction between the user and search engine, *autonomy* means trying to keep the mediator from disappearing. Education can certainly promote a more conscious and competent use of search engines, and there is an argument to be made for the inclusion of critical information literacy into teaching curricula. But we also need to think about *technical means* to better explore the diversity of search results. While query operators – e.g. AND, OR, NOT – are most certainly powerful tools to access a larger set of sites, they are currently rather limited and there is little or no possibility to weight ranking parameters. Alternative search engines such as *Exalead*[45] – one of the few general-purpose search engines that actually produce result lists that differ significantly from the market leader's – allow searching with regular expressions, but there remains much room for improvement in extending users' control over the search process. While using query parameters undoubtedly requires a certain expertise, there are ways to deepen the search process without making it overly complex. Two examples:

- *Clusty*[46] is a search engine that divides results into thematic clusters that users can use to navigate up to 500 results at a time. The cluster list provides a first overview over the search subject and may direct users in new directions by showing aspects that they were not aware of before.
- *TermCloud Search*[47] is a search interface designed to map a topic rather than provide the shortest way between a query and a document. Using the simple *tagcloud principle* – keywords are shown in different sizes according to relevancy – the goal is to make users aware of the concepts surrounding their query and to encourage exploration rather than quick answers.

These two examples are quite simple, but there is enormous potential in search technology and interface design approaches that understand search as part of the knowledge building process and actively promote learning, plurality, and user interaction. Emphasizing the mediation process instead of making it disappear can, at the same time, strengthen users' autonomy and promote access to deeper regions of the index. In recent years, however, exploding costs have become an important roadblock for innovation, because a modern search engine is not just an elaborate piece of software, but also an impressive feat of datacenter design and deployment. Indexing a steadily growing Web and executing billions of searches per day is a daunting task, even if many queries are purely navigational (users typing "ebay" into the browser search field to get to ebay.com). To guarantee fast response time world-wide, a company has to build a network of datacenters, with each node within physical proximity to a central Internet hub to reduce the packet travel route. Promoting experimentation and innovation will have to include measures that help dealing with these infrastructure issues.[48] On the organizational level, this can be done in several different ways, but I would like to quickly explore a route that implies using established companies' infrastructure.

Applications like *Clusty* and *termCloud Search* use so called APIs (*Application Programming Interfaces*) to get a set of results from different search engines in machine-readable form (e.g. XML), apply some form of processing (e.g. re-ranking the results), and display the results in a customized fashion (e.g. result clusters). While this is a great way to experiment and implement ideas without having to invest in server infrastructure, there are important limitations. First, the number of results per request is rather low – Google serves only up to eight, Yahoo and Microsoft 50 – and while an application can load several result sets at the same time, there are practical limits; *Clusty* stops at 500, *termCloud Search* at 250 to keep response time acceptable. Second, the contractual provisions of API terms of use are strongly slanted in favor of service providers. While this is not a problem for experimentation, building a business on a search API may be a risky affair, as technical details and legal specifications may be changed at will. While there are robust licensing models on the content side such as *Creative Commons*, developers using APIs still hope for a more standardized and accountable way to clear up legal uncertainties.

In order to resolve the technical limitations of API based experimentation and enable "deep" experimentation that not only re-ranks results but implies alternative ranking methods, "sandbox" solutions are conceivable.[49] This would mean running search applications by external developers in a protected environment ("sandbox") on datacenter infrastructure run by Google Inc. and other companies, allowing programmers to interface directly with the index, bypassing *PageRank* and other ranking techniques.

We can imagine several intermediate stages between the current API-based approach and a full-fledged search sandbox that vary in difficulty of implementation, economic feasibility, and their ability to effectively encourage innovation and broader access to search results. But whatever the precise approach, without proactive lawmaking any technical solution is at the mercy of service providers. French regulations on cultural diversity, which compel television companies to invest a certain percentage of their revenue in cinema production, could be seen as a rough model for thinking about how it might be possible to bind shared-resources requirements. The project of democratizing search is difficult to imagine without at least some involvement by public authorities.

Conclusion

The goal of this text was to explore both the normative and practical side of how to protect the Web's capacity to be "a valuable collision space between official and unofficial accounts of reality"[50] in light of search engine mechanisms that emphasize popularity and convenience above all else. The issue is part of a larger debate on how to govern technology that is performing tasks algorithmically, and on a very large scale, which used to require human judgment such as the selection and consideration of information. When we examine mechanisms like link analysis, we find that these technical procedures do not divide the world along the same lines as we are culturally trained to do, which leads to considerable conceptual uncertainty – already at the level of analysis and even more so when it comes to normative reasoning. As we have seen, extending democratic principles to the governance of information technology is a delicate business that forces us to go back to some of the basic questions of political organization. The complexity of the socio-technical configurations in search and other areas of "cultural" IT will continue to increase in the coming years, and the task of establishing clear lines of techno-normative thinking is not going to get any easier. In this article I have tried to show how one can move from the critical analysis of technology to explicit recommendations without omitting a discussion of the political frame of reference that orients both. For this is the core of the problem: to "democratize search" we will have to incorporate a clear conceptual grasp of the technology, to reexamine our understanding of democracy, and to build bridges between these two on the levels of critique, design, and policy.

Notes

1. The concept roughly holds that capitalism, after passing through a mercantile and an industrial phase, has entered a new stage where the production of wealth is increasingly based on the production of immaterial goods. Theoretical work on the concept of "cognitive capitalism" has gathered around the journal *Multitudes*, driven by authors like Yann Moulier Boutang, Maurizio Lazzarato, Antonio Negri, Paolo Virno, and others.
2. Deborah Fallows, "Search Engine Users", Pew Internet & American Life Project, published January 23, 2005, http://www.pewinternet.org/pdfs/PIP_Searchengine_users.pdf.
3. In this article, I distinguish between *Google Search* (http://www.google.com), a Web search engine, and Google Inc., the company that owns and operates this service. Google Inc. offers many other products, such as online office applications, video sharing sites, an email service, an online social network, etc.; it generates virtually all of its revenue through advertisements placed on its own sites as well as on thousands of partner sites.
4. Eszter Hargittai, "The Social, Political, Economic, and Cultural Dimensions of Search Engines: An Introduction", *Journal of Computer-Mediated Communication* 12, no. 3 (2007), http://jcmc.indiana.edu/vol12/issue3/hargittai.html.
5. Lucas Introna and Helen Nissenbaum, "Shaping The Web: Why The Politics of Search Engines Matters", *Information Society* 16, No. 3 (2000): 169-185; Susan Gerhart, "Do Web Search Engines Suppress Controversy", *First Monday* 9, No. 1 (2004), http://www.firstmonday.org/issues/issue9_1/gerhart/index.html.
6. Bernhard Rieder, "Networked Control: Search Engines and the Symmetry of Confidence", *International Review of Information Ethics* 3 (2005), http://www.i-r-i-e.net/inhalt/003/003_rieder.pdf; Theo Röhle, "Machtkonzepte in der Suchmaschinenforschung", in *Die Macht der Suchmaschinen / The Power of Search Engines* ed. Marcel Machill and Markus Beiler (Cologne: Herbert von Halem Verlag, 2007), 127-142.
7. Hartmut Winkler, "Suchmaschinen. Metamedien im Internet", *Telepolis*, Mars 12, 1997, http://www.heise.de/tp/r4/artikel/1/1135/1.html; Introna and Nissenbaum, 2000
8. FTC Bureau of Consumer Protection, "Commercial Alert Complaint Letter", FTC, http://www.ftc.gov/os/closings/staff/commercialalertattatch.shtm.
9. Alejandro Diaz, "Through the Google Goggles: Sociopolitical Bias in Search Engine Design", in *Web Search: Multidisciplinary Perspectives*, ed. Amanda Spink and Michael Zimmer (Berlin: Springer, 2008), 11-34.
10. Winkler, 1997
11. Introna and Nissenbaum, 2000
12. Matthew Hindman and Kostas Tsioutsiouliklis and Judy A. Johnson, "'Googlearchy': How a Few Heavily-Linked Sites Dominate Politics on the Web" (paper presented at the Annual Meeting of the Midwest Political Science Association, Chicago, Illinois, April 3-6, 2003).
13. The basic difference is that with a box we know, at least, where the system starts and where it ends. Modern IT is generally so intertwined that we can often no longer determine the limits of the system. E.g., we can only guess at the level of interaction and data exchange between the different services offered by Google Inc.
14. Rieder, 2005
15. In March 2008 *comScore* announced that 80% out of all searches in Europe are conducted on sites owned by Google Inc.: comScore, "comScore Releases March 2008 European Search Rankings", http://www.comscore.com/press/release.asp?press=2208.
16. This holds true not only for static content (e.g. http://www.example.com/example.html) but

149

also for sites that generate pages from a database (e.g. http://www.example.com/example.php?pid=354).
17 The part of the Web accessible by following links; information that can be found only by querying search fields is part of the *deep Web*.
18 Clifford Geertz, *The Interpretation of Cultures* (New York: Basic Books, 1973), 5.
19 The SCI is now part of the *Web of Science* database, maintained by *Thomson Scientific*.
20 Larry Page et al., "The PageRank Citation Ranking: Bringing Order to the Web", Technical Report, Stanford InfoLab, 1999, http://ilpubs.stanford.edu:8090/422/
21 Robert Adler and John Ewing and Peter Taylor, "Citation Statistics", Report from the International Mathematical Union (IMU) in cooperation with the International Council of Industrial and Applied Mathematics (ICIAM) and the Institute of Mathematical Statistics (IMS), published June 12, 2008, http://www.mathunion.org/fileadmin/IMU/Report/CitationStatistics.pdf
22 Introna & Nissenbaum, 2000
23 Google Inc., "Technology Overview", http://www.google.com/corporate/tech.html
24 The phrasing changed in mid-2008 probably in preparation for the *SearchWiki* feature that allows users to manually move sites to the top. The referenced passage can still be found on the Internet Archive at http://web.archive.org/web/20071228101625/www.google.com/intl/en/corporate/tech.html.
25 Scott Huffman, "Search Evaluation at Google", Official Google Blog, posted September 15, 2008, http://googleblog.blogspot.com/2008/09/search-evaluation-at-google.html.
26 Bing, Pan et al., "In Google We Trust: Users' Decisions on Rank, Position, and Relevance", *Journal of Computer-Mediated Communication* 12, No. 3 (2007), http://jcmc.indiana.edu/vol12/issue3/pan.html.
27 Winkler, 1997
28 Introna & Nissenbaum, 2000
29 Marissa Mayer, "The Future of Search", *Official Google Blog*, posted September 10, 2008, http://googleblog.blogspot.com/2008/09/future-of-search.html.
30 Pan et al., 2007
31 Bernhard Rieder, "Métatechnologies et délégation. Pour un design orienté-société dans l'ère du Web 2.0" (PhD diss., Université de Paris 8, 2006), http://tel.archives-ouvertes.fr/tel-00179980/.
32 Winkler, 1997
33 Jimmy Wales, "Free Speech, Free Minds and Free Markets" (talk at the Ford Hall Forum, Suffolk University, Boston, Massachusetts, September 11, 2008), http://fora.tv/2008/09/11/Jimmy_Wales_-_Free_Speech_Free_Minds_and_Free_Markets
34 Howard Zinn, *Passionate Declarations: Essays on War and Justice* (New York: Perennial, 2003), 6.
35 John Rawls, *Justice as Fairness. A Restatement* (Cambridge MA: Harvard University Press, 2001), 3.
36 Thierry Vedel, "L'idée de démocratie électronique. Origines, visions, questions", in *Le désenchantement démocratique*, ed. Pascal Perrineau (La Tour d'Aigues: Editions de l'Aube, 2003), 243-266.
37 Richard Rogers, *Information Politics on the Web* (Cambridge MA: MIT Press, 2004), 28.
38 John Rawls, *A Theory of Justice* (Cambridge MA: Harvard University Press, 1971); 225.
39 Jürgen Habermas, "Preisrede anlässlich der Verleihung des Bruno-Kreisky-Preises für das politische Buch 2005" (talk at the University of Vienna, Austria, March 9, 2006), http://www.renner-institut.at/download/texte/habermas2006-03-09.pdf
40 Diaz, 2008
41 There is considerable doubt, however, when it comes to banning and negative ranking para-

meters. Google search states that "[l]inks to web spammers or bad neighborhoods on the web" might reduce rank, but these definitions remain vague. Cf. Google Inc., "Link schemes", http://www.google.com/support/webmasters/bin/answer.py?hl=en&answer=66356
42 Akira Kawaguchi and Abbe Mowshowitz, "Bias on the Web", *Communications of the ACM* 45, no. 9 (2002): 56-60.
43 Article 29 Data Protection Working Party, "Opinion on Data Protection Issues Related to Search Engines", European Commission, published April 4, 2008, http://ec.europa.eu/justice_home/fsj/privacy/docs/wpdocs/2008/wp148_en.pdf
44 Introna & Nissenbaum, 2000
45 http://www.exalead.com/search
46 http://clusty.com
47 http://software.rieder.fr/termcloud
48 Some authors and technologists have suggested peer-to-peer methods for solving the datacenter problem. While this is certainly an interesting direction to pursue, I remain very skeptical about whether such an approach can produce the response time needed to compete with a well-maintained datacenter infrastructure. The most promising attempt, for the moment, seems to be FAROO, http://www.faroo.com.
49 Rieder, 2005
50 Rogers, 2004

Google's PageRank

Diagram of the Cognitive Capitalism and Rentier of the Common Intellect

Matteo Pasquinelli

> At the heart of [Google] is the PageRank algorithm that Brin and Page wrote while they were graduate students at Stanford in the 1990. They saw that every time a person with a Web site links to another site, he is expressing a judgment. He is declaring that he considers the other site important. They further realized that while every link on the Web contains a little bit of human intelligence, all the links combined contain a great deal of intelligence – far more, in fact, that any individual mind could possibly possess. Google's search engine mines that intelligence, link by link, and uses it to determine the importance of all the pages on the Web. The greater the number of links that lead to a site, the greater its value. As John Markoff puts it, Google's software "systematically exploits human knowledge and decisions about what is significant". Every time we write a link, or even click on one, we are feeding our intelligence into Google's system. We are making the machine a little smarter – and Brin, Page, and all of Google's shareholders a little richer.
> — Nicholas Carr, *The Big Switch*[1]

Reversing the Panopticon: Google as a machinic parasite of the common intellect (or *value production*).

A large part of Google criticism focuses only on the *imperial* nature of its monopoly such as its dominant position, privacy issues, censorship, and global dataveillance. Studies about the *molecular* economic engine at the core of this dominion are rare, however. Whereas many critical texts about Google abuse Foucauldian jargon and indulge in the visualization of a digital Panopticon, its power originates more precisely in an economic matrix that is drawn by the cabalistic formula of *PageRank* — the sophisticated algorithm that determines the importance of a webpage and the hierarchy of Google's search engine results.[2] *PageRank* is intuitive enough to be understood by non-specialists, as is shown in the following passages, but a "political economy" of this apparatus is yet to come.

If the *biopolitical* dimension of Google is widely debated (and often articulated in the above-mentioned post-structuralist jargon), what is missing is a *bioeconomic* analysis to explain how Google extracts value from our lives and the common intellect and transforms it into *network value* and wealth. Justified concerns asides, there is an abuse of a Foucauldian paradigm that highlights only one side of the problem, as Google's power is not given as a metaphysical being, but originates from a technological platform and business model. As Paolo Virno puts it, to understand biopolitics we should begin from the potentiality of our living bodies and from labor power: biopolitical structures come later as an apparatus to capture this potentiality.[3] The metaphor of the *Panopticon* must be reversed: Google is not simply an apparatus of dataveillance from above, but an apparatus of value production from below. Specifically, Google produces and accumulates value through the *PageRank* algorithm and by the rendering of a common knowledge – this is the core question. The political economy of Google starts with the political economy of *PageRank*.

The first description of Google's *PageRank* and the kick-off of Sergey Brin and Lawrence Page's business adventure was presented in their paper "The Anatomy of a Large-Scale Hypertextual Web Search Engine" in 1998.[4] The *PageRank* algorithm introduced a revolutionary change in Information Retrieval technologies and in the search engine panorama of the late 90s: the apparently flat data ocean of the Internet was shaped by Google in dynamic hierarchies according to each website's visibility and importance. The ranking of a web page can be quite intuitively understood: its rank value is determined by the number and quality of incoming links. Particularly, a link coming from a node with a high rank has more value than a link coming from a node with a low rank.

While in the late 90s search engines like Yahoo were still hand-indexing the web and organizing it according to the tree structure typical of traditional encyclopedic knowledge, Google provided a formula to trace a semantic value across a dynamic and chaotic hypertext. *PageRank* started to describe web pages according to their popularity and the search engine returned a hierarchy of results according to this rank. Apart from Yahoo's trees and Google's rankings, there are many other techniques of Information Retrieval.[5] The software of the *PageRank* algorithm, despite its intuitive dimension, is in practice a highly complex construct intelligible only to professional mathematicians: in the present text its understanding is kept at an accessible level to sketch a first political economy of this apparatus.

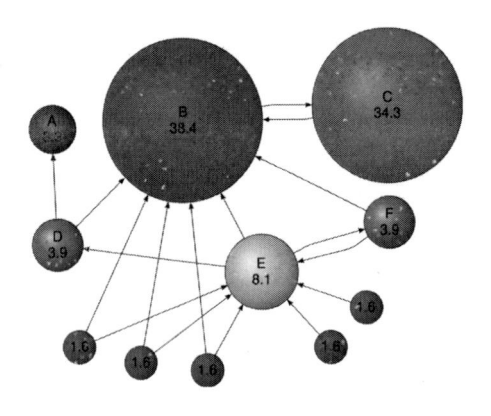

Pic. 1 – A visual example of rank value calculated by PageRank.
Source: http://en.wikipedia.org/wiki/PageRank[6].

The above diagram has no resemblance with the centralized structure of the *Panopticon* described by Foucault in *Discipline and Punishment*.[7] The liquid and hypertextual nature of the web (and more generally of the noosphere) needs to be illustrated using a different structure. A diagram of cognitive capitalism can be intuitively traced if in the structure of a hypertext each symmetrical link is replaced by an asymmetrical vector of energy, data, attention, or value. What *PageRank* unveils and measures is this asymmetrical constitution of any hypertext and network.

Originally, *PageRank* was inspired by the academic citation system. The "value" of an academic publication is notoriously calculated in a very mathematical way according to the number of citations that an article receives from other articles. Consequently, the general rank of an academic journal is the sum of all the incoming citations received by its articles. As Brin and Page explain:

> Academic citation literature has been applied to the web, largely by counting citations or back links to a given page. This gives some approximation of a page's importance or quality. PageRank extends this idea by not counting links from all pages equally, and by normalizing the number of links on a page.[8]

This bookish genealogy of *PageRank* should not be underestimated. A similar way to describe value can be applied to any *cognitive object* and is also *native* to the society of the spectacle and its glossy economy of brands. In a mass media regime, the value of a commodity is produced mainly by a condensation of attention and collective desire driven by mass information and advertisement. Similar processes of such a "condensation of value" can be seen in almost any field, from academic publications to commercial brands, or as in this text, in the ranking of web sites. As the digital colonization gave an online presence to any offline entity, this matrix of social and value relations then migrated online and has become digitally traceable and measurable by search engines. *PageRank*, in particular, describes the attention value of any object to such extent that it has become the most important source of visibility and authority even in comparison with mass media. *PageRank* ultimately provides a formula of value accumulation that is hegemonic and compatible across different media domains: an effective diagram to describe the *attention economy* and the *cognitive economy* in general.

The notion of *attention economy* is useful to describe how (part of) the value of a commodity is produced today via a media-driven accumulation of social desire.[9] Other schools of thought may refer to it as *cultural capital* (Pierre Bourdieu), *collective symbolic capital* (David Harvey) or *general intellect* (especially in post-Operaismo, with a more cognitive spin). Before the Internet, this process was described as a generic collective drive – with the Internet, the structure of the network relations around a given object can be easily traced and measured. *PageRank* is the first mathematical formula to calculate the *attention value* of each node in a complex network and the general *attention capital* of the whole network. What is the nature of the value that is measured by *PageRank*? More interestingly each link and vector of attention is not simply an instinctive gesture, but a concretion of intelligence and often a conscious act. It is fashionable to describe the network society as a conurbation of *desiring flows,* but those flows are dense with knowledge and also belong to the activity of a common intelligence.

In the introductory quotation at the beginning of this article, Nicholas Carr described very well how Google's *PageRank* works, how it feeds on our collective intelligence, and how value is produced and accumulated starting from this common intellect. *PageRank* thus establishes its own attention economy, but a great part of this attention capital is more precisely built on intellectual capital, as each link represents a concretion of intelligence. In this sense Google is a parasitic apparatus designed to capture the value produced by the common intelligence.[10]

PageRank: a diagram of cognitive capitalism (or: *network value*).

Can network theory exist without a notion of network value — a notion of value specific to the network ecosystem and economy? Measuring the cognitive density of the internet, *PageRank* unveils precisely a mechanism that is responsible for setting a rank value for each node of the web. This rank value set by Google is unofficially recognized as the currency of the global attention economy and crucially influences the online visibility of individuals and companies and subsequently their prestige and business. This attention value is then transformed into monetary value in different ways. If the *PageRank* algorithm occupies the inner core of Google's hegemonic matrix, its revenues come from the advertisement platform *AdWords* that exploits this dominant position (99% of revenues are derived from advertisement according to the 2008 Annual Report).[11] The *PageRank* algorithm plus gigantic data centers (running 24-hour and constantly indexing the web) provide a monopolistic position for Google advertisement channels.

The ways through which Google generates value deserve a more attentive analysis, since Google itself does not produce any content, which distinguishes it from traditional mass media. Specifically, Google captures millions of websites and users through its advertisements syndication program *AdSense*. *Google AdSense* provides a light infrastructure for advertising that infiltrates each interstice of the web as a subtle and mono-dimensional parasite, extracting profit without producing content. Money enters the cycle in *AdWords* and is then distributed through *AdSense* to single bloggers or web companies. Within the economy of the Internet, both the traffic of a web site and the redistribution of value are extensively governed today by *PageRank*. *PageRank* is at the core of the attention economy of the Internet as well as at the core of a *general economy of prestige* that affects other domains (take for instance academic reputation, music industries, etc. — many are examples of the symbiosis between the Internet and show business).

What *PageRank* identifies and measures is *network value* in a very numeric form. If commodity is traditionally described by *use value* and *exchange value*, *network value* is a further layer attached to the previous ones to describe its "social" relations. This term is ambiguous for many as it might mean simply a "value of networks" (as in Benkler's much-celebrated "wealth of networks").[12] More precisely, a notion of *network surplus value* should be advanced.[13] Indeed, *PageRank* produces what Deleuze and Guattari described as *machinic surplus value* referring to the surplus value accumulated through the cybernetic domain, or the transformation of a *surplus value of code* in a *surplus value of flux*.[14] Through

PageRank, Google has not simply conquered a dominant position in the storage of web indexes, but also the monopoly of the production of this *network value*.

The *PageRank* diagram shows an important aspect about the relation between two nodes of a network. This relation is never symmetrical, rather it is asymmetrical: each link features one direction like an arrow, each link represents an exchange of desire, attention and knowledge that is never symmetrical. This relation is never binary and equal, but actually *ternary*, as there is always a third node influencing it, and then an accumulation of value is directed in another direction. A network is never flat and horizontal. The digital *ontology* is always influenced by external values and material networks, by the analog world of labor and life (that is the influence of the bio-political and bio-economic field). A network is never symmetrical and homogeneous, it is a topological surface rippled in molecular vortices. Between the *vertical* hierarchies of traditional knowledge and the much celebrated *horizontal* networks of today's knowledge production, this *vortical* dimension shows how the two axes are always connected and how dynamic hierarchies continue to follow us into the digital realm. Google's *PageRank* installed itself precisely on this nexus that shapes the collective sphere of knowledge and the Internet in molecular vortices of value.

By bringing together the semantic topology of *PageRank*, the *vortical* accumulation of value affecting networks, and the notion of *machinic surplus value*, we can start to sketch a new diagram of the knowledge economy, or more precisely of cognitive capitalism (the capitalist dimension of Google being self-evident).

Political economy in the age of Google: introducing the notion of cognitive rent.

The previous paragraphs have tried to show how value is collectively produced within the network and then captured by the *immaterial factory* of Google. After value *production* has been introduced, it is important to clarify stages and modes of its *accumulation*. Using Google as a case study helps to illuminate the more general question of how cognitive capitalism extracts surplus-value and "makes money". To understand today's knowledge economy and the cultural industries, it is important to distinguish different business models and possibly to visualize a machinic assemblage of different regimes of accumulation and not simply one typology.

In a basic overview, today's knowledge economy is currently described according to two dominant paradigms: on one side, intellectual property and, on the other, cultural capital. The definition of Creative Industries, for instance, stresses the "exploitation of intellectual property",[15] whereas the much-celebrated "creative economy" – a concept developed by Richard Florida – is actually based on the exploitation of the general human capital of a given city.[16] Similarly, for decades Italian post-Operaismo has underlined the productive nature of the *general intellect* of the industrial workers once and of the post-Fordist multitudes now.[17] In this reading, the collective production of knowledge is constantly parasited by the corporations of cognitive capitalism, as once factories extracted surplus value from workers' living labor. Opposite this, approaches like Benkler's notion of "social cooperation" or Lessig's "free culture" completely obliterate the dimension of surplus value. All these schools of thought should be confronted with the same question: how is surplus value extracted and accumulated within today's knowledge economy?

Critical discourse is indeed monopolized by an emphasis on intellectual property and on the conflict between the global copyright regime and the anti-copyright movements. In contrast, Google itself is a clear example of a technological empire that was built with no need of a strict copyright regime. Google is clearly a supporter of *free* content produced by the *free* labor of the Internet users. The focus on intellectual property must shift to the issue of *cognitive rent* to understand how surplus is extracted and accumulated in the digital sphere.

Monopolies of intellectual property are clear enough today. Music corporations are fighting precisely to defend this regime from the assault of digital culture. This regime can be described in terms of rent over intellectual property or *cognitive rent,* as media corporations simply exploit the copyright of artworks that were produced by artists and have today virtually no cost of reproduction. Also, Google works on the basis of a concept of cognitive rent, but it does not involve any intellectual property. So which kind of cognitive rent is embodied by Google? After reversing the model of the *Panopticon,* it is also necessary to reverse some basic interpretations of network and knowledge economies to understand how Google became *Googlepoly.*

A new understanding of rent recently advanced by post-Operaismo reveals the parasitic dimension of cognitive capitalism in a helpful way. In an article published in 2007 in *Posse* magazine, Antonio Negri and Carlo Vercellone establish rent as the central mechanism of the passage from industrial capitalism to cognitive capitalism.[18] In classical economic theory, rent is distinguished from profit. Rent is the *parasitic* income an owner can earn just by possessing an asset and is traditionally associated with land property. Profit, on the other hand, is meant to be *productive* and is associated with the power of capital to generate and extract a surplus (from commodity value and the workforce). Yet Vercellone criticizes the idea of "good productive capitalism" by highlighting the turn towards rent as profit as the characteristic trait of current economy.[19] Vercellone accordingly provides a slogan for cognitive capitalism: "rent is the new profit". In this way, Google can be understood as a global rentier that is exploiting the new lands of the Internet with no need for enclosures and no need to produce content. The rent form is reappearing in the post-industrial age as a parasitic apparatus over new material and immaterial spaces.

For Negri and Vercellone the central axis of contemporary valorization is the "expropriation of the common through rent". This explains the ongoing pressure for a stronger intellectual property regime: copyright is one of the strategic evolutions of rent to expropriate the commons and reintroduce artificial scarcity. Today, according to Negri and Vercellone as well as many other authors, speculation is directed toward intellectual property, forcing artificial costs on cognitive goods that can paradoxically be reproduced or copied virtually for free. The composite case of intellectual property, however, must be further illuminated, as rent may not necessarily arise from the new knowledge enclosures, but also from the exploitation of a common cognitive space such as in the relation of Google to the whole web sphere. The *PageRank* diagram seems to suggest a sort of *differential rent* along dynamic spaces that would deserve specific investigation.[20]

Conclusions: "Reclaim your page rank" (or: *value reappropriation*).

The only political response to Google would be an alternative ranking system able to undermine the monopoly of today's attention economy and also the monopoly of the accumulation of value controlled by Google. Can such a monopolistic production of network value be reversed in some way? A first option would be to imagine a collective, voluntary, hand-made indexing of the web based on an open protocol (a sort of Wikipedia of network relations described under the FOAF ontology).[21] Google of course cannot be challenged on the scale of its computing power: such a competition would be quite silly and primitive. On the other hand, the idea of an *open source page rank* algorithm would not address the issue of value accumulation and monopoly. Thus, the idea of an *OpenRank* algorithm was soon abandoned.[22] The fatal attraction of the masses for Google seems to rely more on its mystical power to set a *spectacular value* for anything and anybody than on the precision of its results. Rumors say that *PageRank* will soon be replaced by *TrustRank*, another algorithm developed by Stanford University and Yahoo! researchers to separate useful web pages from spam and establish a sort of community trust across the Internet.[23]

The battle against the accumulation of the *PageRank* data is similar to the battle against the accumulation of capitals and monopolies. *PageRank* is to the Internet what primitive accumulation and rent are to capitalism. A critique of the present mode of networking cannot be simply established on the predictable narrative of the good network against the bad monopoly. A political response can be imagined only if the nature of the molecular *dispositif* that produces the *network value* is understood. *PageRank* cannot be easily neutralized. Thus, all the new fashionable schools of peer-to-peer cooperation and "social production" through the Internet will never represent a decent political alternative until they address the issue of the production and accumulation of *network surplus-value*.

Notes

1 Nicholas Carr, *The Big Switch: Rewiring the World, from Edison to Google* (New York: W.W. Norton, 2008).
2 "PageRank" (without space) is a trademark and patent owned by Google.
3 Paolo Virno, *A Grammar of the Multitude* (New York: Semiotexte 2004), pp. 81-84: "In my opinion, to comprehend the rational core of the term 'bio-politics', we should begin with a different concept, a much more complicated concept from a philosophical standpoint: that of labor-power. [...] What does 'labor-power' mean? It means *potential* to produce. Potential, that is to say, aptitude, capacity, *dynamis*. Generic, undetermined potential: where one particular type of labor or another has not been designated, but *any* kind of labor is taking place, be it the manufacturing of a car door, or the harvesting of pears, the babble of someone calling in to a phone 'party-line', or the work of a proof-reader. [...] Having said this, we still have to address a crucial question: why is life, as such, managed and controlled? The answer is absolutely clear: because it acts as the substratum of a mere faculty, labor-power, which has taken on the consistency of a commodity. [...] One should not believe, then, that bio-politics includes within itself, as its own distinct articulation, the management of labor-power. On the contrary: bio-politics is merely an effect, a reverberation, or, in fact, one articulation of that primary fact—both historical and philosophical—which consists of the commerce of potential as potential."
4 Sergey Brin and Lawrence Page, "*The Anatomy of a Large-Scale Hypertextual Web Search Engine*", 1998. http://infolab.stanford.edu/~backrub/google.html
5 See: Amy N. Langville and Carl D. Meyer, *Google's PageRank and Beyond: The Science of Search Engine Rankings*, Princeton University Press, 2006. And: Michael W. Berry and Murray Browne, *Understanding Search Engines: Mathematical Modeling and Text Retrieval* (Philadelphia: Society for Industrial and Applied Mathematics, 1999).
6 Wikipedia comments this image in this way: "Mathematical PageRanks (out of 100) for a simple network (PageRanks reported by Google are rescaled logarithmically). Page C has a higher PageRank than Page E, even though it has fewer links to it: the link it has is much higher valued. A web surfer who chooses a random link on every page (but with 15% likelihood jumps to a random page on the whole web) is going to be on Page E for 8.1% of the time. (The 15% likelihood of jumping to an arbitrary page corresponds to a damping factor of 85%.) Without damping, all web surfers would eventually end up on Pages A, B, or C, and all other pages would have Page-

Rank zero. Page A is assumed to link to all pages in the web, because it has no outgoing links." Source: http://en.wikipedia.org/wiki/PageRank, 12 March 2009.

7   Michel Foucault, *Surveiller et punir. Naissance de la prison* (Paris, Gallimard, 1975); trans.: *Discipline and Punish: The Birth of the Prison* (New York: Pantheon, 1977).
8   Sergey Brin and Lawrence Page, "*The Anatomy of a Large-Scale Hypertextual Web Search Engine*", 1998. http://infolab.stanford.edu/~backrub/google.html
9   Herbert Simon, "Designing Organizations for an Information-Rich World", in M. Greenberger (ed.), *Computers, Communication, and the Public Interest*, Baltimore: Johns Hopkins Press, 1971. See also: T. Davenport and J. Beck, *The Attention Economy: Understanding the New Currency of Business*, Harvard Business School Press, 2001.
10 This model of capturing the network capital of each node and user can be applied generically to the whole Internet and, for instance, to social networks as well (like Facebook and MySpace, where the most important number is precisely the figure of "friends" shown on each personal page).
11 "AdWords is Google's flagship advertising product and main source of revenue ($16.4 billion in 2007). AdWords offers pay-per-click (PPC) advertising, and site-targeted advertising for both text and banner ads. The AdWords program includes local, national, and international distribution. Google's text advertisements are short, consisting of one title line and two content text lines." [Source: Wikipedia entry "Adwords", 11 March 2009]
12 Yochai Benkler, *The Wealth of Networks: How Social Production Transforms Markets and Freedom* (New Haven: Yale University Press, 2006).
13 This network-value should be distinguished from the traditional definition: Metcalfe's law of "network value" states that the value of a telecommunications network is proportional to the square of the number of connected users of the system (n2).
14 Gilles Deleuze and Félix Guattari, *L'Anti-Oedipe. Capitalisme et schizophrénie* (Paris: Minuit, 1972). Translation: *Anti-Oedipus: Capitalism and Schizophrenia* (Minneapolis: University of Minnesota Press, 1983)
15 Originally, the precise 1998 definition adopted by the Creative Industries Task Force set up by Tony Blair stated: "Those industries that have their origin in individual creativity, skill and talent and which have a potential for wealth and job creation through the generation and exploitation of intellectual property."
16 See: Richard Florida, *The Rise of the Creative Class: And How It's Transforming Work, Leisure, Community and Everyday Life* (New York: Basic Books, 2002)
17 See: Paolo Virno, *A Grammar of the Multitude. For an Analysis of Contemporary Forms of Life* (New York: Semiotexte, 2004).
18 Antonio Negri, Carlo Vercellone, "Il rapporto capitale/lavoro nel capitalismo cognitivo", in *Posse*, "*La classe a venire*", Nov. 2007. Web: www.posseweb.net/spip.php?article17
19 As Vercellone explains in a previous study: "According to a widespread opinion in Marxian theory that stems from Ricardo's political economy, rent is a pre-capitalist inheritance and an obstacle to the progressive movement of capital's accumulation. On this premise, real, pure, and efficient capitalism is capitalism with no rent." In: Carlo Vercellone, "La nuova articolazione salario, rendita, profitto nel capitalismo cognitivo", in *Posse*, "*Potere Precario*", 2006; trans. by Arianna Bove, "The new articulation of wages, rent and profit in cognitive capitalism", Web: www.generation-online.org/c/fc_rent2.htm
20 See my taxonomy of rent in: Matteo Pasquinelli, *Animal Spirits: A Bestiary of the Commons* (Rotterdam: NAi Publishers / Institute of Network Cultures, 2008).
21 FOAF (an acronym of Friend of a Friend) is a machine-readable ontology describing persons, their activities and their relations to other people and objects. Anyone can use FOAF to describe

him or herself. FOAF allows groups of people to describe social networks without the need for a centralized database. See: www.foaf-project.org

22 See: www.openrank.org
23 Gyöngyi, Zoltán; Hector Garcia-Molina, Jan Pedersen. "Combating Web Spam with TrustRank", in: *Proceedings of the International Conference on Very Large Data Bases*, 2004

The Power of Classification
Culture, Context, Command, Control, Communications, Computing

Konrad Becker

How do things relate to each other? What is essential to one thing in relation to another? How do subjective meaning and generalized or objectified attributions of sense interrelate? What does it mean for our sense of self and how we relate to each other? What is meaning, how does it develop? These questions have puzzled humankind for ages. In an era of digital information, of human-machine interfaces and robotic data spiders, surfing in the vast space of electronic data all on their own, they become vastly relevant. Proteus, an early sea-god in Greek mythology, can foretell the future. But he answers only to someone who is capable of capturing him and changes his shape to avoid this. More than ever, in a time of information explosion, it is not enough that data is useful, it also needs to be findable and accessible. Even though it can be quite hard to define the difference between similar and dissimilar objects, it is significantly even more difficult for abstractions and ideas. However, finding information is not the opposite of losing it, but an active effort to recognize interconnections in systems of meaning. Searching is an act of imagination, an approximation of expected outcomes, where findings inscribe themselves into the future.

Dragons of Chaos and Social Fiction

Ancient cultures had concepts of an ocean of information and a deep-sea monster dwelling in its dark expanse. The Black Winged Night of the Dragon of Chaos, the "vast and dark void" of Tiamat, from whose dismembered body the cosmos emerged and the world was formed. These demonic creatures mirror anxieties associated with a space of chaotic and unstructured information, untouched by the logocentric rays of solar deities and the light of reason. As we are adrift on the seas of knowledge, navigation is at the root of modern sciences. Cybernos, the steersperson of the seafaring ancient Greeks, maneuvering the nautical routes with the help of bright stars in the sky, lent its name to the science of cybernetics. This discipline of control and feedback, first applied in the field of ballistic course-plotting, stood at the beginning of many present-day information and communication technologies. Trying to produce intelligent maps of the world, these maps often reveal more about their authors than the territory they describe. Classification, elemental in mapping conceptual spaces of knowledge, typically mistakes transient social fictions for real and physical unchangeable facts. It happens time and again, particularly in relation to race, gender, social institutions, and any other domains where there is a vested interest in the making of realities.

Self-fulfilling Voodoo Categories

Names give an advantage to those who know them, the ability to call forth, to evoke or even to command the powers related to a name. There has always been an intimate relation between knowledge and control, and it is a power to have the authority to name something. Problem solving involves a process of naming things and issues and framing the context to attend to them. To bring order into the classes of names and hierarchies of designations is not only a practical or formal scientific issue, but a religious one as well. Categorization is type of cognitive voodoo related to deep-rooted beliefs that the world is/was created by the use of language, by the spelling out of names, and consequently that the universe can be influenced by a correct use of name and order. And it can be – but not quite that simply. Luckily, creating shared worldviews and producing ideological conceptual fields is more complex. Conjurers of classification, trying to force their hubristic will onto the world, may underrate the forces at work in the minds of others. They become victims of wishful thinking regarding the level of agreement that can possibly be achieved. Fortunately, for a start, the world is not necessarily compliant to voodoo categorization. Rigid standardization is actually hard to come by in a world where research is an ongoing process with changing definitions and a constant drift of understanding. It is a meshed up reality of unexpected shifts in perspective and dynamic interrelations with ever varying trajectories of power. Reaching a consensus about a standard first requires an agreement, and that can't possibly happen where conformity does not exist. Nonetheless, expert "scientific" classification can be used to advance an agenda, to create a reality that in itself forms an effective case for a particular interpretation of reality. Cataloging schemes are hardly the discovery of a true "natural order", but authored, and the purpose is chosen, not given. Categorization in a field of knowledge doesn't necessarily document a given reality, but produces knowledge in a particular interpretation of perception. Classification systems are notoriously off track, but evidently good for the game of self-fulfilling projections of ideological power.

All the Print that Fits, or Not

While the ordering and structuring of knowledge has always been central to the findability of past information, at least since the library of Alexandria, a sorting concept like alphabetic order by author is a much more recent fashion. Today's dominant library classification system conserves the 19th century worldviews of one Mr. Dewey and his limited grasp of realities beyond a white Protestant US middle class. The inventor of the Decimal Classification System of books was fond of the metaphor of an army to restore order in a chaotic mob of information, to impose a hierarchical structure and to force ideas into military style organization charts. Melvyl Dewey was making bold assertions about the world when, in 1876, he threw all non-Christians into one single category, listed very last in all categories about religion. Designers of the Soviet library's catalogue system produced similarly strong ideological statements about the world when they established the top category "Works of the classical authors of Marxism-Leninism". This demonstrates the problem of mapping catalogue systems onto one another, or attempting to match classification schemes – they each portray a different universe. The US Library of Congress classification system had to put a "former" label in front of their Soviet Union category, and still ranks tiny countries like "Austria" or "Switzerland" on the same level of relevance as the continents of Africa and Asia. These funny distortion effects of reality and relevance are also rooted in the need to find physical objects, books or atlases on shelves. When the software of concept and classification meets with the hardware of the tangible, and the immaterial interacts with the physical, it can produce unexpected results. Compared with smart automated search and indexing technologies, the traditional categorization systems loose out in finding things in large digital resources. But obscured by obsolete habits and outdated strategies from earlier efforts to structure knowledge, attempts to categorize information and research resources in the electronic realm can be highly inadequate. Digital information needs no shelf and the question arises whether predefined categorizations are such a good idea after all. A main reason for Google's success was that there is no virtual shelf, no awkward pre-constructed file system. But with shelf space, even if it distorts the space of knowledge in curious ways, at least it is easy to see if it's full or empty.

Mentalist Catalogues and Fortune Cookies

Professional catalogue and categorization workers strive to avoid what is context-dependent and temporary at all costs, but always end up in the middle of it. Trying to establish law and order in the information sphere, some warriors of categorization seem oblivious to the nature of transient realities and the fuzzy inflections of meaning. Cataloguers' interests and requirements necessarily dominate over the more objective need of navigating the complexity of the world. They breed cognitive management technologies blind to cultural and subjective ambiguity and the slipperiness of context-dependent statements. Ideas of an objective ordering of abstract space are based on a religious notion of immaculate purity. They feed on dangerous ideologies of cybernetic control that imagine the manifest world to be reducible to a single viewpoint. Language is a complex temporal and spatial dynamic of signs and representation in relation to signified objects. In general linguistics there are no positive terms, only differences. Those working on categorization and building the ontology of classification systems intended to provide stable continuation over time have to organize the world ahead. Categorizing things in advance means to forecast the future, which is the magical practice of oracles, clairvoyant seers or spiritist mediums. And it is exactly the traps of categorization that mentalists and cold readers exploit in their illusionist stage shows. Organizational schemes deteriorate with time and scale, and the cost of support for highly managed centralized large volumes soon becomes prohibitive. Even though demand-driven systems like Google are fortunate not have to use advance predictions and projections of what one needs to know, the massive scale of data remains a key technology challenge.

Modern Ghost Logic

For complex information systems, it is essential that machines not only respond and interact with humans, but with each other as well. What are they talking about behind our backs? Semantic computer networks run on ontologisms and first order logic reducing logical inference down to simple rules. Syllogisms are a form of logical argument described by Aristotle as "… certain things being stated, something other follows of necessity from their being so." The classic example is: Humans are mortal. Greeks are human. Therefore, Greeks are mortal. This kind of Cartesian logic not only sounds stiff and technical, but based on absurd absolutes invariably leads to ridiculous conclusions. Clay Shirky gives the following example: If – Count Dracula is a Vampire + Count Dracula lives in Transylvania + Transylvania is a region of Romania + Vampires are not real – then the only logical conclusion from such a set of statements is that Romania isn't real. Sometimes the move from the logical to the silly is closer than it appears. Computers are very well adjusted to syllogisms, but the world can't be reduced to unambiguous statements that can be effortlessly recombined. At the dawn of the 20th century, Sherlock Holmes significantly propagated the suggestion that brilliantly smart people arrive at unavoidable conclusions by connecting antecedent facts: "When you have eliminated the impossible, whatever remains, however improbable, must be the truth." Holmes' inventor Arthur Conan Doyle not only popularized the value of deductive reasoning, but was also deeply engaged in fairy photography, conversations with ghosts and a range of other spooky entities. Doyle was an enthusiastic follower of late 19th century Spiritualism, a complex socio-cultural adaptation to the advancements in science and new technologies. Holmes is part of this response to a beginning modernity, where the irrational and the rational meet at the dawn of mass societies. The cocaine-driven pseudo-rationalism of logical deduction was a hysterical reaction to an ambiguous world filled with libidinal ectoplasm and an explosion of things from industrial-scale production machines. Painting pictures of a simplified world in a narrowed down logic is soothing and somewhat comforting. Unfortunately, the unnerving daily reality – from ancient times to high tech societies and urban angst – mostly involves incomplete, inconclusive or uncertain and highly context-dependent information. Machines are good at logical reasoning that works well in places like index tables, and this is where computer assisted automation is largely useful and effective. Humans handle information based on "feelings", popular heuristics, intuition, paranoia, wild speculations, and peer pressure or group dynamics. People rely on imitation, tradition or repetition and many other methods, but rarely on syllogistic reasoning or deductive logic.

Do Ideas Dream of Electric Sheep?

In its philosophical origins, the term ontology means the study of entities and their relations in a systematic account of existence. This tradition, less concerned with what is than with what is possible, asks, "What exists?" The object is a purely speculative purpose, not to facilitate action but to advance understanding. Ontological implications of categorization are highly problematic and ideas of "natural" classification betray essentialism beneath an epistemological cover. Ontology, which is about making clear and explicit statements about entities in a particular domain, has variable definitions in itself. Computer sciences and the field of digital knowledge management/classification have now taken this word "ontology", and have applied it to the problem of machine intelligible information and an explicit specification of a conceptualization. Their organizing of collections of entities, things or concepts into related groups and hierarchical trees is based on such categorization and classification. Philosophers like to accuse each other of category errors, a semantic or ontological error. As in "colorless green ideas sleep furiously"; properties are ascribed to things that supposedly could not have that property. Similarly, it is seen as a mistake to conceptualize the mind as an object of immaterial substance, because it appears meaningless for a dynamic set of dispositions and capacity. Unfortunately there is no agreement on how to actually identify category mistakes. Ontologisms call for domains with central and legitimate authority, a confined stable corpus with limited entities and clear edges suitable for formal categories. Strictly regulated realms of juridical systems are just such an example. They require participants to be highly trained cataloguers, along with high levels of expertise and user coordination and authoritative reference sources for decision making. Closed ontological domains of hierarchical nature are typical for religious systems. It is not only psychotic personalities, institutionalized or not, who try to bring order into the world with endless and bizarre lists or Byzantine systems of classification in private cosmologies. These are also the base for a critical psychological discipline of controlled paranoia, Cabbalist analytical methodologies, and other gymnastics of the mind. Furthermore, there are long traditions specializing in experimentally induced deliriums of interpretation and artificially produced individual delusions of reference. These include techniques for the cathartic shattering of categories through the paradox and the breakup of false identifications in the perplexities of Zen riddles.

Blind Taxonomies and Orders of the Imagination

Mnemonic devices and memory hooks do not work because they are objective. On the contrary, the ancient Ars Memoria applies narrative structuring of the imagination and a visual anchoring of information to the geometry of thought. Typologies and taxonomies do not make assertions that can be judged true or false, but rather they are tools for the organization and stabilizing of thoughts about a shared reality. Geekish dreams of an "Ontology of Everything" aside, most proponents of semantic webs do seem sufficiently aware that building a top-down ontology or taxonomy that works for everyone and describes everything is not an option. They assert that this research enables local communities of interest to create their own ontology – and is not pursued for the enforcement of a New World Order of authoritarian classification. The reification of typologies is not unusual, but building taxonomies in the naïve belief that they represent the hierarchical structure of reality can be considered as rather unenlightened. In the real world of vast domains of proliferating entities that overlap in multiple ways, unstable and without clear boundaries, ontological structuring does not work well in broad access for non-expert users. The desired level of consistency in a normative classification setting influences the balance between complexity, simplification and scale. Either there is broad agreement in a narrow band of users, or slight agreements in broad groups.

Stereotypes and the Exploitation of Subjectivity

The distributed use of tags in flat hierarchies enables a new heterogeneity with large amounts of specific intelligence that improves organizational value with scale and time. Triggered by users with similarities in classifying, collaborative tagging may disproportionately reinforce each other's views, predisposition and foregone conclusions. Specialist blindness, enthusiastic favoritism, tribal fads, gangland attitudes or stereotype prejudices can develop a strong dynamic of skewing issues based on a questionable validity of judgment. But if tagging remains transparent, it allows preserving individual, conflicting or even heretical viewpoints without having to force them into the straitjacket of temporal mainstream opinions. It accommodates statistical distributions where infrequent events frequently make up a majority. The total volume of the long tail of events with low popularity can exceed that of those with high popularity, and Internet ventures have leveraged this for their business. This outreach to the obscure and far out, disconnecting the service model from the peak-idiocy blockbuster demand curve, has certainly made media programming somewhat more intelligent. It has also contributed to the commercial exploitation of cultural niche markets and marks the transition from the traditional disciplinarian modes of preconfigured categories towards the new societies of control; from educational indoctrination to the fluid mining of cognitive response and reaction flows in opinion poll perception management. The so called "Web 2.0 interfaces" enable the commodification of subjectivity where social networks are exploited and then licensed back to the user.

Digital Eyes and the Hidden Gods

"The perfect search engine would be like the mind of God," Google co-founder Sergey Brin once said. Accordingly, digital search engines aim for maximum reach and maximum recall. In the beginning is the search term, but Google wants to process all the information in the world and "understand exactly what you mean". Without users, there is no mind of God. Google has now become the mainstream oracle of choice, the waves of *zeitgeist* queries breaking on the rocks of solidified identities. A recent USC study by the "Center for the Digital Future" found that a majority believes that "most or all of the information produced by search engines is reliable and accurate". Increasingly, people rely on online resources for their routine intake of daily news instead of traditional print newspaper. Clearly, the issue of ranking and the intrinsic ordering of information and the underlying measuring and organization system prove to be a factor in forming worldviews. Imagination, shaped by the information we consume, in turn predetermines what we are looking for. *Google News* is by now a classic example of online news aggregation. Google's ranking logics and indexing methods result in exclusion, and their news service hardly qualifies for a pluralism of viewpoints. Search results based on skewed but hidden mechanics of classification lack in inclusiveness, fairness and scope of representation. Their ranking practices are a trade secret, and when alternative information suddenly vanishes from top search results, there is simply no way of finding out why. It is a decentralized system, where all users become transparent to deep marketing data-mining practices and motivational research, but with an impenetrable center where at the core remains a hidden god. While a corporation may run its server systems on open source software, any political or economic influence remains hidden and the key providers of search and retrieval technology are completely unaccountable to questions of censorship and manipulation. In an age where access to information is largely controlled by a few companies, this is one of the most problematic aspects of the search engines.

Playgrounds for Spooks

Search, data mining and information retrieval technologies are in high demand by state or business intelligence agencies, and spooks are on the board of all major commercial operations. These technologies are indispensable in security operations, risk management and for Command, Control, Communications, Computing and Intelligence (C4I) systems. They can be used for humanitarian aims or rescue missions, but in an asymmetric digital war on terror, information sorting and retrieval can be turned into virtual or physical search and destroy operations. This is the playground for the *Total Information Awareness* officers and their panoptic Eye of Providence: subverting search engine capabilities for their all-seeing Eye's massive surveillance of personal information flowing across the digital networks, breeding information paranoia and data panic to haunt the crossroads of search technologies. And the liberty to engage in social, cultural and intellectual activities free from oversight, in privacy and autonomy vanishes from sight. Data mining and retrieval applications are developed in vastly expensive software suites that are then beyond the reach of civil society organizations, independent researchers or critical initiatives. These powerful applications are not supported as tools for the public, but are used as weapons against this public by those who can afford it. Further development of semantic technology will enhance the uncanny ability to identify, understand and manipulate individuals without their knowledge or awareness. In the name of diversity, accessible and transparent applications are required, and the cryptology of open secrets must remain open source. A dynamic system of heterogeneous multiplicity including peer-to-peer exchange interfaces and open source search strategies, scalable personal information crawlers and anonymous engines are needed, as well as decentralized cluster architectures without central servers. Tools of cultural intelligence production should be in the hands of the many and not the privilege of the few. A truly free market of competing ideas requires access to the tools of computer aided analyzing and inferring, and a democratic diversity of making sense means the broad accessibility of automated information processes.

Augmented Cyborg Cognition

Many experts see advancements in information processing moving towards a stronger human-computer symbiosis in a range of fields that include bio-cybernetics and cognitive sciences. Human system integration is the buzzword for new human/machine interfaces in speed and depth enhanced information retrieval and decision making. Augmented Cognition wants to beat human cognitive limitations through adaptive computation. An adaptive user interface involves sensors for determining user state and emotions, and inference engines and classifiers to evaluate incoming sensor information. Computational systems continually adapt to their users and through sensing, learning, and inferences understand trends, patterns, and situations relevant to context and goals. Away from systems of linear or static text and the electronic typewriter towards advanced statistical text analytics, information mining and enhanced pattern recognition. Obviously the jet fighter pilot is currently the prototypical cyborg. But both pilots and the information workers on the ground have to filter relevant information from vast amounts of data in no time and act on the results. It appears only natural that DARPA is a leading player in a technology that shapes the future of warfare and information dominance. Since any sufficiently advanced technology is indistinguishable from magic, without a practical understanding of how it operates, this emerging technology remains a black art. Arcane sciences of high-powered and excessively funded labs set out to influence information landscaping.

Embedded Information Politics

Futuristic applications and computational complexity aside, technologies of the mind are political philosophy masked as neutral code. Innocent utilities that blend into the routine of everyday work and leisure, shading, blinding or subtly bending our perception in various ways, weave cognitive threads into the fabric of reality. Deliberately designed to yield results in a limited frame of reference, or naïve mechanisms of ideologies in specific domains, these cognitive tools are always political. Classification is not merely a retrieval tool, but also an embedded element of the ongoing construction of a work context and its associated dynamic processes and mechanisms. The logic of everyday language and political rhetoric typically evolve from a hierarchy of semantic objects, where its assumptions are presented as god-given and "natural". However, in the daily reality of info overflow it is imperative to acknowledge both arbitrariness and willful design, and that hierarchies are not miraculously produced by nature itself. What is at stake is nothing less than the informational constitution of societies and their institutions. Throughout the heterogeneous fields of search research and the formation of applied sciences at the foundations of a democratic public, cultural intelligence is the thread to look for.

Visibility

The Googlization Question
Towards the Inculpable Engine?

Richard Rogers

Googlization and the service-for-profile model

The illustration of Google by Jude Buffum may be read as a short-hand reference for "googlization", a term introduced in 2003 to describe the growing "creep" of the media company's search technologies and aesthetics into more and more Web applications and contexts, not to mention tradition-rich institutions such as the library.[1] (See Figure One.) In a post on his book-in-progress blog, the *Googlization of Everything*, the media scholar Siva Vaidhyanathan writes that Google has "altered the rules of the game for at least six major industries: advertising, software applications, geographic services, e-mail, publishing, and Web commerce itself".[2]

Figure One: Responses to Googlization. Illustration by Jude Buffum, 2008

Googlization connotes media concentration – an important political economy style critique of Google's taking over of one service after another online. Within the study of media, more specifically, googlization also could be interpreted as an analysis of Google as mass media, inviting thought about how broadcast media of old are classically critiqued. For example, is there a strict separation between the producer/distributor and the consumer of the media? Engine users generally do not provide feedback about the query returns. Are the financial and technical barriers of entry into the area so high as to forestall newcomers from entrance? New search engines emerge, but the industry has matured. And every major engine employs an algorithm that seeks to emulate Google's *PageRank*. There is what could be termed algorithmic concentration. Is the programming, or content delivered, seeking to appeal to the largest possible audience? Search engine returns, as is argued below, do not necessarily put on display a plurality of viewpoints from a diversity of voices. Rather, the sources often appear quite familiar and established. From those characteristics and others, one could begin to consider the value of mass media critique applied to Google.[3]

What else is googlization? Vaidhyanathan points out that the services appear to be gratis. Yet, when we use "Web search, email, Blogger platforms, and YouTube videos, Google gets our habits and predilections so it can more efficiently target advertisements to us".[4] To googlization scholars and others studying Google, especially in surveillance studies, the search engine company's is a personal information economy business, where the standard exchange is service for profile.[5] Thus googlization, as a process, implies the fanning out of the service-for-profile model both by Google, into its other, non-search areas, as well as by its followers and emulators. The question for googlization scholars is both the extent of such a "creep" as well as its consequences.

That is, to study googlization, and its further spread, one would enquire into whether the service-for-profile model is transforming other media, including the "older" media and perhaps off-line trades. Building on the work of the communications scholar Joseph Turow, as well as the surveillance studies scholar David Lyon, I described one consequence of the phenomenon of the personal information economy as having to know you, in order to sell to you, in the retail industry.[6] The questions surrounding the increasing mediatization of retail, including customer relationship management and especially loyalty cards, relate to giving discounts only in exchange for profilable information. Coupons yield to cards swiped. In department stores, geo-identifiers (e.g., zip code) are keyed in prior to check out.

In his study of niche economies, Turow argues that advertising, with the Internet, is gradually turning away from mass broadcast of the television age to "direct", a form of salesmanship that historically has relied on the personal attention of the door-to-door seller or the visiting market representative.[7] Without the human contact now, building a relationship lies in the form of technology chosen to collect user data and subsequently to personalize salutations, alerts, adverts as well as recommendations. The customization code referred to here is distinct from more mundane means of making the desktop, avatars and mobile communications environments one's own through modification, where the user places her own skins and templates on a page, or associates a ringtone with a particular individual. Google's "direct" is an algorithmic, relational design approach that places relevant information in precious spaces. In a sense, the software also enters the user into personal communication with the database. Here "the personal" should not be understood in the customary, official sense, such as one having to enter date and place of birth, gender, etc. into form fields. Rather, the database contains one's "flecks", content about interests and habits (e.g., from search queries) that are employed to glean a profile on the basis of a small collection of information pieces.[8] Crucially, piecing it together only partially de-anonymizes the user. That is, there is no army of salesmen becoming acquainted with the customers, as deployed by modern "direct" companies such as Amway selling Nutrilite. Rather, the profiling of tastes follows from one's key words (from search history) and geography (from the IP address). The question for googlization scholars thus concerns the uptake of such identifiers into more and more services.

How may one further inquire into what happens when an industry has been "googlized"? More conceptually, there occurs what may be described as a mode switch from consultational to registrational interactivity.[9] In consultational interactivity, the user queries and chooses from pre-loaded information, as in a library catalogue. One consults what is already there, and user anonymity does not come into play (unless books are borrowed, and anonymity is dealt with through data retention laws). There are no dynamic recommendations. With registrational interactivity, the information delivered is dependent on one's personal settings, be they preferences such as language, safe search and the quantity of results (in a lighter version), or on one's histories of sessions, searches, purchases, etc., in a deeper variation. As personal settings and personal histories fuse, the search engine's acquaintance with the user would ultimately provide the uncanny, as if it knew what you were looking for and desiring all along. The effects, and affect, of personalization on search may be studied by striving to train a logged-in Google account to return only sources that are desired, such as only anti-fur groups for a fur query, instead of purveyors of the pelts and hides.

Back-end googlization

Research into what may be termed the uncanniness of search engine returns suited to one's predilections and desires has found forms of the familiar, albeit somewhat different from the expected. In early research, which has been followed up by the search engine critical design group, Metahaven, engine results are scrutinized not only for what they include and exclude, which is the classical, info-political critique.[10] Beyond looking into levels of source plurality and diversity in the medium once celebrated for its egalitarian spirit, the info-political work also scrutinizes the kinds of stories search engine results tell. The idea of fashioning a story from search engine returns harkens to the writings of literary hypertext theorists, following Jorge Luis Borges's short story written in 1941, where the path the surfer takes is considered a means of authorship.[11] Here, however, the search engine is the authoring device, as it provides the current sources considered relevant and timely. The usage of the term timeliness is different from the journalistic sense, where news should be on top of events. Similarly, but in a Web-specific sense, timeliness refers to an acceptable refresh or posting frequency. What do all these timely sites with high inlink counts add up to? Examining the specific set of sources delivered in the returns, what stories do they tell?

I critiqued Google by comparing the results of a query for terrorism to the source set one is accustomed to hearing on the evening news.[12] Instead of providing a collision space for alternative accounts of reality, Google furnished the familiar, in that the storyline about the war on terrorism has been repeated frequently on television by showing clips from the U.S. White House. Whitehouse.gov was among the top results for the query terrorism in 2003, together with cia.gov, fbi.gov and other establishment sources, including *CNN* and *Al Jazeera*. The familiarity of results put paid to the notion of a reputational free-for-all on the Web. Google had become journalistic, sourcing like elite media and well-resourced agenda-setters. The findings became starker in Metahaven's experiment. In July 2008 a Google.com query for Karadžić furnished, in the following order, "Wikipedia, *BBC News*, *Google News*, *Yahoo News*, *The Guardian*, *Reuters*, *MSNBC*, *Interpol*, *YouTube* and *Google Blog Search*".[13] With the exception of Interpol, the entire source set is media and leaning towards the self-referential.

Thus the crucial question is, which kinds of sources are being recommended for a particular query? Put differently, how may one think through the kind of recommendation engine Google is? One may argue that Google, for its majority of user types (searchers and Webmasters) as opposed to its advertisers, has always provided an indication of the state of source dominance per area of inquiry. Google is a status-authoring device. Given all the pages that reference a key word, the search engine delivers those "deserving" to be listed as the top sources. Thus, apart from seeing the source set as the story, one also may view the engine results as telling a second kind of story – the current status of the topic or issue in question through the organizations currently representing it, on the record, in the engine returns. Compare queries made in Google in 2004 for "climate change" and for RFID, in terms of the types of actors present in the top returns. For "climate change", there are U.N. scientists, governmental agencies, and other establishment actors. For the RFID (radio frequency identification) query, the actor types are the trade press, corporations, lone activists and electronics tinkerers. A comparison of the actor composition provides an indication of the maturity of the issue, with RFID in an emerging, more polarized discursive space (hopes and fears), and climate change more settled (policy processes). By 2008 the RFID engine return space contains a somewhat different population of actors, with non-governmental organizations (epic.org and eff.org), mainstream media as well as a governmental agency making an appearance. Comparing the actor composition in engine returns for the same query over time shows changing states of play for an issue, according to the sources at the top of the returns.

Generally speaking, the lesson for googlization scholars is the resonance of such novel status-making across other platforms. Has the back-end algorithm taken over from the traditional status-makers, the publishers, editors and other classic adjudicators? One case study to build upon concerns the Web directory, the human-edited projects, including Yahoo's and the Open Directory Project's, which have sought to organize the Web by topic. Yahoo's Web directory is the prototypical example, once compared to Shiyali Ramamrita Ranganathan's 1933 Colon Classification system.[14] In the well-cited piece published in 1998, the "Internet cataloguer" Aimee Glassel argues that Yahoo is Ranganathanian, in the sense that it does not endlessly create new, unique topic areas – building out that flat ontological list – as in the Dewey Decimal System (or encyclopedias more generally), but rather has broad top-level categories and facets that constitute them. From the mid-nineties to the end of the twentieth century, prior to Wikipedia's entry onto the Web in 2001, it was a model to emulate, not only for the entire Web, but also nationally, with such efforts as Startpagina in the Netherlands.

For all the innovation and imitation that it spawned, the Yahoo directory met its fate in October 2002, when it was replaced as Yahoo's default engine – by Google returns. Subsequently, in February 2004, Yahoo cut the ribbon on its very own algorithmic machine, designed by in-house engineers, to yield results not so unlike Google's. Giving way to the familiar "'organic" results of the dominant engine, it put its hand-made directory aside. Was Yahoo, in a sense, googlized?

Front-end Googlization

On the front-end, Yahoo's portal approach remained, with its bountiful services, text and images, or clutter, if one's sensibilities are trained by Google's aesthetics. What had changed at Yahoo? Casting an eye not on the front-page, but on Yahoo's engine results page, Search Engine Watch writes:

> How does the new Yahoo search engine differ from Google? The presentation of the results is very similar. Yahoo has wisely opted to keep things looking mostly the same, with a few exceptions. There's a link to the cached copy of each indexed page – now being served from Yahoo, not Google. Just about everything else on search result pages looks the same.[15]

Having the same look as Google was thought desirable, certainly in terms of the single search box, front and center. In his lament about the loss of the butler at Ask Jeeves as well as the longer march of engines joining the "logo, form, button" aesthetic, Derek Powezek, a designer of Technorati's interfaces, argues that too many engines have asked the question, "What would Google do?"[16] His argument could be interpreted as a concern for interface googlization. Indeed, in describing the "googlization meme", John Battelle, author of a well-known book on Google, argues that attention should be paid to the increasing homogeneity on the homepage. Reducing it to a single search box could be construed as the pinnacle of the merging of usability and functionality.

> Everybody loves using Google. Therefore, doesn't everybody want the same simple design on every site they visit? (…) People are calling this approach Home Page Googlization.[17]

The fascination is with Google's simple search box, including its two main buttons, Web search and its homage to hyperspace, I'm feeling lucky. That second button is an anomaly for the googlization critique, in the sense that neither has it spread across engines, nor is it linked up with the source of revenue, advertising. I'm feeling lucky skips the results page.

Where the second interface, the results page, is concerned, a critical study should include what could be dubbed Results Page googlization. Despite the arrival of Kartoo in 2002 and other engines "visualizing" returns, listed results dominate, with a default of ten per page, and each entry comprising title, description or teaser text, and hyperlink per entry.

Studying the input field (search box) and the output (the list) has detracted attention from the tabs, however. In its first ten years, recently celebrated, Google has made subtle changes to its front-page real estate. There have been upgrades and downgrades of such services as Froogle and Groups, as *Google Labs* and other acquired projects see the light of day, only to be de-emphasized later. Paying attention to the tabs in a longitudinal study is one way to step back-stage and come to grips with Donald Norman's classic Google critique: "Is Google simple? No. Google is deceptive. It hides all the complexity by simply showing one search box on the main page."[18] Norman, the design and usability scholar, is referring to the absence of transparency in two respects – the interface lacks an overview of the services on offer, and also, perhaps more to the point, masks the organizational structure. Google thus becomes a new case of a "social hieroglyphic".[19] In a variation on the Marxist language, one could argue that it makes invisible the social relations behind its commodity, and at the same time naturalizes it, making it seem like second nature.[20] Search engine returns, at least those that are not sponsored, are "organic". It is here that the contribution of Henk van Ess, the investigative journalist and search engine observer, is of special interest. The URL discovered in 2005, http://eval.google.com, prompted a cause célèbre and exchanges with company representatives, posted online, for van Ess found that Google hires humans (students) to check the search engine results for reliability.[21] Finding that the results are manufactured arouses excitement, not only because of its association with the Mechanical Turk or the climax of *The Wizard of Oz*, when the curtain is drawn back to reveal a human. But it also complexifies the simple search box, removing its reductionism. As pure algorithmic logic recedes, Google's back-end becomes messier.

Where another of its significant relationships with humans is concerned, Google more generally has been in sync with Yahoo on one project of crucial importance to librarians and editors. Google followed Yahoo by downgrading its directory. In March 2004, Google moved its directory (the engine built on top of the Open Directory Project, dmoz.org) off its front-page, demoting the directory tab to the "more" button. In 2006, Google's directory was placed under "even more". By late 2007, when Google.com's menu moved upper left, the "even more" tab item was gone, though it did return (again without the directory) in 2008.

Googlization studies are thus inquiries into how subtle interface changes imply a politics of knowledge, in particular the de-privileging mechanisms through the relegation of editorial services to further depths of a Website. The burying of the directory in both Yahoo and Google signals a much larger transformation – the demise of the expert human editors of the Web. (Paid "Internet cataloguing" positions also disappear.) Just as poignantly, for library scientists, is another consequence of the rise of the back-end algorithm for directory innovation, very much unlike in the alphabetical, egalitarian spirit and also unlike Ranganathanian's top-level categories with constitutive elements forming a whole. By 2007 Yahoo had changed the default output of its directory. The alphabetical listing was replaced by a ranking of sources based on "popularity".

> By default, Directory site listings are presented sorted by popularity and relevance. Sites that are most popular with users or the most relevant to the category appear at the top of the site listings. The order of websites or web documents is based upon Yahoo! Search Technology.[22]

That search has supplanted browsing (and surfing) is a larger Web phenomenon, often attributed to usefulness rather than to googlization. The bottom-up user has needs over those of the top-down cataloguers.[23] In another of the many inversions brought about by new media, the audience has taken over from the tour guide. Everybody holds the red umbrella. But for the googlization project the further question has to do with the impact of user empowerment over that of editorial expertise or algorithmic purity.[24] Search is becoming personalized, whereby results are tailored to one's tastes, based on search history and the results clicked. To achieve it, the search engine user is being "recorded", also in the sense of the words Google has chosen for the settings. One pauses search history and resumes it. Playing back one's history is encapsulated in the feed option. As the veteran search engine observer Danny Sullivan writes, one of the greater significances of personalized search is that "the days of everyone seeing the same results for any particular query are growing more numbered."[25] The story authored by the search engine results is now partly of one's own writing, as certain sites that one visits frequently are boosted a few places upwards. Sullivan tells of his gratification in seeing his own articles rather high in the rankings for certain favorite queries, and wondering if his work is as highly ranked for other users.

The Inculpable Engine

For media scholars one of the questions has been how to reinterpret the idea of the gatekeeper, the powerful editor controlling the stories that are fit to print, in light of the link networks determining rankings and search histories boosting favorite sources in personalized search. Without taking algorithmic tweaks and major overhauls into account, a straightforward discussion of new forms of gatekeeping would follow from cases of sites being de-indexed. The "Google Guy", Matt Cutts, blogs about them, telling readers about "webmaster best practices", Google guidelines with admonitions about baiting crawlers with "engine spam", such as back-door pages. Perhaps of greater import are particular glimpses into the workings of the Google bots provided by Cutts. Writing about a mother crawl in 2006, called bigdaddy, he relates that there are "sites where our algorithms had very low trust in the inlinks or the outlinks of that site. Examples that might cause that include excessive reciprocal links, linking to spammy neighborhoods on the web (...)."[26] The valuation of one hyperlink as one vote no longer applies; not all links are of equal value. It is a useful corrective.

The excessive reciprocal interlinking explanation may help with the following. As a case in point about the varying values of links, in 2007 researchers and I began logging Google results for the query 9/11 with a focus on *911truth.org*, a source that is referred to as a conspiracy site in various contexts, including through the tags the site has been given by Del.icio.us users (see Figure Two). Beyond *911truth.org*, two other sites' rankings are highlighted, *The New York Times* (nytimes.com), and the New York City government (nyc.gov). In 2007, from March through the anniversary of 9/11, *911truth.org* routinely makes the top ten in the results for the query. *The New York Times* and the New York City government are well below the fold, coming in under result rank 50 and 100 respectively. One of the purposes of the work is to put on display particular organizations' rankings for a query, in an effort to switch the view of Google results, and think through the cognitive changes that Google has brought about. (Thus googlization studies also become interested in the evolution of one's ideas about relevant sources.) Normally, the top ten results (or the top 20, 30, 50, 100, depending on one's preferences) constitute the population of sources one would consult. One does not normally think to oneself, why is *The New York Times* not present on my results page? Where is the New York City government in the results for my 9/11 query? Having figured so significantly in the event itself, shouldn't the New York City Fire Department be there? Such questions are precluded, for instead the Google results make up the world of relevance.

Query:	http://911truth.org
Method:	Delicious Tags per URL	December 2008

Delicious Tags for 911truth.org   **Digital Methods Initiative**   19 December **08**

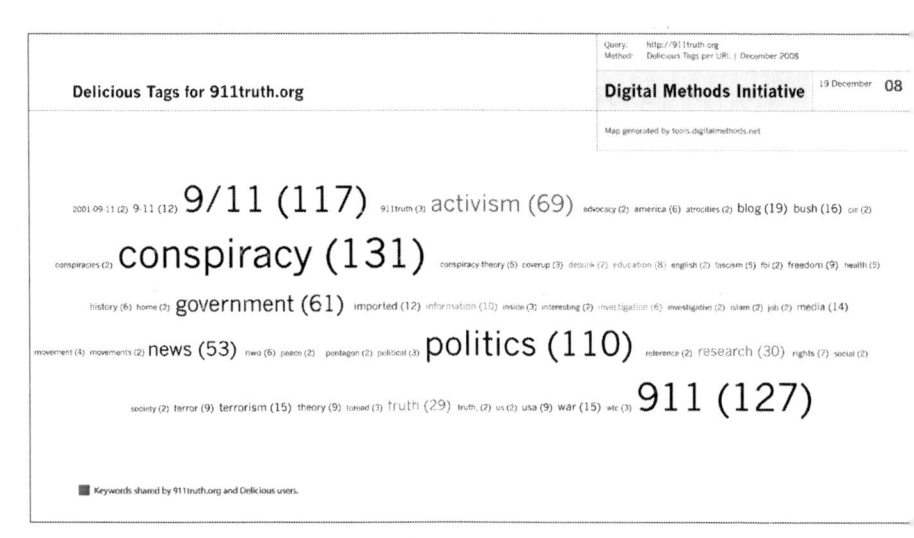

Map generated by tools.digitalmethods.net

2001-09-11 (2) 9-11 (12) **9/11 (117)** 911truth (3) activism (69) advocacy (2) america (6) atrocities (2) blog (19) bush (16) cia (2)
conspiracies (2) **conspiracy (131)** conspiracy-theory (5) coverup (3) debunk (2) education (8) english (2) fascism (5) fbi (2) freedom (9) health (5)
history (6) home (2) government (61) imported (12) information (10) inside (3) interesting (2) investigation (6) investigative (2) islam (2) job (2) media (14)
movement (4) movements (2) news (53) nwo (6) peace (2) pentagon (2) political (3) **politics (110)** reference (2) research (30) rights (7) social (2)
society (2) terror (9) terrorism (15) theory (9) tinfoil (3) truth (29) truth. (2) us (2) usa (9) war (15) wtc (3) **911 (127)**

■ Keywords shared by 911truth.org and Delicious users.

Figure Two: Delicious Tags for 911truth.org. Analysis by Michael Stevenson. Graphic: Digital Methods Initiative, Amsterdam, 2008.

Of greater importance, the research project documented the sudden disappearance of *911truth.org* from the results. Some ten days after 11 September 2007, *911truth.org* dropped precipitously from a top 5 source, to 200, and then off the chart, returning some two weeks later to its usual top placement. (see Figure Three)

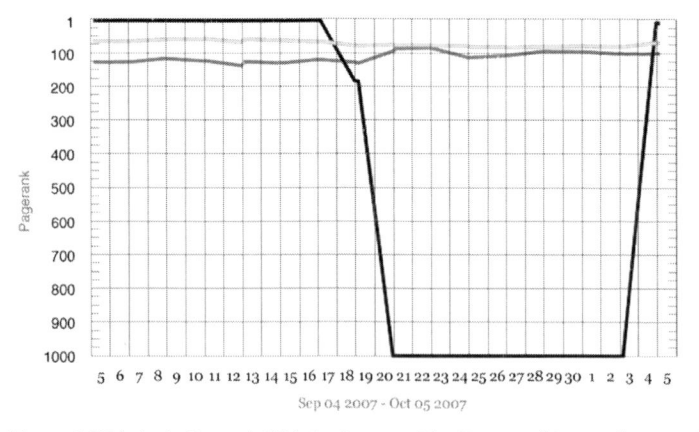

Figure Three: A Website is Gone. A Website Returns. The Drama of 911truth.org in Search Engine Space. A comparison of the Pagerank of 911truth.org (highest on Sept.5), nytimes.com (second on Sept.5) and nyc.gov (lowest on Sept.5) Data source: Google.com. Graphic: Issue Dramaturg, Govcom.org Foundation, Amsterdam, 2007.

One possible explanation is that *911truth.org*, as a franchise site, has chapter affiliates such as *ny911truth.org*, *sf911truth.org* and *vancouver911truth.org* that routinely link to the parent site, and did so with a flourish around the 9/11 memorial day, signaling what Matt Cutts called excessive reciprocal linking. For the researchers and me charting the sudden drop in ranking, the question arises as to the stability of the source set in search engine returns. Is there volatility in the returns in the sense that what one receives today may be rather different from the next? (That results change over time is of interest to those researching the current status of the subject matter, according to the source set or actor composition returned, as argued above.)

I would like to conclude with a major implication of personalization. To Danny Sullivan's point that customized search removes returns common to all searchers for the same query, I would like to add that personalization takes the search engine off the hook, because the "blame" or responsibility for the results is partly one's own. Critical examinations of search results for their politics of information provision turn inward. For those viewing Google as mass media, the previous lack of user feedback has been built in.

Acknowledgments

The author would like to thank the members of the Digital Methods Initiative, Amsterdam, http://www.digitalmethods.net/, as well as the organizers of the Deep Search conference, Vienna, November, 2008.

Notes

1 Alex Salkever, "Google Here, There, and Everywhere", *BusinessWeek Online*. December 16, 2003 http://www.businessweek.com/technology/content/dec2003/tc20031216_9018_tc047.htm (accessed 22 December 2008); John Battelle. "The 'Creeping Googlization Meme'", *John Battelle's Searchblog*, December 16, 2003 http://battellemedia.com/archives/000145.php (accessed 22 December 2008)
2 Siva Vaidhyanathan, "Where is this book going?," *The Googlization of Everything Blog*, September 25, 2007. http://www.googlizationofeverything.com/2007/09/where_is_this_book_going.php (accessed 22 December 2008)
3 Laura van der Vlies, "*Googlization: A New Form of Mass Media Critique*," M.A. Thesis, Media Studies, University of Amsterdam (2008)
4 Siva Vaidhyanathan (2007)
5 Greg Elmer, *Profiling Machines*, Cambridge, MA: MIT Press (2004); David Lyon. *Surveillance Studies*, London: Polity (2007)

6. Richard Rogers, "Consumer technology after surveillance theory", in: *Mind the Screen: Media Concepts according to Thomas Elsaesser*, eds., Kooijman, Jaap, Pisters, Patricia and Strauven, Wanda. /Amsterdam: Amsterdam University Press, 2008), 288-296
7. Joseph Turow, *Niche Envy*, Cambridge, MA: MIT Press (2006)
8. David Weinberger, *Small Pieces Loosely Joined: A Unified Theory of the Web*, Cambridge, MA: Perseus (2002); Matthew Fuller. *Media Ecologies*, Cambridge, MA: MIT Press (2005)
9. Jens F. Jensen, "Interactivity: Tracking a New Concept in Media and Communication Studies", in: *Computer Media and Communication*, ed. Mayer, Paul (Oxford: OUP, 1999), 160-188.
10. Lucas Introna and Helen Nissenbaum, "Shaping the Web: Why the Politics of Search Engines Matters," *The Information Society*, 16,3 (2000): 1-17; van Elizabeth Couvering, "New Media? The Political Economy of Internet Search Engines", presented at the Annual Conference of the International Association of Media & Communications Researchers, Porto Alegre, Brazil (July 25-30, 2004); Metahaven, *Multipolar Search – EXODVS*, published on the occasion of Pancevo Republic!, 13th Biennial of Art, Pancevo, Serbia (2008)
11. Jorge Luis Borges, "The Garden of Forking Paths", in: *The New Media Reader*, eds., Wardrip-Fruin, Noah and Montfort, Nick, Cambridge, MA: MIT Press (2003), 29-34.
12. Richard Rogers, *Information Politics on the Web*, Cambridge, MA: MIT Press (2004)
13. Metahaven (2008)
14. Aimee Glassel, "Was Ranganathan a Yahoo!?", *InterNIC News*, (March, 1998) http://scout.wisc.edu/Projects/PastProjects/toolkit/enduser/archive/1998/euc-9803.html (accessed 22 December 2008)
15. Chris, Sherman, "Yahoo! Birth of a New Machine" (February 18, 2004) http://searchenginewatch.com/3314171 (accessed 22 December 2008)
16. Derek Powezek, "What Would Google Do?", *Vitamin* (May 14, 2006) http://www.thinkvitamin.com/features/design/what-would-google-do (accessed 22 December 2008)
17. Jarod Spool, "Homepage Googlization", *User Interface Engineering* (April 5, 2006) http://www.uie.com/brainsparks/2006/04/05/home-page-googlization/ (accessed 22 December 2008)
18. Donald Norman, "The truth about Google's so-called 'simplicity'", *Donald Norman's jnd Website* (2004), http://www.jnd.org/dn.mss/the_truth_about.html (accessed 22 December 2008).
19. James Berger, *After the End*, Minneapolis: University of Minnesota Press (1999)
20. Alexander Galloway, *Protocol. How Control Exists After Decentralization*, Cambridge, MA: MIT Press (2004)
21. Henk van Ess, "Google Secret Lab, Prelude", *Henk van Ess's Search Engine Bistro* (June 1, 2005) http://www.searchbistro.com/index.php?/archives/19-Google-Secret-Lab,-Prelude.html (accessed 22 December 2008)
22. Yahoo, "What is the 'By Popularity | Alphabetical' feature shown above site listings?," *Directory Basics FAQ* (2008) http://help.yahoo.com/l/us/yahoo/directory/basics/basics-21.html (accessed 22 December 2008).
23. Clay Shirky, "Ontology is Overrated", *Clay Shirky's Writings About the Internet*, (2005) http://www.shirky.com/writings/ontology_overrated.html (accessed 22 December 2008).
24. Andrew Keen, *The Cult of the Amateur*, New York: Currency Doubleday (2007)
25. Danny Sullivan, "Google Ramps Up Personal Search", *Search Engine Land* (February 2, 2007) http://searchengineland.com/google-ramps-up-personalized-search-10430 (accessed 22 December 2008)
26. Matt Cutts, "Indexing Timeline", *Matt Cutts: Gadgets, Google, and SEO* (May 16, 2006) http://www.mattcutts.com/blog/indexing-timeline/ (accessed 22 December 2008)

Peripheral Forces

On the Relevance of Marginality in Networks

Metahaven

This article is about ranking. Hidden in the search engine, ranking is the elusive, complicated machinery of magic which structures our encounters with information on the Web. Despite the intricate system of ranking, most engines make search look deceptively simple: enter a term into the empty text field where the cursor is blinking, click "search", and a list of results unfolds. Depending on what you entered, the list will be long or short. But no search engine either indexes or shows results without applying some kind of hierarchy to them. This initially seems like a normal, everyday procedure, comparable to the ways we judge between relevant and trivial, foreground and background information in everyday life; after all, our own hierarchies of visibility are also shaped according to certain needs, beliefs, and limitations. Often, the hierarchy applied by ranking rewards what is already popular. Like a forward echo, the search seems to already know what we "want" before we have run the query. The threshold of ranking also tends to suppress less often viewed currents and opinions in broad, public topics.

Redesigning the search engine begins with challenging the principles of relevance and popularity inherent to ranking. In this essay, we argue how ranking mechanisms translate as phenomena of sociability, and how a different take on the sociability of "weak ties" may bring a different appreciation of their relevance to networks.

On the web, choices we make – and links we click – have far-reaching consequences for what others find, see and click. We are not neutral bystanders to an unfolding natural process on which we exert no influence. What we choose to look at and link to is what we reward and recommend to others. What we ignore, we eventually obscure – if others concur. This process entails a form of political power exercised through sociability, where networks, protocols and ranking mechanisms supplant the exercise of direct force, and algorithms become wholesale distributors of visibility and obsolescence. Results displayed at the top of a ranked list are "naturally" considered more relevant than ones at the bottom.

But the properties defined by the algorithm or the values of the 'relevance decision' remain kept from public view and user intervention. Most search engines are designed to cater to the impossibly large target audience of "every other web user". Just as a global fastfood chain offers its clientele little insight into the intricate fabrication of a hamburger, there seems to be no need for the world's mass markets to tweak the controls of its web search results – or so it seems – as long as the results list is stunningly long, impossibly up-to-date and loading at the speed of light. After Google, since that is what we want, that is what we get.

The public's engagement with the web is mostly made on terms of free choice; clicking, tagging, linking and browsing[1] are social actions, often with reciprocal forms of reward – which, in online social networking platforms such as Facebook and MySpace, have become systematized and automated by means of the "friend" ranking as a mutually affirmed social bond. On a larger scale, these forms of reward, subscription and consent constitute a genuine form of "network power". "The idea of network power argues that we are pulled by our choices along avenues smoothed by the prior choices of others,"[2] as David Grewal explains. In networks, power by sociability is immanent.

While networks can be viewed as the natural arena for the exercise of a global free will – producing an aggregative, collective form of giant decision on "what we all want" – we suspect that the most relevant structural components of networks are their gaps. These "structural holes" are not just the limitations of sociability within clusters of mutually affirmed alliances and links; they are also gaps of knowledge and power.[3] We will argue how weak ties spanning structural holes provide a critical alternative to ranking models based on aggregative forms of sociability, by being unpopular, autonomous and peripheral. We will explain the argument by an up-close exploration of the theory of structural holes as developed by Ronald Burt. By way of example, we will assess notions of social power present in U.S. president Barack Obama's election campaign, as well as his initiatives for the reinvention of the U.S. government's relationship to the people. These will ultimately be structurally compared to the semi-independent terrorist cells which constitute the Al Qaeda network after central command has been taken down.

From relevance to authority, and back

Ranking mechanisms may constitute a form of power both more sneaky and more structural than old-fashioned coercion; the affirmative force of sociability, present in the reciprocal processes of cross-linking and tagging, may have become the vehicle of a kind of power which suppresses alternatives without coercion being needed.

Currently the hierarchy of relevance applied by ranking algorithms propels a hierarchy of influence: the initial relevance of results topping the list is reaffirmed by the public's browsing behavior. The more relevant a result, the easier it is found and clicked on, and the more it eventually will get seen, read and linked to. Such a ranking process risks constituting a self-fulfilling prophecy of relevance. The most well known example of this type of algorithm – or mode of decision-making – is called *PageRank*, the algorithm of the Google search engine. Google's founders Sergey Brin and Larry Page state that

> a user might prefer a news story simply because it is linked directly from the *New York Times* homepage. Of course such a story will receive quite a high PageRank simply because it is mentioned by a very important page. This seems to capture a kind of collaborative trust, since if a page was mentioned by a trustworthy or authoritative source, it is more likely to be trustworthy or authoritative.[4]

When Brin and Page assert that "quality or importance seems to fit within this kind of circular definition"[5,] they refer to "a kind of peer review"[6] – borrowing the name from the process by which impartial experts scrutinize the work of fellow scholars; often, the same assumption is made when the efficiency of algorithms is tested on academic datasets where citations count as links.
Brin and Page continue:

> [I]f a web page has a link off the Yahoo home page, it may be just one link but it is a very important one. This page should be ranked higher than many pages with more links but from obscure places. (…) [A] page has a high rank if the sum of the ranks of its backlinks is high. This covers both the case when a page has many backlinks and when a page has a few highly ranked backlinks.[7]

The Google founders leap across these two contradictory logics — the academic peer and the social actor. With the *PageRank* model, "more important and central web pages are given preference".[8] Since highly ranked links exert more influence on the distribution of authority, there is a higher payoff for "proximity" to the authoritative source.

Nevertheless the web culture of the amateur is not bound to academic impartiality. Unlike the academic processes of peer reviewing and referrals, web users are social actors who don't need to discuss or verify prior assumptions. Actors often seek to bond with others "like them" and confirm what they already consider true or valuable. In other words, there is an incentive to link with others who share certain (ideological) standards – or simply the same protocol. The advent of blogs, amateur journalism, social tagging and other forms of user-generated content puts any prior definition of authoritative sources under further pressure. Because of their basis in the handshake of protocol and the aggregation of user benefits in joining mutually affirmative standards of cross-linking, blogs and social networking platforms are acquiring a high level of *PageRank* despite the fact that they do not possess factual authority comparable to *The New York Times*. In other words, what began as a peer reviewed quality standard is transforming into a "peer pressured" sociability standard. Links function as a way for users to associate themselves with what they like, voting for those they agree with; linkage – sociability – is becoming the stand-in for authority. It follows that dense social spheres, tied by consent, often disregard the unpopular information offered by the weak ties at their peripheries.[9]

Politics of structural holes

In his book *Structural Holes: The Social Structure of Competition,* Ronald Burt addresses precisely these features which reinforce central actors. Running counter to the aggregative logic of authority, Burt argues for the relevance of weak ties. In his approach, social cohesion is an indicator of redundancy. He sees a high probability that tightly-knit clusters circulate the same information among their actors. Burt is particularly concerned with defining the conditions under which a networked actor may benefit from putting other actors into contact.

> Structural holes are the gaps between non-redundant contacts. As a result of the hole between them, [once bridged] the two contacts provide network benefits that are in some degree additive rather than overlapping.[10]

The main cost of aggregative sociability lies in the redundancy of information. There are also structural constraints on the freedom to opt out or relate to unpopular and peripheral ideas. At the level of the wholesale distribution of visibility via algorithms, the capacity of peripheral ideas to surface in a list of results becomes structurally affected by the relative weight of heavily cross-linked, socially coherent spheres of consent, combined with the algorithmic preference for these spheres as more "authoritative". This preference was first based on an "extrinsic" definition of authority taken from printed media and the academic peer review, but then gradually became "intrinsic" to the aggregative economy of linking on the web, with standards of sociability supplanting old-fashioned authority. Therefore, the "design of consent" of Google's list – in particular the first 10 results – harnesses a preference for sources, many of which have become authoritative via their social structure (like Wikipedia).

The disregard that social networks tend to display for Burt's structural holes translates into a further suppression of marginalized ideas, some of which may hold valid criticality of the popular theses. The structure of a critical argument and its difference from the mainstream may be linguistic or semantic in nature. For example, the name "Radovan Karadzic", on English-language news sites, is mostly surrounded by a "semantic escort" of words like "criminal", "tribunal" and "Bin Laden", whereas on Serbian-language blogs words like "narodni" and "heroj" ("national" and "hero") may be more frequent.[11] The critical knowledge at hand is *not* that Karadzic is not a criminal, but that users get confronted with both agreement and disagreement with the general thesis – whether or not they consider Karadzic a criminal. With the broad adoption of the web, opposing points of view can be directly consulted rather than just being heard of. The challenge of a search engine algorithm emulating something of a peer review need not avoid the inherent partiality bound to political questions. If sources of alternative views are systematically irrelevant because of their lack of authority-sociability (formalized through semantics), the "giant decision" through Google-like ranking becomes dependent on actors able to — both semantically and socially — reframe an issue on a large scale.

The propagation model rewarding central actors with more influential "votes" produces as a consequence that, when an actor's ranking increases, his increase in authority propagates to his neighboring actors; all linked actors get gradually promoted along. This situation, where self-interest promotes "peer-interest", has an impact on social formations such as online communities but also on political practice.

Studies on how social actors influence each other's political views revealed similar effects even prior to the use of social networking platforms for large-scale political campaigns, such as the one for the election of Barack Obama. They show that voting patterns are highly influenced by the choices made by one's acquaintances, resulting in cascading effects along the social hierarchy.[12] The political scientist Cass R. Sunstein warns that these "cybercascades" might lead to the fragmentation of public discourses, with a further polarization into completely disconnected political spheres. Sunstein speaks of "communication worlds" where people "hear echoes from their own voices and wall themselves off from others";[13] each sphere is reaffirming its own bias towards like-minded convictions.

The "mere exposure" effect means that [group] polarization is likely to be a common phenomenon in a balkanized speech market. (...) To the extent that these exposures are not complemented by exposure to competing views, group polarization will be the inevitable consequence.[14]

Through bypassing group polarization, current ranking models deflect these "cybercascades" away from each other, avoiding their confrontation. Organizational models based on sociability — rather than authority — rely on aspects that have not yet been adopted by the search engines market. In the next paragraphs we will see how these networks have fully integrated the consequences of fragmentation, making these aspects the key incentives for building their networks.

Campaign strategy

When Barack Obama ran for the U.S. presidency in 2008, his campaign displayed an unprecedented ability to reach, influence and mobilize actors who were peripheral to the Democratic points of view, or to the elections at large. The cunning of Obama's team, directed by David Plouffe, was to address the division not from within his camp but from its border with Republican and undecided voters. This campaign turned voters into social actors by relying foremost on their own abilities at communicating, linking and forging other actors. "Neighbor to neighbor canvassing actions" were organized in every quarter, town, city and throughout all states. To succeed, an actor had to get others' consent at voting for the same candidate. By including new voters as part of the network, they diffused the social border between the two camps. Field organizer Patrick Frank, addressing campaigners, tells them to "[b]uild yourself a team and be organizers too. There's no end to it."[15] The diffused process is taken under control, but unlike other campaigns, the structural advantage of small, autonomous clusters is played out. Gene Koo drafts the following model:

> The superstructure of the campaign is traditional, top-down command-and-control (with information flowing upwards, of course). At the roots the campaign – as is typical for most volunteer efforts – comprises ad hoc mesh networks. It's in inserting strong, tightly-knit teams that the campaign has made the greatest innovation.[16]

The model is optimized since redundant information is intentionally kept within the tightly-knit teams; the only critical information that is coming from the top-down hierarchy is for avoiding overlap. The teams can fully act on their structural autonomy and social opportunities. This means that the political practice of inclusion and exclusion to and from the decisive demos[17] is no longer in the hands of a representative system of authority. A new level is inserted, formed by clusters of actors pushing local snowball effects. Koo writes that "each team, as a whole, functions like a paid staffer, with similar responsibilities and accountability".[18] Their advantage is that "the teams also have a deeper and wider network"[19,] since each actor can rely on his own network of contacts. The teams are close enough to others so as to easily deal with new information, which allows them to broker bridges between conflicting ideas. Their autonomy abounds with structural holes, and their crucial role in the campaign is to connect otherwise disparate spheres of actors.[20]

Centrality-based ranking would have a hard time detecting these clusters as the key components of the campaign, simply because they are at the periphery of their social sphere. Community organizers and field managers have much more authority than the teams and ad-hoc volunteers; they exert their power and take decisions which have far-reaching influence. Their role is to manage the network internally, from its central positions. They have to avoid information overlaps which would otherwise make them "structurally equivalent" for the campaign.[21] Regardless of their communication, they rely on the small teams and volunteers for accessing new (outside) information.

Cancelling out central power

Along with the notion of "authority" that influenced Brin and Page's model for Google search, Jon Kleinberg has also introduced the concept of "principal and non-principal communities". Kleinberg's model situates each actor in a community and measures an actor's relevance ranking according to that community's size. Large (principal) communities tend to suppress actors engaged in smaller ones. Brin and Page did not include the mechanisms Kleinberg proposed to avoid this effect[22] into Google; actors engaged in small, peripheral communities typically have low PageRanks. The difference between these two models can be traced when comparing the campaign structure, facilitated through the social networking site my.barackobama.com, with the one used in the social-governmental web site: change.gov. Change.gov was developed for Obama's transition to the U.S. presidency. It repeated on a governmental level the social voting logic by putting to use the "user generated content" of the people itself as a source of policy change. The principle of Change.gov is a PageRank devoid of influential differences; since it is a direct voting system, there is no social network through which authority can propagate. As advanced by Kleinberg and Burt, the cost of the excess of centrally-oriented actors is the circulation – and dominance – of redundant information. Regardless of the influence that each tightly-knit social cluster would be able to cover, as long as they remain non-principal and non-overlapping, all new (formerly weak) ties would be non-redundant. The actors who are the least constrained socially and the most autonomous in their ideas are the ones dealing with outside, conflictual information. Peripheral actors occupy the border between the two political spheres.

Spanning bridges

Valdis Krebs, chief scientist and founder of orgnet.com, has extensively studied political instances when bridging affects political choices. In an article published in the book *Extreme Democracy* he assesses how weak ties function across spheres holding different political views.

> Not only do individuals have [motivational] thresholds, but communities and networks also have thresholds. These are barriers to minor opinions taking hold. Opinions and information that run counter to the dominant view within the network are usually dismissed.[23]

By looking at how actors' motivations affect their ability to influence their acquaintances, this study reveals how the threshold for accepting new opinions is a property of the community rather than one of each actor independently. Ronald Burt questions the role that motivation would have on the behavior of actors in networks and their engagement in communities. Whether actors engage in relations because they are motivated or because the opportunity presents itself is, for Burt, a non-issue. He considers "motivation and opportunity as one and the same", since an actor is author of his network just as the nature of the actor's environment is.

> [A] network rich in entrepreneurial opportunity surrounds a player motivated to be entrepreneurial. At the other extreme, a player innocent of entrepreneurial motives lives in a network devoid of entrepreneurial opportunity.[24]

This means that a network can be emergent or adjusted in order to exploit the advantages of structural holes. Krebs proposes to evaluate the returns of Plouffe's ground strategy in a sharp comparison with previous elections. During the 2004 US elections the *New York Times* published an article based on a cluster analysis of online book purchases, which corroborates Sunstein's polarization argument.

> [Krebs] calls this pattern the "echo chamber" effect: for the most part, he found, buyers of liberal books buy only other liberal books, while buyers of conservative books buy only other conservative books.[25]

Krebs ran the same analysis towards the end of the 2008 elections. This time the graph showed a new tendency for books read by both liberals and conservatives. Interestingly these books were mostly read at the periphery of each political sphere.

> The anti-Obama books – *The Obama Nation* and *The Case against Barack Obama* – are mostly being read by people who are already against Obama. One of the anti-Obama books is connected to one of the [bridging] books. (…) Could some undecided voters be reading this to make up their mind on Obama?[26]

Here, weak ties stretch over those parts of the network where we find content that is unknown to the center of each group. In political terms, bridging these holes and strengthening these ties translates as conflict or friction. As Sunstein argues, such outside information — unpopular within one's sphere — is essential for bridging polarized fragments of public discourses. Obama plans to carry out his politics along the same logic. When accepting the presidency on November 4th 2008, he proclaimed that "I will listen to you, especially when we disagree."[27]

Burt understands relations not only in their positive properties — such as their informational benefits — but also in the constraints limiting the level of structural autonomy. He asserts that the most dramatic change in structural autonomy happens with the first signs of constraints.

> [S]tructural holes have their greatest effect as unconstrained actions begins to be constrained. Once action is constrained beyond a low level … further increases in constraint are almost superfluous.[28]

The opportunity for bridging is higher for non-central, unconstrained and peripheral positions, since they are able to play conflicting demands against each other, while non-conflicting demands end up in a self-referential core. This core is enclosed by the alignment of the structural holes around actors. In more recent works, Burt compares structural holes to "network closures",[29] which at a higher scale of collectivity are the sum of holes, the structural periphery and social border of a consensual sphere of actors. Closely following Burt, Jon Kleinberg has recently developed an optimized algorithmic model testing the extent to which social differences can be resolved when all actors use their network power to bridge the holes surrounding them.

> [T]he symmetry-breaking [is] putting different nodes at different social levels in which they obtain different payoffs. (…)[S]ince the advantages of bridging decreases rapidly with the number of people doing it, there are "first-mover" advantages that translate into broken symmetry in equilibrium.[30]

Kleinberg's model pushes structural holes to extreme states of equilibrium. His findings corroborate with studies having similar aims; using different methods, these reveal that social stratification is a key example of stable networks even when actors keep acting on their structural opportunities. At the other extreme of political strategies, there are networks of terrorist cells; although these fully rely on the structural holes between their cells, the latter are only rarely acted upon. Krebs provides a much-cited argument in his study of Osama bin Laden's Al Qaeda structure, as the design of stealth networks and their ability to function even without central command at all.

> In a normal social network, strong ties reveal the cluster of network players – it is easy to see who is in the group and who is not. In a covert network, because of their low frequency of activation, strong ties may appear to be weak ties.[31]

Krebs shows how weak ties — which typically connect actors that are socially distant from each other — when used for coordinated action, are able to bridge "deep structural holes". The depth of a structural hole increases with the weakness of the tie between actors of different cells.[32] Once overcome, deep holes function as "ports of information" with the benefit of exclusive access.[33] Krebs further explains the strategy behind fostering strong yet dormant relations.

The hijacker's network had a hidden strength — massive redundancy through trusted prior contacts. The ties forged in school, through kinship, and training/fighting in Afghanistan made this network very resilient.[34]

Both Obama and Osama's use of network power can be explained through the lens of structural holes; both have highly resilient networks since their key components are highly autonomous. But their difference lies in their use of standards – the central conventions common to all of a network's actors. With his definition of network power, David Grewal distinguishes mediating standards from membership standards:

> [A] mediating standard is a standard that governs access to others by its very nature; some particular social activity is inherently regulated by it … they form a part of that very activity itself. [A membership] standard is not necessarily basic or inherent to a given activity … but rather establishes an ideal or target.[35]

Grewal asserts that mediating standards are self-enforced, which explains why the activity of networking – and bridging structural holes – empowers those engaged in it, while the network gets richer and more diverse in information. With membership standards, revealing the network's structure presents a risk for its own activity and survival.

Search design

A tentative conclusion to our structural comparison comprises two negations. Obama's network seems to be driven by a renewed ideology with a consistent brand identity. Following Grewal's prescriptions, this network is governed by a mediating standard; one becomes part of the network through networking. The system itself is self-referential, but all efforts go into the setting of the ad-hoc peripheral meshes to absorb potential conflict at the border of the political sphere. Osama's network, by contrast, is composed of isolated cells separated by dormant ties. Such a structure is designed to create endless opportunities for the setting of powerful strategies by bridging any number of cells. Osama's network need not rely on active peripheral networking structures, since it is governed by a membership standard. In this article we argue that the most critical network positions lay at the periphery and in between the dominant spheres of information networks. Current models of ranking are unable to capture the power of weak ties, making their design less suited for searching for actors with peripheral yet substantial social engagement. Future search engine designs have to confront both the back-end – with the algorithm, and the front-end – with the user interface, with the weak ties and structural holes in networks. With game-changing ranking algorithms no longer based on central cores but on peripheral forces, the design of search engines is at a promising new inroad for change. Users need to be made more aware of what the currents are around the page they are looking at, clicking on, and choosing. They need to be able to grasp where the borders between these social currents persist, and where they consent or diverge. Ultimately, network power induced by ranking models that value the spanning of social bridges, will hold an incentive for resolving polarized views instead of reinforcing them.

Notes

1 Yuting Liu, Bin Gao, Tie-Yan Liu, et al., "Microsoft Research Asia, BrowseRank: Letting Web Users Vote for Page Importance" (*Proc. 31st Annual International ACM SIGIR Conference*, 2008), 451-8
2 David S. Grewal, Network Power: The Social Dynamics of Globalization (New Haven: Yale University Press, 2008), 140
3 Ronald S. Burt, Structural Holes: The Social Structure of Competition (Cambridge: Harvard University Press, 1992), 7
4 Larry Page, Sergey Brin, Rajeev Motwani, and Terry Winograd, "The PageRank citation ranking: Bringing order to the web", technical report (Stanford: Stanford University, 1998), 11
5 Ibid.
6 Ibid, 15
7 Ibid, 3
8 Ibid, 15
9 Mark Granovetter, "The Strength of Weak Ties", in *American Journal of Sociology* Vol. 78 Issue 6 (Chicago: University of Chicago Press, 1973), 1360-80
10 Burt, 1992, 47
11 Metahaven, "Multipolar Search: EXODVS" (Pancevo Republic! 13th Biennial of Art, Pancevo, Serbia, 2008) Under development together with Tsila Hassine, this model follows prior research conducted at the Lab for Media Search at the National University of Singapore
12 James H. Fowler, "Turnout in a Small World", in A. Zuckerman (ed.) *Social Logic of Politics* (Philadelphia: Temple University Press, 2005), 21
13 Cass R. Sunstein, *Republic.com* (Princeton: Princeton University Press, 2002), 44
14 Ibid, 66
15 Zack Exley, "The New Organizers: What's really behind Obama's ground game" (*Huffington Post*, 2008), http://www.huffingtonpost.com/zack-exley/the-new-organizers-part-1_b_132782.html
16 Gene Koo, 2008, "A network analysis of the Obama 08 campaign", http://blogs.law.harvard.edu/anderkoo/2008/10/14/a-network-analysis-of-the-obama-08-campaign/

17 Jacques Rancière, *Disagreement: Politics and Philosophy*, translated by Julie Rose (Minneapolis: University of Minnesota Press, 1998), 10.
18 Koo, 2008.
19 Ibid.
20 Burt, 1992, 30. By bridging between conflicting demands, these teams set the conditions for what Burt refers to as the "tertius gaudens". The "tertius" is the third who benefits from the disunion of others. On page 48 he states the following. "In the swirling mix of preferences characteristic to social networks, where no demands have absolute authority, the tertius negotiates for favorable terms. (…) Structural holes are the setting of tertius strategies. Information is the substance. Accurate, ambiguous, or distorted information is moved between contacts by the tertius."
21 Burt, 1992, 19
22 Jon M. Kleinberg, "Authoritative Sources in a Hyperlinked Environment", *IBM Research Report* RJ 10076 (Proc. ACM-SIAM Symposium on Discrete Algorithms, 1997), 15.
23 Jon Lebkowsky and Mitch Ratcliffe, *Extreme Democracy* (Lulu.com, 2005), 119
24 Burt, 1992, 36
25 Emily Eakin, "Study Finds a Nation of Polarized Readers" (*The New York Times*, March 13 2004), http://query.nytimes.com/gst/fullpage.html?res=9F01EFD6103EF930A25750C0A9629C8B63
26 Valdis E. Krebs, "New Political Patterns" (orgnet.com, 2008), http://www.orgnet.com/divided.html
27 Barack Obama's speech as president-elect of the United States, Chicago, 4 November 2008
28 Burt, 1992, 94
29 Ronald S. Burt, *Brokerage and Closure: An Introduction to Social Capital* (Oxford: Oxford University Press, 2005)
30 Jon M. Kleinberg, Siddharth Suri, Éva Tardos and Tom Wexler, "Strategic Network Formation with Structural Holes" (*Proc. 9th ACM Conference on Electronic Commerce*, 2008), 3.
31 Valdis E. Krebs, *Mapping Networks of Terrorist Cells* (Connections 24-3, 2002), 49
32 Burt, 1992, 42
33 Ibid, 43
34 Krebs, 2002, 49-50
35 Grewal, 2008, 22-3

How to Follow Global Digital Cultures

Cultural Analytics for Beginners

Lev Manovich

From "New Media" to "More Media"

Only fifteen years ago we typically interacted with relatively small bodies of information that were tightly organized in directories, lists and a priori assigned categories. Today we interact with a gigantic, global, not well organized, constantly expanding and changing information cloud in a very different way: we Google it.

The rise of search as the new dominant way for encountering information is one manifestation of the fundamental change in our information environment.[1] We are living through an exponential explosion in the amounts of data we are generating, capturing, analyzing, visualizing, and storing – including cultural content. On August 25, 2008, Google's software engineers announced that the index of web pages, which Google is computing several times daily, has reached 1 trillion unique URLs.[2] During the same month, YouTube.com reported that users were uploading 13 hours of new video to the site every minute.[3] And in November 2008, the number of images housed on Flickr reached 3 billion.[4]

The "information bomb", already described by Paul Virilio in 1998, has not only exploded.[5] It has also led to a chain of new explosions that have together produced cumulative effects larger than anybody could have anticipated. In 2008 the *International Data Corporation* (IDC) predicted that by 2011, the digital universe would be ten times the size it was in 2006. This corresponds to a compound annual growth rate of 60%.[6] (Of course, it is possible that the global economic crisis that began in 2008 may slow this growth – but probably not too much.)

User-generated content is one of the fastest growing parts of this expanding information universe. According to the IDC 2008 study, "approximately 70% of the digital universe is created by individuals."[7] In other words, the amount of media created by users easily competes with the amounts of data collected and created by computer systems (surveillance systems, sensor-based applications, datacenters supporting "cloud computing", etc.) So if Friedrich Kittler -- writing well before the phenomena known as "social media" – noted that in a computer universe "literature" (i.e. texts of any kind) consists mostly of computer-generated files, the humans are now catching up.

The exponential growth of the number of non-professional media producers in 2000s has led to a fundamentally new cultural situation and a challenge to our normal ways of tracking and studying culture. Hundreds of millions of people are routinely creating and sharing cultural content – blogs, photos, videos, map layers, software code, etc. The same hundreds of millions of people engage in online discussions, leave comments and participate in other forms on online social communication. As mobile phones with rich media capabilities are becoming ever more available, this number is only going to increase. In early 2008, there were 2.2 billion mobile phones in the world; it was projected that this number will rise to 4 billion by 2010, with the main growth coming from China, India, and Africa.

Think about this: today the number of images uploaded to Flickr every week is probably larger than all the objects contained in all the art museums in the world.

The exponential increase in the number of non-professional producers of cultural content has been paralleled by another development that has not been widely discussed. And yet this development is equally important in understanding what culture is today. The rapid growth of professional educational and cultural institutions in many newly globalized countries since the end of the 1990s -- along with the instant availability of cultural news over the web and ubiquity of media and design software – has also dramatically increased the number of culture professionals who participate in global cultural production and discussions. Hundreds of thousands of students, artists, designers, musicians have now access to the same ideas, information and tools. As a result, often it is no longer possible to talk about centers and provinces. (In fact, based on my own experiences, I believe the students, culture professionals, and governments in newly globalized countries are often more ready to embrace the latest ideas than their peers in "old centers" of world culture.)

If you want to see the effects of these dimensions of cultural and digital globalization in action, visit the popular web sites where the professionals and students working in different areas of media and design upload their portfolios and samples of their work – and note the range of countries that the authors come from. Here are examples of these sites: xplsv.tv (motion graphics, animation), coroflot.com (design portfolios from around the world), archinect.com (architecture students projects), infosthetics.com (information visualization projects). For example, when I checked on December 24, 2008, the first three projects in the "artists" list on xplsv.tv came from Cuba, Hungary, and Norway.[8]

Similarly, on the same day, the set of entries on the first page of coroflot.com (the site where designers from around the world upload their portfolios; it contained 120,000+ portfolios by the beginning of 2009) revealed a similar global cultural geography. Next to the predictable 20th century Western cultural capitals -- New York and Milan – I also found portfolios from Shanghai, Waterloo (Belgium), Bratislava (Slovakia), and Seoul (South Korea).[9]

The companies which manage these sites for professional content usually do not publish detailed statistics about their visitors – but here is another example based on the quantitative data that I do have access to. In the spring of 2008 we created a web site for our research lab at the University of California, San Diego: softwarestudies.com. The web site content follows the genre of "research lab site", so we did not expect many visitors; we also have not done any mass email promotions or other marketing. However, when I examined the *Google Analytics* stats for softwarestudies.com at the end of 2008, I discovered that we had visitors from 100 countries. Every month people from 1000+ cities worldwide check out the site. The statistics for these cities are even more interesting. During a typical month, no American cities made it into "top ten list" (I am not counting La Jolla, which is the location of UCSD where our lab is based). For example, in November 2008, New York occupied 13th place, San Francisco was at 27th place, and Los Angeles was at 42nd place. The "top ten" cities were from Western Europe (Amsterdam, Berlin, Porto), Eastern Europe (Budapest), and South America (Sao Paulo). What is equally interesting is that the list of visitors per city followed a classical "long tail" curve. There was no sharp break anymore between "old world" and "new world," or between "centers" and "provinces."[10]

All these explosions which have taken place since the late 1990s – non-professionals creating and sharing online cultural content, culture professionals in newly globalized countries, students in Eastern Europe, Asia and South America who can follow and participate in global cultural processes via the web and free communication tools (email, Skype, etc) – have redefined what culture is.

Before, cultural theorists and historians could generate theories and histories based on small data sets (for instance, "classical Hollywood cinema", "Italian Renaissance", etc.). But how can we track "global digital cultures" with their billions of cultural objects and hundreds of millions of contributors? Before, you could write about culture by following what was going on in a small number of world capitals and schools. But how can we follow the developments in tens of thousands of cities and educational institutions?

Introducing Cultural Analytics

The ubiquity of computers, digital media software, consumer electronics, and computer networks led to the exponential rise in the number of cultural producers worldwide and the media they create – making it very difficult, if not impossible, to understand global cultural developments and dynamics in any substantial detail using 20th century theoretical tools and methods. But what if we can use the same developments – computers, software, and availability of massive amounts of "born digital" cultural content – to track global cultural processes in ways impossible with traditional tools?

To investigate these questions – as well as to understand how the ubiquity of software tools for culture creation and sharing changes in what "culture" is theoretically and practically – in 2007 we established the *Software Studies Initiative* (softwarestudies.com). Our lab is located at the campus of the University of California, San Diego (UCSD) and is housed inside one of the largest IT research centers in the U.S. -- the *California Institute for Telecommunications and Information* (www.calit2.net). Together with the researchers and students working in our lab, we have been developing a new paradigm for the study, teaching and public presentation of cultural artifacts, dynamics, and flows. We call this paradigm *Cultural Analytics*.

Today sciences, business, governments and other agencies rely on computer-based quantitative analysis and interactive visualization of large data sets and data flows. They employ statistical data analysis, data mining, information visualization, scientific visualization, visual analytics, simulation and other computer-based techniques. Our goal is start systematically applying these techniques to the analysis of contemporary cultural data. The large data sets are already here – the result of the digitization efforts by museums, libraries, and companies over the last ten years (think of book scanning by Google) and the explosive growth of newly available cultural content on the web.

We believe that a systematic use of large-scale computational analysis and interactive visualization of cultural patterns will become a major trend in cultural criticism and culture industries in the coming decades. What will happen when humanists start using interactive visualizations as a standard tool in their work, the way many scientists do already? If slides made possible art history, and if a movie projector and video recorder enabled film studies, what new cultural disciplines may emerge out of the use of interactive visualization and data analysis of large cultural data sets?

From Culture (few) to Cultural Data (many)

In April 2008, exactly one year after we founded the *Software Studies Initiative*, NEH (*National Endowment for Humanities*, the main federal agency in the U.S. which provides grants for humanities research) announced a new "*Humanities High-Performance Computing*" (HHPC) initiative that is based on a similar insight:

> Just as the sciences have, over time, begun to tap the enormous potential of High-Performance Computing, the humanities are beginning to as well. Humanities scholars often deal with large sets of unstructured data. This might take the form of historical newspapers, books, election data, archaeological fragments, audio or video contents, or a host of others. HHPC offers the humanist opportunities to sort through, mine, and better understand and visualize this data.[11]

In describing the rationale for *Humanities High-Performance Computing* program, the officers at NEH start with the *availability of high-performance computers* that are already common in the sciences and industry. While we share their vision, our starting point for Cultural Analytics is complementary – it is the *widespread availability of cultural content* (both contemporary and historical) *in digital form*. Of course, massive amounts of cultural content and high-speed computers go well together – without the latter, it would be very time consuming to analyze petabytes of data. However, as we discovered in our lab, even with small cultural data sets consisting of hundreds, dozens or even only a few objects, it is already viable to carry out Cultural Analytics: that is, to quantitatively analyze the structure of these objects and visualize the results revealing the patterns which lie below the unaided capacities of human perception and cognition.

Since Cultural Analytics aims to take advantage of the exponential increase in the amount of digital content since the middle of the 1990s, it will be useful to establish a taxonomy for the different types of this content. A taxonomy of this kind may guide the design of research studies as well as being used to group these studies once they start to multiply.

To begin with, we have vast amounts of *media content* in digital form – games, visual design, music, video, photos, visual art, blogs, web pages. This content can be further broken down into a few categories. Currently, the proportion of "born digital" media is increasing; however, people also continue to create analog media (for instance, when they shoot on film), which is later digitized.

We can further differentiate between different types of "born digital" media. Some of this media is explicitly made for the web: for example, blogs, web sites, layers created by users for *Google Earth* and *Google Maps*. But we also now find massive amounts of "born digital" content (photography, video, music) online, which until the advent of "social media" was not intended to be seen by people worldwide – but which now ends up online on social media sites (Flickr, YouTube, etc.) To differentiate between these two types, we may refer to the first category as "web native", or "web intended". The second category can be then called "digital media proper".

As I already noted, YouTube, Flickr, and other social media sites aimed at average people are paralled by more specialized sites which serve professional and semi-professional users: xplsv.tv, coroflot.com, archinect.com, modelmayhem.com, deviantart.com, etc.[12] Hosting projects and portfolios by hundreds of thousands of artists, media designers, and other cultural professionals, these web sites provide a live snapshot of contemporary global cultural production and sensibility – thus offering a promise of being able to analyze the global cultural trends with a level of detail that was previously unthinkable. For instance, as of August 2008, deviantart.com has eight million members, 62+ million submissions, and was receiving 80,000 submissions per day.[13] Importantly, in addition to the standard "professional" and "pro-ams" categories, these sites also host content from people who are just starting out and/or are currently "pro-ams", but who aspire to be full-time professionals. I think that the portfolios (or "ports" as they are sometimes called today) of these "aspirational non-professionals" are particularly significant, if we want to study contemporary cultural stereotypes and conventions since, in aiming to create "professional" projects and portfolios, people often inadvertently expose the codes and the templates used in the industry in a very clear way.

Another important source of contemporary cultural content – and at the same time a window into yet another cultural world different from non-professional users and aspiring professionals – are the *web sites and wikis created by faculty* teaching in creative disciplines to post and discuss their class assignments. (Although I don't have direct statistics on how many sites and wikis for classes are out there, here is one indication: a popular wiki creation software pbwiki.com has been used by 250,000 educators.[14]) These sites often contain *student projects* – which provides yet another interesting source of content.

Finally, beyond class web sites, the sites for professionals, aspiring professionals and non-professionals, and other centralized content repositories, we have *millions of web sites and blogs by individual cultural creators and creative industry companies*. Regardless of the industry category and the type of content people and companies produce, it is now taken for granted that you need to have a web presence with your demo reel and/or portfolio, descriptions of particular projects, a CV, and so on. All this information can be potentially used to do something that was previously unimaginable: to create dynamic (i.e. changing in time) maps of global cultural developments that reflect activities, aspirations, and cultural preferences of millions of creators.

A significant part of the available media content in digital form was originally created in electronic or physical media and has been digitized since the mid-1990s. We can call such content "born analog". But it is crucial to remember that what has been digitized in many cases are only the canonical works, i.e. a tiny part of culture deemed to be significant by our cultural institutions. What remains outside of the digital universe is the rest: provincial nineteenth century newspapers sitting in some small library somewhere; millions of paintings in tens of thousands of small museums in small cities around the world; thousands of specialized magazines in all kinds of fields and areas which no longer even exist; millions of home moves…

This creates a problem for Cultural Analytics, which has a potential to map everything that remains outside the canon – to begin generating "art history without great names". We want to understand not only the exceptional, but also the typical; not only the few cultural sentences spoken by a few "great men", but the patterns in all cultural sentences spoken by everybody else; in short, what is outside a few great museums rather than what is inside and what has already been extensively discussed too many times. To do this, we will need as much of previous culture in digital form as possible. However, what is digitally available is surprisingly little.

Here is an example from our research. We were interested in the following question: What did people actually paint around the world in 1930 – outside of a few "isms" and a few dozen artists who entered the Western art historical canon? We did a search on artstor.org, which at the time of this writing contains close to one million images of art, architecture and design from many important US museums and collections, as well as the 200,000+ slide library of the University of California, San Diego where our lab is located. (This set, which at present is the largest single collection in artstor, is interesting in that it reflects the biases of art history as it was taught over a few decades when color slides were the main media for teaching and studying art.) To collect the images of artworks that are outside the usual Western art historical canon, we excluded from the search Western Europe and North America. This left the rest of the world: Eastern Europe, South-East Asia, East Asia, West Asia, Oceania, Central America, South America, etc. When we searched for paintings done in these parts of the world in 1930, we only found a few dozen images. This highly uneven distribution of cultural samples is not due to artstor, since it does not digitize images itself – it only makes available images that are submitted by museums and other cultural institutions. So what the results of our search reflect is what museums collect and what they think should be digitized first. In other words, a number of major US collections and a slide library of a major research university (which now has a large proportion of Asian students) together contain only a few dozen paintings done outside the West in 1930, which have been digitized. In contrast, searching for Picasso returned around 700 images. If this example is any indication, digital repositories may be amplifying the already existing biases and filters of modern cultural canons. Instead of transforming the "top forty" into "the long tail," digitization can be producing the opposite effect.

Media content in digital form is not the only type of data that we can analyze quantitatively to potentially reveal new cultural patterns. Computers also allow us to capture and subsequently analyze many dimensions of human cultural activities that could not be recorded before. Any cultural activity – surfing the web, playing a game, etc. -- which passes through a computer or a computer-based media device leaves traces: keystroke presses, cursor movements and other screen activity, controller positions (think of Wii controller), and so on. Combined with camera, a microphone, and other capture technologies, computers can also capture other dimensions of human behavior such as body and eye movements and speech. And web servers log yet other types of information: which pages the users visited, how much time they spend on each page, which files they downloaded, and so on. In this respect, *Google Analytics*, which processes and organizes this information, provided a direct inspiration for the idea of Cultural Analytics.

Of course, in addition to all this information which can be captured automatically, the rise of social media since 2005 has created a new social environment where people voluntarily reveal their cultural choices and preferences: rating books, movies, blog posts, software, voting for their favorites, etc. Even more importantly, people discuss and debate their cultural preferences, ideas and perceptions online. They comment on Flickr photographs, post their opinions about books on amazon.com, critique movies on rottentomatoes.com, review products on epinions.com, and enthusiastically debate, argue, agree and disagree with each other on numerous social media sites, fan sites, forums, groups, and mailing lists. All these conversations, discussions and reflections, which before were either invisible or simply could not take place on the same scale, are now taking place in public.

To summarize this discussion: because of digitization efforts since the mid-1990s, and because the significant (and constantly growing) percentage of all cultural and social activities that passes through or takes place on the web or networked media devices (mobile phones, game platforms, etc.), we now have access to unprecedented amounts of both "cultural data" (cultural artifacts themselves) and "data about culture". All this data can be grouped into three broad conceptual categories:
- Cultural artifacts ("born digital" or digitized).
- Data about people's interactions with digital media (automatically captured by computers or computer-based media devices)
- Online discourse around (or accompanying) cultural activities, cultural objects, and creation process voluntarily created by people.

There are other ways to consider this recently emerged cultural data universe. For example, we can also make a distinction between "cultural data" and "cultural information":
- Cultural data: photos, art, music, design, architecture, films, motion graphics, games, web sites – i.e., actual cultural artifacts that are either born digital or are represented through digital media (for examples, photos of architecture).
- Cultural information: cultural news and reviews published on the web (web sites, blogs) – i.e., a kind of "extended metadata" about these artifacts.

Another important distinction, which is useful to establish, has to do with the relationships between the original cultural artifact/activity and its digital representation:
- "Born digital" artifacts: representation = original.
- Digitized artifacts that originated in other media – therefore, their representation in digital form may not contain all the original information. For example, digital images of paintings available in online repositories and museum databases normally do not fully show their 3D texture. (This information can be captured with 3D scanning technologies – but this is not commonly done at this moment.).
- Cultural experiences (experiencing theater, dance, performance, architecture and space design; interacting with products; playing video games; interacting with locative media applications on a GPS enabled mobile device), where the properties of material/media objects that we can record and analyze is only one part of an experience. For example, in the case of spatial experiences, architectural plans will only tell us a part of a story; we may also want to use

video and motion capture of people interacting with the spaces, and other information.

The rapid explosion of "born digital" data has not passed unnoticed. In fact, the web companies themselves have played an important role in making it happen so they can benefit from it economically. Not surprisingly, out of the different categories of cultural data, born digital data is already being exploited most aggressively (because it is the easiest to access and collect), followed by digitized content. Google and other search engines analyze billions of web pages and the links between them to make their search algorithms run. *Nielsen Blogpulse* mines 100+ million blogs to detect trends in what people are saying about particular brands, products and other topics its clients are interested in.[15] *Amazon.com* analyzes the contents of the books it sells to calculate "Statistically Improbable Phrases" used to identify unique parts of the books.[16]

In terms of media types, today text receives most attention – because language is discrete and because the theoretical paradigms to describe it (linguistics, computational linguistics, discourse analysis, etc.) have already been fully developed before the explosion of the "web native" text universe. Another type of cultural media, which is also starting to be systematically subjected to computer analysis in large quantities, is music. (This is also made possible by the fact that Western music has used formal notation systems for a very long time.) A number of online music search engines and Internet radio stations use computational analysis to find particular songs. (Examples: Musipedia, Shazam, and other applications which use acoustic fingerprinting.[17]) In comparison, other types of media and content receive much less attention.

If we are interested in analyzing cultural patterns in other media besides text and sound, and also in asking larger theoretical questions about cultures (as opposed to more narrow pragmatic questions asked in professional fields such as web mining or quantitative marketing research – for instance, identifying how consumers perceive different brands in a particular market segment[18]), we need to adopt a broader perspective. Firstly, we need to develop techniques to analyze and visualize the patterns in different forms of cultural media – movies, cartoons, motion graphics, photography, video games, web sites, product and graphic design, architecture, etc. Second, while we can certainly take advantage of the "web native" cultural content, we should also work with other categories such as those listed above ("digitized artifacts which originated in other media"; "cultural experiences"). Thirdly, we should be self-reflective. We need to think about the consequences of thinking of culture as data and of computers as the analytical tools: what is left outside, what types of analysis and questions are privileged, and so on. This self-reflection should be part of any Cultural Analytics study. These three points guide our Cultural Analytics research.

Cultural Image Processing

Cultural Analytics is thinkable and possible because of three developments: digitization of cultural assets and the rise of web and social media; work in computer science; and the rise of a number of fields which use computers to create new ways of representing and interacting with data. The two related fields of computer science – image processing and computer vision –- provide us with the variety of techniques to automatically analyze visual media. The fields of scientific visualization, information visualization, media design, and digital art provide us with the techniques to visually represent patterns in data and interactively explore this data.

While people in digital humanities have been using statistical techniques to explore patterns in literary text for a long time, I believe that we are the first lab to start systematically using image processing and computer vision for the automatic analysis of visual media in the humanities. This is what separates us from 20th century humanities disciplines that focus on visual media (art history, film studies, cultural studies) and also 20th century paradigms for quantitative media research developed within social sciences, such as quantitative communication studies and certain works in the sociology of culture. Similarly, while artists, designers and computer scientists have already created a number of projects to visualize cultural media, the existing projects that I am aware of rely on existing metadata such as Flickr community-contributed tags[19]. In other words, they use information about visual media – creation date, author name, tags, favorites, etc. – and do not analyze the media itself.

In contrast, Cultural Analytics uses image processing and computer vision techniques to automatically analyze large sets of visual cultural objects to generate numerical descriptions of their structure and content. These numerical descriptions can then be graphed and also analyzed statistically.

While digital media authoring programs such as *Photoshop* and *After Effects* incorporate certain image processing techniques, such as blur, sharpen, and edge detecting filters, motion tracking, and so on, there are hundreds of other features that can be automatically extracted from still and moving images. Most importantly, while *Photoshop* and other media applications internally measure properties of images and video in order to change them – blurring, sharpening, changing contrast and colors, etc. – at this time they do not make available to users the results of these measurements. So while we can use *Photoshop* to highlight some dimensions of image structure (for instance, reducing an image to its edge), we can't perform more systematic analysis.

To do this, we need to turn to more specialized image processing software, such as open source *imageJ*, which has been developed for life sciences applications and which we have been using and extending in our lab. MATLAB, popular software for numerical analysis, provides many image processing applications. There are also specialized software libraries of image processing functions, such as *openCV*. A number of high-level programming languages created by artists and designers in the 2000s, such as *Processing* and *openFrameworks*, also provide some image processing functions.

While certain common techniques can be used without the knowledge of computer programming and statistics, many others require knowledge of C or Java programming. Which of the algorithms can be particularly useful for cultural analysis and visualization? Can we create (relatively) easy-to-use tools which will allow non-technical users to perform automatic analysis of visual media?

These are the questions we are currently investigating. As we are gradually discover, despite the fact that the fields of image processing and computer vision have existed now for approximately five decades, the analysis of cultural media often requires the development of new techniques that do not yet exist.

To summarize: the key idea of Cultural Analytics is the use of computers to *automatically analyze cultural artifacts in visual media extracting large numbers of features which characterize their structure and content*. For example, in the case of a visual image, we can analyze its grayscale and color characteristics, orientations of lines, texture, composition, and so on. Therefore, we can also use another term to refer to our research method – *Quantitative Cultural Analysis* (QCA).

While we are interested in both content and structure of cultural artifacts, at present automatic analysis of structure is much further developed than the analysis of content. For example, we can ask computers to automatically measure gray tone values of each frame in a feature film, to detect shot boundaries, to analyze motion in every shot, to calculate how the color palette changes throughout the film, and so on. However, if we want to annotate the film's content – writing down what kind of space we see in each shot, what kinds of interactions between characters are taking place, the topics of their conversations, etc., the automatic techniques to do this are more complex and less reliable. For many types of content analysis, at present the best way to is annotate media manually – which is obviously quite time consuming for large data sets. In the time it will take one person to produce such annotations for the content of one movie, we can use computers to automatically analyze the structure of many thousands of movies. Therefore, we started developing Cultural Analytics by developing techniques for the analysis and visualization of structures of individual cultural artifacts and large sets of such artifacts – with the idea that once we develop these techniques we will gradually move into the automatic analysis of content.

Deep Cultural Search

In November 2008 we received a grant that gives us 300,000 hours of computing time on US Department of Energy supercomputers. This is enough to analyze millions of still images and video – art, design, street fashion, feature films, anime series, etc. This scale of data is matched by the size of visual displays that we are using in our work. As I already mentioned, we are located inside one of the leading IT research centers in the U.S. – the California Institute for Telecommunication and Information Technology (Calit2). This allows us to take advantage of the next-generation visual technologies – such as *HIperSpace*, currently one of the highest resolution displays for scientific visualization and visual analytics applications in the world. (Resolution: 35,640 by 8,000 pixels. Size: 9.7m x 2.3m.)

One of the directions we are planning to pursue in the future is the development of visual systems that would allow us to follow global cultural dynamics in real time. Imagine a real-time traffic display (à la car navigation systems) – except that the display is wall-size, the resolution is thousands of times greater, and the traffic shown is not cars on highways, but *real-time cultural flows* around the world. Imagine the same wall-sized display divided into multiple windows, each showing different real-time and historical data about cultural, social, and economic news and trends – thus providing *a situational awareness for cultural analysts*. Imagine the same wall-sized display playing an animation of what looks like an earthquake *simulation* produced on a super-computer – except in this case the "earthquake" is the release of a new version of popular software, the announcement of an important architectural project, or any other important cultural event. What we are seeing are the effects of such "cultural earthquakes" over time and space. Imagine a wall-sized computer graphic showing *the long tail* of cultural production that allows you to zoom in to see each individual product together with rich data about it (à la real estate map on zillow.com) – while the graph is constantly updated in real time by pulling data from the web. Imagine a visualization that shows how other people around the word remix new videos created in a fan community, or how a new design software gradually affects the kinds of forms being imagined today (the way Alias and Maya led to a new language in architecture). These are the kinds of tools we want to create to enable a new type of cultural criticism and analysis appropriate for the era of cultural globalization and user-generated media: three hundred digital art departments in China alone; approximately 10,000 new users uploading their professional design portfolios on coroflort.com every month; billions of blogs, user-generated photographs and videos; and other cultural expressions which are similarly now created at a scale unthinkable only ten years ago.

To conclude, I would like to come back to my opening point – the rise of search as a new dominant mode for interacting with information. As I mentioned, this development is just one of many consequence of the dramatic and rapid increase in the scale of information and content being produced, which we have experienced since the middle of the 1990s. To serve the users search results, Google, Yahoo, and other search engines analyze many different types of data – including both metadata of particular web pages (so-called "meta elements") and their content. (According to Google, its search engine algorithm uses more than 200 input types.[20]) However, just as *Photoshop* and other commercial content-creating software do not expose to users the features of images or videos they are internally measuring, Google and Yahoo do not reveal the measurements of web pages they analyze – they only serve their conclusions (which sites best fit the search string), which their propriety algorithms generate by combining these measures. In contrast, the goal of Cultural Analytics is to enable what we may call "deep cultural search" – to give users the open source tools so they themselves can analyze any type of cultural content in detail and use the results of this analysis in new ways.

Notes

1 This article draws on the white paper Cultural Analytics that I wrote in May 2007. I am periodically updating this paper. For the latest version, visit http://lab.softwarestudies.com/2008/09/cultural-analytics.html.
2 http://googleblog.blogspot.com/2008/07/we-knew-web-was-big.html.
3 http://en.wikipedia.org/wiki/YouTube.
4 http://blog.flickr.net/en/2008/11/03/3-billion/
5 Paul Virilio, *Information Bomb*. (Original French edition: 1988.) Verso, 2006.
6 IDC (International Data Corporation), *The Diverse and Exploding Information Universe*. 2008. (2008 research data is available at http://www.emc.com/digital_universe.)
7 Ibid.
8 http://xplsv.tv/artists/1/, accessed December 24, 2008.

9   coroflot.com, visited December 24, 2008. The number of design portfolios submitted by users to coroflot.com grew from 90, 657 on May 7, 2008 to 120,659 on December 24, 2008.
10 See softwarestudies.com/softbook for more complete statistics
11 http://www.neh.gov/ODH/ResourceLibrary/HumanitiesHighPerformanceComputing/tabid/62/Default.aspx.
12 The web sites aimed at non-professionals such as Flickr.com, YouTube.com and Vimeo.com also contain large amounts of media created by media professionals and students: photography portfolio, independent films, illustrations and design, etc. Often the professionals create their own groups – which makes it easier for us to find their work on these general-purpose sites. However, the sites specifically aimed at the professionals also often feature CVs, descriptions of projects, and other information not available on general social media sites.
13 http://en.wikipedia.org/wiki/DeviantArt.
14 http://pbwiki.com/academic.wiki, accessed December 26, 2008.
15 "BlogPulse Reaches 100 Million Mark" < http://blog.blogpulse.com/archives/000796.html>.
16 http://en.wikipedia.org/wiki/Statistically_Improbable_Phrases.
17 http://en.wikipedia.org/wiki/Acoustic_fingerprint
18 http://en.wikipedia.org/wiki/Perceptual_mapping.
19 These projects can be found at visualcomplexity.org and infosthetics.com.
20 http://www.google.com/corporate/tech.html.

Author Information

Konrad Becker is an author, artist and producer in the field of culture and information technology. Director and co-founder of the Institute for New Culture Technologies/t0, and of Public Netbase from 1994 to 2006, he started World-Information.Org, a cultural intelligence agency. Publications include: *Strategic Reality Dictionary* (2009) *Tactical Reality Dictionary* (2002) and *Politik der Infosphäre* (2002). www.t0.or.at, world-information.org, global-security-alliance.com

Robert Darnton taught at Princeton from 1968 until 2007, when he became Carl H. Pforzheimer University Professor and Director of the University Library at Harvard. He has written and edited two dozen books, including *The Business of Enlightenment: A Publishing History of the Encyclopédie* (1979, an early attempt to develop the history of books as a field of study), and *The Forbidden Best-Sellers of Prerevolutionary France* (1995, a study of the underground book trade). His latest book, *The Devil in the Holy Water, or The Art of Slander in France, 1650-1800* will be published in 2009.

Paul Duguid is an adjunct professor in the School of Information at the University of California, Berkeley, and a research fellow at Queen Mary, University of London. He is co-author, with John Seely Brown, of *The Social Life of Information* (2000).

Joris van Hoboken is a PhD researcher at the Institute for Information Law (IViR) at the University of Amsterdam. His research focuses on search engine freedom, in other words on the implications of the fundamental right to freedom of expression for the governance of Web search engines. He is a former co-director for Bits of Freedom, a Dutch digital civil rights organization and holds graduate degrees in law and theoretical mathematics.

Claire Lobet-Maris, a sociologist, is professor at the Faculty of Computer Science, University of Namur, Belgium. Her research focusses on the development and use of information and communication technologies (ICT) in organisations. She also directs CITA (Cellule Interfacultaire de Technology Assessment), a research team specialized in the social and economic assessment of information and communication technologies.

Geert Lovink is the founding director of the Institute of Network Cultures, is a Dutch-Australian media theorist and critic. In 2004 he was appointed as Research Professor at the Hogeschool van Amsterdam and Associate Professor at University of Amsterdam. He is a founder of Internet projects such as nettime and fibreculture. His recent book titles are *Dark Fiber* (2002), *Uncanny Networks* (2002) and *My First Recession* (2003) and *Zero Comments* (2007).

Lev Manovich is a Professor in Visual Arts Department, University of California -San Diego, a Director of the Software Studies Initiative at California Institute for Telecommunications and Information Technology (Calit2), and a Visiting Research Professor at Godsmith College (University of London), De Montfort University (UK) and College of Fine Arts, University of New South Wales (Sydney). His books include *Software Takes Command* (released under CC license, 2008), *Soft Cinema: Navigating the Database* (2005), and *The Language of New Media* (2001) which is hailed as "the most suggestive and broad ranging media history since Marshall McLuhan."

Christine Mayer studied History and English Language and Literature at the University of Vienna and University College London. She brings her experiences from teaching in varied fields (adult education, university, secondary school, teacher training) to her new post at the Institute for New Culture Technologies/t0, where she is mainly responsible for research, translations, and editorial work.

Katja Mayer holds a MA from the University of Vienna, where she studied sociology, physics and philosophy. Before starting to work as IT consultant, she was employed at Public Netbase Vienna, where she was responsible for content development, research and production of lecture series and exhibitions. Currently she is teaching at the Department of Social Studies of Science, University of Vienna, and she is writing her dissertation entitled: *Imag(in)ing Networks* on aesthetic engagements in Social Network Analysis.

Metahaven is a studio for research and design based in Amsterdam and Brussels, consisting of Gon Zifroni, Daniel van der Velden and Vinca Kruk. The collective investigates graphic design, information networks, branding and architecture from their overlapping discourses. Metahaven's work is exhibited as part of the traveling exhibition *Forms of Inquiry: the Architecture of Critical Graphic Design* at the Architectural Association, London, and in *On Purpose: Design Concepts* at Arnolfini, Bristol. In the context of the ISEA2008, Metahaven developed *Exodvs*, an internet search prototype visualizing content which is conventionally overridden by popularity-based ranking algorithms. www.metahaven.net

Matteo Pasquinelli is a writer, curator and researcher at Queen Mary University of London. He wrote the book *Animal Spirits: A Bestiary of the Commons* (2008) and edited the collections *Media Activism* (2002) and *C'Lick Me: A Netporn Studies Reader* (2007). He writes frequently on French philosophy, media culture and Italian post-operaismo. Since 2000 he has been editor of the mailing list Rekombinant. rekombinant.org/mat

Bernhard Rieder holds a Ph.D. in information science and is an assistant professor at Paris VIII University's hypermedia department where he teaches digital anthropology and Web programming. Combining a background in the humanities with the practice of software development, his work is centered on the ethics and politics of technology and particularly the design of digital machinery.

Theo Röhle is a PhD candidate at the department for Media and Communication Studies, University of Hamburg. He worked as a part-time assistant lecturer at the universities of Stockholm and Hamburg. His research interests are located at the intersection of media theory, surveillance studies and the politics of code. More information can be obtained at www.netzmedium.de.

Richard Rogers holds the Chair in New Media & Digital Culture at the University of Amsterdam. He is Director of Govcom.org, the group responsible for the Issue Crawler, and the Digital Methods Initiative, reworking method for Internet research. Rogers is author of *Information Politics on the Web* (2004), editor of Preferred Placement (Jan van Eyck, 2000) and author of *Technological Landscapes* (1999). Current research interests include Internet censorship, googlization, the Palestinian-Israeli conflict as well as the technicity of content.

Felix Stalder is a lecturer in the Theory of the Media society at the Zurich University of Arts. His work focusses on the intersection of cultural, political and technological dynamics. He is a founder of Openflows, a long-time moderator of the nettime mailing list, and a board member of the institute for new cultural technologies in Vienna. With the institute, co-organized, among others, the *Deep Search* conference (2008), and the *World Information City Conferences*, Bangalore (2005) and Paris (2009). He has published most recently *Open Cultures and the Nature of Networks* (2005), *Manuel Castells and the Theory of the Network Society* (2006), and, as co-editor, *Media Arts Zurich* (2008). felix.openflows.com